Nonviolent Revolutions

NONVIOLENT REVOLUTIONS

Civil Resistance in the Late 20th Century

Sharon Erickson Nepstad

OXFORD
UNIVERSITY PRESS

Oxford University Press, Inc., publishes works that further
Oxford University's objective of excellence
in research, scholarship, and education.

Oxford   New York
Auckland   Cape Town   Dar es Salaam   Hong Kong   Karachi
Kuala Lumpur   Madrid   Melbourne   Mexico City   Nairobi
New Delhi   Shanghai   Taipei   Toronto

With offices in
Argentina   Austria   Brazil   Chile   Czech Republic   France   Greece
Guatemala   Hungary   Italy   Japan   Poland   Portugal   Singapore
South Korea   Switzerland   Thailand   Turkey   Ukraine   Vietnam

Published by Oxford University Press, Inc.
198 Madison Avenue, New York, New York 10016

www.oup.com

Oxford is a registered trademark of Oxford University Press

Library of Congress Cataloging-in-Publication Data
Nepstad, Sharon Erickson.
Nonviolent revolutions : civil resistance in the late 20th century / Sharon Erickson Nepstad.
    p.   cm.
Includes bibliographical references and index.
ISBN 978-0-19-977820-1 (hardback : alk. paper)—ISBN 978-0-19-977821-8 (pbk. : alk. paper)
1. Government, Resistance to—History—20th century. 2. Revolutions—History—20th century. I. Title.
JC328.3.N47   2011
323'.044—dc22   2011015264

Printed in the United States of America
on acid-free paper

To my parents,
Millard and Virginia Erickson

CONTENTS

ACKNOWLEDGMENTS

There are many individuals who have made this book possible. While I have been thinking about this project for many years, it was a fellowship from the Kroc Institute for International Peace Studies and the Center for the Study of Religion and Society at Notre Dame University that gave me the uninterrupted time to pursue it. I am grateful to Robert Johansen, Hal Culbertson, Scott Appleby and Dan Myers at the Kroc Institute and to Christian Smith at the Center for the Study of Religion and Society for the opportunity to be a Visiting Fellow in such a vibrant intellectual community. I especially thank those at the Kroc Institute who gave me excellent feedback on this study in its earliest stages and who made my family feel so welcomed during our stay at Notre Dame.

At the University of New Mexico, special thanks go to Christina Jensen and Nancy Rice. Their skillful handling of administrative matters meant that I was able to continue working on the manuscript. I deeply value their friendship, support, and sage advice on a variety of issues, both academic and personal. I am particularly thankful to Christina Jensen, who read an early draft of the book and provided useful editorial suggestions.

I have been fortunate to work with many fine people at Oxford University Press. I thank the Culture and Politics Series editors, Clifford Bob and James Jasper, for their support. I also wish to thank the three anonymous reviewers, whose insightful suggestions helped me hone and refine my analysis. I am particularly indebted to Cliff Bob, who read the manuscript several times; his exceptional editing abilities and sound advice have strengthened the book considerably. Additionally, I thank James Cook, who deftly guided the manuscript through the review and publication process and did so with humor and grace. I am grateful to Joy Matkowski, for her skillful copyediting, and to Jaimee Biggins for managing the production process.

Finally, I thank my family. I thank my parents for their support. I thank my sister Kathryn for her remarkable friendship over all these years. I thank my sister Sandra, who is always in my heart. Most of all, I express my deepest gratitude to my daughters, who occasionally practice nonviolent resistance to my authority and who always remind me of how fortunate I am. Linnea and Malaya: it is you I cherish most.

PREFACE

Although it is seldom stated, scholars' interests are often rooted in their biographical experiences. This is certainly true for me, as my interest in the revolutionary potential of nonviolence dates back to when, as an undergraduate, I first read about Gandhi. I was intrigued with his ability to transform morally principled pacifism into a strategic form of civil resistance that enabled him to defeat one of the strongest militaries of his era. The movement to liberate India demonstrated that nonviolence was a pragmatic alternative to war. Yet in the 1980s, as civil wars erupted throughout the world, I wondered how well we could adapt his strategies to repressive regimes in Latin America, Asia, Africa, and Eastern Europe. Then, with utter awe, I watched the Philippines' "bloodless revolution" unfold in the winter of 1986. Within days, Filipinos ousted a dictator who had been in power for 20 years and had established a reputation for brutality, corruption, and repression.

Shortly after the Philippine revolt, I began working for a peace organization in West Germany that, among other things, supported churches in East Germany that were promoting disarmament, human rights, and democracy. Their work was always accompanied by concerns over the omnipresent surveillance of the Stasi, the East German secret police, and the repressive consequences of activism. Yet they continued on, despite the fact that their organizing efforts appeared to have no direct influence on the government. But in the summer and fall of 1989, an unanticipated citizen uprising shook the East German state. Those of us in West Germany watched the news each night, amazed at the rapid change we were witnessing. Within a few short months, the Berlin Wall was gone, and the East German state disintegrated.

My experience in Germany convinced me that nonviolent action could be tremendously powerful, even in highly repressive regimes—a belief that was further reinforced as a wave of nonviolent revolts subsequently transformed numerous Eastern Europe regimes. But how did it happen? Could other groups living under authoritarian systems replicate this? And what were the critical factors that led to victory, or at least helped groups avoid defeat? This last question weighed heavily on many of us since just a few months earlier the world had watched Chinese students and workers occupy Tiananmen Square, bravely calling for change. But their story ended tragically, not triumphantly. Why were Filipinos and East Germans successful while Chinese resisters were not? This book is an attempt to provide some preliminary answers to these questions.

OTHER STUDIES OF NONVIOLENCE

Since the 1980s, scholarly literature on nonviolent change has expanded. Adding to the many fine works on principled nonviolence—the moral and ethical refusal to use violence—recent research has focused on the strategic use of nonviolent methods for social and political purposes. Yet the literature in this field reveals a divide. On the one hand, there is a group—mainly nonviolence practitioners and advocates—who argue that a sound strategy can enable civil resisters to win in just about any conditions. On the other hand, another group—mostly social scientists—believes that structural conditions (e.g., the degree of repression, level of political openness, and extent of societal divisions) have a significant influence on a movement's outcome.[1]

I maintain that both conditions and strategy matter. Social, economic, and political conditions can facilitate or thwart the emergence and expansion of nonviolent uprisings. As following chapters show, certain events often trigger public outrage and heighten long-standing grievances, making people receptive to unarmed revolutionary movements. Moreover, conditions matter because unanticipated political changes can provide new opportunities or obstacles for challengers, who may rethink their strategic plans in light of these shifting circumstances. Yet no movement succeeds solely on the basis of favorable structural conditions; strategic actions are critical in determining whether resisters achieve their goals. In this study, for instance, I find that the one factor distinguishing successful from failed uprisings is a strategic one: those movements that undermined troops' loyalty were the ones who succeeded in overthrowing the state. Thus to focus solely on strategy or conditions provides only part of the picture of when nonviolent uprisings are likely to win.

In this book, I also underscore the importance of rulers' countermoves. A chess game is not won or lost by the skill of just one player but rather of both. Much of the strategic nonviolence literature acknowledges this, echoing Thomas Schelling's assertion:

The tyrant and his subjects are in somewhat symmetrical positions. They can deny him most of what he wants—they can, that is, if they have the disciplined organization to refuse collaboration. And he can deny them just about everything they want—he can deny it by using his force at his command. They can deny him the economic fruits of their own activity. They can deny him the satisfaction of ruling themselves. They can confront him with chaos, starvation, idleness and social breakdown, but he confronts them with the same thing. . .. It is a bargaining situation in which either side, if adequately disciplined and organized, can deny most of what the other wants; and it remains to see who wins.[2]

In reality, however, many studies of strategic nonviolence offer only a one-sided focus, emphasizing what movements do while largely ignoring dictators' strategies. This, too, provides an incomplete picture since some well-planned nonviolent revolts have failed because rulers out-maneuvered resisters. For example, two authoritarian leaders examined in this study found ways to neutralize the effects of international sanctions and use them to their advantage. These same rulers developed techniques to keep their troops loyal, thereby diminishing the chance of defections. Shrewd counterstrategies, I argue, were the main reason these regimes endured in the face of widespread civil resistance.

This book also differs from other studies of strategic nonviolence in that it takes a comparative approach. Many earlier works are descriptive, documenting successful civil resistance movements.[3] The primary goal of these books is to demonstrate that nonviolence is a practical and effective form of political struggle. Yet by only examining successful cases and ignoring the failed ones, it is impossible to discern the critical factors that lead a nonviolent revolution to victory.[4] Additionally, we miss the opportunity to learn from failed movements' experiences and to glean lessons about how unarmed uprisings are defeated. To build and test theory on this topic, comparative studies are needed that pair successful and failed nonviolent revolts.

METHODOLOGY

To do this type of comparative work, I followed Mill's method of difference,[5] whereby I selected nonviolent revolts that had differing outcomes: three of the cases I examine were successful (East Germany, Chile, the Philippines), and three were not (China, Panama, Kenya). I define success simply as the removal of an existing regime or ruler. While all of the victorious movements in this study culminated in a transition to democracy, I do not include democratization in my definition of success. It is true that most nonviolent revolutions in recent history have aimed to establish a democratic form of governance, but such movements can also usher in other political systems. The citizen-based Iranian Revolution of 1979, for instance, ousted a monarchy and replaced it with an Islamic theocracy.[6] I also limit my definition of success for another reason: overthrowing an existing regime and building a new regime entail distinct processes. In other words, the factors that help a movement defeat a political ruler must be differentiated from the factors that enable resisters to successfully establish a new political system. When researchers conflate these processes, we lose analytic clarity and obfuscate causal dynamics. Therefore, I focus only on the factors associated with regime overthrow and demise, not regime construction.

My definition of success may lead some readers to question whether the victorious movements in this study can genuinely be considered successful, given their postrevolutionary records. This is a legitimate concern. As I witnessed the process of East and West Germany uniting, I was keenly aware that many of those who overturned the East German government did not want to relinquish the gains of socialism or be completely absorbed into the capitalist-driven Federal Republic of Germany. For many activists, reunification was not their goal, although it was the ultimate outcome. Similarly, critics will note that Filipinos ousted their dictator, but their postrevolution presidents did little to change economic and social structures, and thus the nation's problems persisted. While these are indeed important points, it is beyond the scope of my research here to address the long-term achievements of those governments ushered in through nonviolent methods.[7] In this book, I am primarily interested in the factors that lead to nonviolent regime change, not comprehensive social, cultural, and economic transformation. In other words, the focus of this book is on political revolutions, not social revolutions.[8]

So why did I choose to examine these six political revolutionary movements? As Table P.1 indicates, there have been literally dozens of nonviolent revolts in recent history. To determine which cases to include in this research, I first focused on movements that had clearly divergent outcomes of either succeeding or failing. In other words, I eliminated those cases—such as South Korea, Nepal, and Bangladesh—that could be considered partial successes because they achieved reforms but not regime transformation.

I also selected cases that had sufficient similarities to make them appropriate for comparison, enabling me to "control" for other factors that could influence movement outcomes.[9] The following criteria, therefore, guided my choices. First, I decided to focus solely on citizen uprisings against their own regimes since domestic struggles may have a different dynamic than struggles against foreign occupying forces.[10] Hence I disregarded cases such as the West Bank and Gaza, as well as the Baltic States' struggle for

Table P.1: MAJOR NONVIOLENT REVOLUTIONARY MOVEMENTS, 1978–2011

Country	Peak Years of Struggle	Outcome
Iran	1978–1979	success
El Salvador	1979–1981	failure
Bolivia	1978–1982	success
Pakistan	1983	failure
Philippines	1983–1986	success
Chile	1985–1988	success
South Africa	1983–1990	success
Sudan	1985	success
Haiti	1985	success
South Korea	1987	reforms
Burma	1987–1988	failure
Tibet	1987–1989	failure
Panama	1987–1989	failure
West Bank & Gaza	1987–1990	failure
Baltic States	1987–1991	success
China	1989	failure
Czechoslovakia	1989	success
East Germany	1989	success
Nepal	1989–1990	reforms
Bangladesh	1989–1990	reforms
Mali	1989–1992	success
Kenya	1989–1992	failure
Niger	1991–1992	failure
Madagascar	1991–1993	success
Indonesia	1998	success
Serbia	2000	success
Philippines	2001	success
Georgia	2003	success
Ukraine	2004	success
Kyrgyzstan	2005	success
Lebanon	2005	success
Burma	2007	failure
Armenia	2008	failure
Tunisia	2011	success
Egypt	2011	success

Note: Adapted from Zunes (1994) and Schock (2005); all dates are approximate.

independence from the Soviet Union. Second, I selected cases occurring in the late Cold War era (specifically the 1980s) to control for major differences in geopolitical dynamics of other time periods.[11] Thus, while a flurry of nonviolent revolts happened at the start of the 21st century—including Serbia, Georgia, the Ukraine, Kyrgyzstan, Lebanon, Tunisia, and Egypt—these took place in a very different post-Soviet environment and hence are not suitable for comparison with Cold War era movements. Third, I selected cases according to regime type. Since some have argued that certain regime types are more susceptible to revolutionary challenges,[12] I wanted to see if the dynamics of nonviolent revolt are the same when citizens resist a socialist regime as compared with a military dictatorship or a personal dictatorship.

Of course, there are limitations to this research design. Despite careful efforts to construct comparisons that illuminate causal dynamics, social scientists can never fully control all the potential intervening influences. I readily acknowledge another limitation—namely, that the inclusion of other cases might generate alternative conclusions. Thus, while I discern factors that are linked with successful or failed revolts in these six cases, I cannot claim that these factors hold true universally. The results might have looked different if I had, for instance, studied revolutionary movements in Czechoslovakia, Haiti, Mali, Pakistan, Niger, and Burma.

My intent, therefore, is not to develop a definitive explanation for all nonviolent uprisings' successes and failures. Rather, I use this comparative method to generate plausible theoretical claims that will advance research into this relatively understudied topic.[13] I hope my findings are sufficiently thought provoking that other researchers will test them against additional cases, thereby expanding our knowledge of the key causal factors and dynamics involved in civil resistance.

DATA SOURCES

The data for this study are mostly derived from secondary sources and archived newspaper accounts. While primary data are preferable, I am fortunate that many excellent works include interviews with movement participants. Since most were published shortly after the revolts occurred, participants' recollection of events is more accurately captured in these secondary sources than it would be if I conducted interviews now, decades after the uprisings ended. Nonetheless, I am certain that historians and area specialists will be less than fully satisfied with my reliance on secondary sources, the lack of new empirical data, and my cursory overviews of each case. In defense of this method, I wish to emphasize that my purpose here is to offer new analysis of nonviolent revolutions rather than new historical narratives. Hence I underscore the words of T. H. Marshall, who long ago wrote:

> Sociologists must inevitably rely extensively on secondary authorities, without going back to the original sources. They do this partly because life is too short to do anything else when using the comparative method, and they need data assembled from a wide historical field; and partly because original sources are very tricky things to use.... It is the business of historians to sift this miscellaneous collection of dubious authorities and to give others the results of their careful professional assessment. And surely they will not rebuke the sociologists for putting faith in what historians write.[14]

TERMS

Before turning to the six case studies and the literature on revolutionary change, I would like to clarify my use of the terms *nonviolence* and *revolution*. For many, nonviolence connotes passivity or neutrality, and thus the term *nonviolent revolution* seems an oxymoron.[15] However, as Gandhi, King, and numerous others have emphasized, this is a complete misunderstanding: nonviolence is a civilian-based form of struggle that employs social, economic, and political forms of power without resorting to violence or the threat of violence.[16] Although armaments are not used, civil resistance can nonetheless be equally disruptive since it occurs outside the parameters of institutional methods of political change, such as lobbying or legislating.[17]

Yet a quick browse through the nonviolence literature reveals that a variety of terms are used to describe this method of struggle. For example, some authors dislike the term *nonviolence* since it is more suggestive of what is not involved (violence) than what is involved (resistance by other means). Others reject the term *peaceful resistance* since it obfuscates the contentious and disruptive nature of these movements. As an alternative, many recent studies refer to *civil resistance*[18]—a term Gandhi frequently employed. One will also find scholars who discuss "people power" or "unarmed insurrections."[19] Although these terms are generally synonymous, I primarily refer to these movements as nonviolent revolutions or civil resistance.

Some readers may also be perplexed that I describe the following cases as revolutions (or attempted revolutions) since many assume that this term refers to armed struggle. Of course, the "classic revolutions"—such as the French Revolution (1789), the Russian Revolution (1917), and the Chinese Revolution (1949)—did transpire through acts of violence, as did many revolutions in the late 20th century, such as Angola (1974) and Nicaragua (1979). Moreover, revolutionary leaders have often argued that overthrowing a state can occur only through violent means. For instance, Mao Zedong stated:

> A revolution is not a dinner party, or writing an essay, or painting a picture, or doing embroidery; it cannot be so refined, so leisurely and gentle, so temperate, kind, courteous, restrained and magnanimous. A revolution is an insurrection, an act of violence whereby one class overthrows another. . ... Proper limits have to be exceeded in order to right a wrong, or else the wrong cannot be righted."[20]

But in the late 20th century, numerous movements demonstrated that people are capable of overturning long-standing regimes without bloodshed. Timothy Garton Ash has argued that these movements have marked "the birth of a new genre of revolution, qualitatively different from the Jacobin-Bolshevik model of 1789 and 1917."[21] Like armed revolutions, unarmed revolutions entail the mass mobilization of people who erupt into public spaces, aiming to overturn established rulers and transform political institutions.[22] But nonviolent revolts are distinct from violent revolts in a couple of ways. They employ different "weapons," such as noncooperation, strikes, boycotts, and the subversion of regime supporters' loyalty. They also differ because traditional armed revolutions have mostly mobilized members of the peasantry or working class to fight in rural settings; in contrast, many recent unarmed revolutions have mobilized cross-class coalitions to fight in urban centers.[23] Hence our conception of revolution has changed as the character of insurrectionary movements has evolved.[24]

Various terms have been coined to denote this new genre of revolt. Some call them *velvet revolutions*—a phrase first used to describe the political transformation of Eastern Europe in 1989.[25] Others have dubbed them *negotiated revolutions*[26] or *refolutions*, indicating that they include elements of reform and revolution.[27] More recently, the term *color revolutions* has become increasingly popular. This term is derived from the many nonviolent revolutionary movements that used a color to symbolize their cause. For instance, the 1986 Philippine "people power" movement was represented in yellow, the 2004 Ukraine movement adopted the color orange, and the 2007 resistance in Burma is known as the "saffron revolution," denoting the color of rebellious Buddhist monks' robes. In this book, I refer to them simply as nonviolent revolutions. But whichever terms are used, it is my hope that readers will gain a deeper appreciation of what civil resistance is about, how it works, and how it has changed the way people struggle for social and political change.

Nonviolent Revolutions

CHAPTER 1

Nonviolent Power and Revolutionary Change

F ew people thought that Philippine dictator Ferdinand Marcos could be quickly removed from office. During his twenty years as president, Marcos had repeatedly demonstrated that he would take any measures to retain power. He had altered the constitution to repeal term limits, declared martial law and suspended elections, and given orders to imprison tens of thousands of political activists, many of whom were tortured. A vivid illustration of his brutality occurred in 1983, when oppositional leader Benigno Aquino flew back to the Philippines after years in exile. Just seconds after he disembarked from the plane, Aquino was shot by government forces.[1] The message of the assassination was clear: Marcos would not tolerate any opposition.

As reports of the regime's human rights abuses expanded, Marcos held elections to generate the appearance of Philippine democracy. Yet they were nothing more than a façade since Marcos secured his electoral victory through vote rigging and fraud. When Marcos stole yet another election in 1986, Filipinos decided that they would take no more. Millions flooded the streets in the capital city of Manila, demanding that Marcos step down. He refused. Consequently, the leaders of the burgeoning civil resistance movement organized a campaign of noncooperation. But before the campaign began, two top-ranking military leaders defected, announcing their mutinous decision on television. Aware that the defectors would soon be arrested and probably executed, Cardinal Jaime Sin called upon faithful Filipino Catholics to protect the two military men. Within hours, a million people had formed a human barricade around them.[2]

An infuriated Marcos sent out tanks to disperse the crowd and apprehend the defected military leaders. Holding crucifixes and statues of the Virgin Mary, the crowd held its ground, offering food and water to the soldiers. Catholic clergy and laypeople began talking with the troops, asking them to lay down their weapons and join the movement. When tank drivers revved their engines in preparation for an assault, a group of nuns kneeled before the armored vehicles to pray the rosary. Unwilling to kill the nuns, and moved by the protesters' appeals, soldiers began defecting. Over the next days, roughly 80 percent of the troops had joined the crowd, and Marcos—left without any power to repress the movement—fled the country.[3] One participant recalled the experience:

> Where in the world will you find a people whose faith is so strong that they believe holding up a statue of the Blessed Virgin before tanks would stop them? Where will you find battle-tested soldiers who stopped their tanks when faced with people at prayer? . . . The tanks turned away. I saw an old woman hugging a dumbfounded Marcos loyalist soldier who had defected. . . . I saw a young man jubilantly holding up his right hand and saying, "I'll never wash this hand. It pushed back a tank." I heard a Swiss journalist remark, "Is this a revolution?" My husband replied, "We Filipinos like to do things differently."[4]

Indeed, the Philippine movement represents a different kind of revolution, whereby citizens engage in an insurrectionary struggle, armed only with techniques of nonviolent resistance. But Filipinos did not invent this form of revolution. Similar methods have been used throughout history, including Gandhi's movement for Indian independence, Portugal's "Revolution of the Carnations," and Iran's revolt against the Shah—to name just a few examples. Yet this new type of revolution has flourished since 1986. Just a couple of years after the Philippine victory, citizens overturned Chile's military dictatorship. Then came the so-called velvet revolutions in Czechoslovakia, East Germany, and other East European regimes. The trend continued into the 21st century with successful nonviolent revolts in Serbia (2000), Georgia (2003), Ukraine (2004), Lebanon (2005), Kyrgyzstan (2005), Tunisia, and Egypt (2011).

These cases indicate that nonviolent methods can produce political transformation—not only in stable democracies with fair and reasonable leaders but also under authoritarian regimes, dictatorships, and corrupt governments. Nevertheless, there is still a widely held belief that violence is the most effective method of achieving political transformation and that successful nonviolent uprisings are rare flukes. This is simply not true. In one recent study, Adrian Karatnycky and Peter Ackerman document that 67 authoritarian regimes were dismantled between 1972 and 2002; more than 70 percent of these were the result of nonviolent civilian uprisings.[5] In other words, civil resistance is not rare but rather quite common. Moreover, another study by Maria Stephan and Erica Chenoweth found that nonviolent uprisings tend to be *more effective* than violent campaigns, not less. Specifically, they found that of the hundreds of resistance campaigns that have occurred over the past century, nonviolent movements were successful 53 percent of the time; in contrast, only 26 percent of groups employing violent tactics achieved their goals.[6]

Given the explosion of nonviolent revolutions in the past 25 years and the successful political transformation that has occurred through civil resistance, it is surprising that relatively few researchers have analyzed this form of struggle. While there is a long tradition of studying armed revolutions, which has resulted in a rich measure of empirical data and theoretical insights, many of these insights do not adequately explain nonviolent revolutions. As the following review of this literature reveals, armed and unarmed revolutions arise out of similar conditions but, once these struggles are underway, nonviolent insurrections exhibit distinctive traits, dynamics, and strategic processes.

CAUSES OF REVOLUTIONS

Armed and unarmed insurrections emerge from similar causes.[7] Specifically, revolutionary movements erupt when five conditions are present.[8] First, there must be *widespread grievances against the state* that generate doubts about the regime's legitimacy. These grievances may be the result of economic decline and material deprivation,[9] but they may also result from fraudulent elections[10] or growing restrictions on civil liberties and democratic rights.

Second, revolutionary movements are likely to arise when *national elites shift their allegiance from the state to the opposition.*[11] Elites may cut ties with regime rulers who are unable to manage a fiscal crisis, exclude them from power, or impose policies that undercut their wealth, status, and privilege. They may also turn against rulers who violate religious beliefs, nationalist aspirations, cultural norms, or standards of justice.[12] There is strong evidence that regimes are unlikely to fall if they enjoy the unified support of national elites.[13] But when this support deteriorates, conditions are ripe for an insurrection.

Third, *people must be angered enough by regime injustices that they are willing to act.* Teodor Shanin wrote, "Social scientists often miss a centrepiece of any revolutionary struggle—the fervour and anger that drives revolutionaries and makes them into what they are. . . . At the very centre of revolutions lies an emotional upheaval of moral indignation, revulsion and fury with the powers-that-be, such that one cannot demur or remain silent, whatever the cost. . . . Without this factor, any understanding of revolutions falls flat."[14]

Fourth, opposition groups must unify around an *ideology of rebellion* that situates this indignation within a social and ideological critique.[15] An effective ideology indicates why the regime is to blame for their suffering (the "diagnosis") and what can be done (the "prognosis"), thereby channeling anger into action.[16] But to link emotions to this type of oppositional ideology, revolutionary leaders need "free spaces"—that is, autonomous places that are relatively independent from the influence of dominant society.[17] Such spaces are particularly crucial in authoritarian regimes, where few public avenues are available to express anger, voice criticisms, debate strategies for social change, and cultivate a "culture of rebellion."[18] Without free spaces, oppositional organizers will have a difficult time transforming indignation into insurgency.

Fifth, *mobilizing organizations* are needed to coordinate, support, and direct the uprising.[19] Often, preexisting organizations—such as labor unions, religious groups, or university clubs—take on this function. In other instances, preexisting groups serve as "movement midwives," assisting in the birth of a new organization by providing financial resources, communication systems, leaders, and recruitment networks.[20] Regardless of how they are formed, to be effective, these organizations must have a unified leadership system that can respond quickly and intelligently to changing circumstances.[21] Organizational leaders must also have sufficient credibility and authority so that their decisions do not generate divisions that could undermine a movement's capacity to act.

FACTORS AFFECTING REVOLUTIONARY OUTCOMES

Structural Conditions

Once a revolutionary movement erupts, its chances of successfully overthrowing the state are shaped, to some degree, by structural conditions. I define *structural conditions* as the macrolevel factors that can tip the balance of power in favor of the movement or the regime, helping one side or the other to secure victory. One type of structural condition includes a nation's preexisting, established features that are beyond the direct control of revolutionary actors.[22] For example, if a regime is economically dependent on other nations, then it is more vulnerable to trade embargoes or aid reductions. Conversely, if a regime is fairly economically self-sufficient, it may be relatively immune to international sanctions.[23] Similarly, some political scientists have argued that regimes with highly institutionalized one-party political systems are less susceptible to elite divisions because rulers have sole discretion over the distribution of valued rewards (such as political positions or material gains). Hence there are significant benefits for elites who remain loyal and potentially tremendous costs for those who do not.[24] This situation—where elites are unlikely to defect—stacks the odds against a movement.

Structural conditions also include new developments and unanticipated events that can suddenly weaken a regime or provide greater momentum to a revolutionary movement, thereby increasing its chances of winning. This type of fluctuating structural condition is what many scholars refer to as "political opportunities."[25] Political opportunities may include shifts in international alliances and agreements,[26] newly called elections,[27] a succession crisis following the retirement of a long-standing ruler,[28] inspiration from successful uprisings in other nations,[29] or public outrage generated by "moral shocks," such as the assassination of a leading opposition figure.[30] Unlike the more fixed type of structural conditions, political opportunities are not necessarily beyond the control of movements since civil resisters can engage in actions that create new possibilities for mobilization.[31]

Clearly, these types of stable and fluctuating structural conditions matter because they make the task of overthrowing an authoritarian regime more or less difficult. However, we must be careful to not grant this factor an undue amount of causal power.[32] Favorable conditions merely create regime vulnerabilities and new possibilities for resistance. In other words, they offer the *potential* for revolutionary change, but people are still needed to turn these opportunities into action. Thus, when an assassination occurs that morally shocks the population, someone must propose a way for people to channel their outrage. When a repressive regime changes its policies to permit free spaces to exist, someone must fill those free spaces with people and cultivate an oppositional culture. When a regime is economically dependent on other nations, a movement can benefit from this vulnerability only if someone persuades the international community to cut off trade and aid. Hence we need to remember: structures do not revolt, people do. Moreover, we ought to recognize that even when conditions are not favorable, revolutionary actions may still be effective. As Peter Ackerman and Christopher Kruegler have noted, "We are all familiar with cases of military conflict in which David beats Goliath despite starting from an objectively inferior position."[33]

The Strategy of Violent Revolution

Any theory of revolutionary success or failure must therefore include an assessment of both structural conditions and revolutionary strategy. I define *strategy* as actors' choices about targets, timing, and tactics.[34] In a

Clausewitz-inspired understanding, I use the term *tactics* to denote the actions taken to win a single campaign (one "battle") and *strategy* to signify the master plan of how to win the struggle ("the war"). Thus tactics involve the small-scale repertoire and subgoals of the movement, and strategy is about how a movement reaches its ultimate aims. But here is where the differences between violent and nonviolent movements become most evident.

The basic strategy of violent revolutions is to create an armed force that gains sufficient strength to defeat the state's military. Defeat may occur through superior destructive capacity or attrition, but once the military capitulates, rulers are left without protection or the capacity to impose their rule. As a result, they either flee or are captured, enabling revolutionary forces to seize political power. As the revolutionary party assumes office, it can then dismantle and rebuild the nation's political, economic, and/or cultural institutions.

This strategy reflects a monolithic conception of state power.[35] That is, armed revolutionaries see the regime as a pyramid-like structure: rock-solid, durable, and virtually indestructible. At the pinnacle of this pyramid are the rulers, who possess political, economic, and social power. At the base of the pyramid are citizens, who have little power and therefore must rely on rulers to take their interests into consideration as they legislate policies and govern the nation. But if rulers become self-interested, corrupt, or oppressive, then there are few options for change. In democratic contexts, citizens can organize electorally to vote in new leaders. Yet in authoritarian settings where legitimate elections are not held or institutional mechanisms for change do not exist, people must either acquiesce or use violent measures to destroy this system. Hence the belief is that in authoritarian settings, the population has only one form of power: violence.

The Strategy of Nonviolent Revolution

Nonviolent revolutionaries also aim to seize power and usher in political transformation, but they operate with an alternative conception of political power. In direct contrast to the monolithic perspective, civil resisters maintain a relational view,[36] which draws on the insights of political philosophers Etienne La Boétie, Hannah Arendt, and Henry David Thoreau. This relational perspective posits that rulers have no intrinsic power; rather, citizens possess various types of power that they may either grant to rulers or withhold.[37] If the population chooses to withhold its power, violent attacks on the state are not necessary; a ruler is rendered impotent, and the regime simply collapses. As La Boétie stated, "Reserve to serve no more, and you are at once freed. I do not ask that you place hands upon the tyrant to topple him over, but simply that you support him no longer, then you will behold him, like a great Colossus whose pedestal has been pulled away, fall of his own weight and break into pieces."[38]

The Gandhian Model

How do nonviolent activists transform this relational theory of political power into revolutionary action? One model reflects the strategy developed by Mohandas Gandhi. Heavily influenced by Thoreau's concept of noncooperation with an evil system, Gandhi argued that British colonizers could not maintain control of India unless Indians cooperated with them. Thus he identified various ways that Indians tacitly supported British rule and then devised a strategic plan to systematically withdraw this support until British control disintegrated. As Indians engaged in general strikes, refused to buy British goods, and ignored unjust laws, the British concluded that it was no longer economically fruitful or politically viable to remain in India. They voluntarily withdrew, granting India independence.[39]

Numerous scholars have studied the Gandhian strategy, discerning six distinct ways that citizens can withdraw their support from regimes.[40] First, citizens can *refuse to acknowledge rulers as legitimate*, thereby stripping them of authority. This often occurs in fraudulent elections when citizens refuse to accept the results, making it difficult for the proclaimed leader to establish credibility at home and abroad. This, in turn, may make the international community less willing to contribute aid or forge alliances with the disputed leader. Second, people can *contest mentalities or ideologies of obedience* that encourage submission to the government. European monarchs claimed a divine right to rule, which minimized uprisings since rebelling against the aristocracy was tantamount to rebelling against God. However, with the onset of Enlightenment thinking, citizens questioned this divine right, ultimately paving the way for democratic challenges. Third, citizens can *refuse to obey laws or cooperate* with a regime. People ultimately decide whether they will comply with a ruler's orders, and history is full of examples of those who refused to do so—from U.S. civil rights activists who broke segregation laws to Polish resisters who surreptitiously changed street signs in the night to confuse occupying Nazi soldiers.[41] Fourth, citizens can *withdraw their material resources* from a regime. When people refuse to pay taxes or purchase governmental goods and services, they deplete a ruler's coffers.

A fifth way that the population can undermine a regime is by *refusing to use their skills to promote and sustain government activities*. In other words, all regimes depend on their citizens to carry out the daily tasks needed to have a functional state. As Robert Helvey argues:

> The President of the United States of America is widely accepted as being the most powerful person in the world. Yet this most powerful ruler knows little or nothing about the complicated tasks of maintaining airplanes and flight schedules, administering maritime law, conducting criminal investigations, collecting taxes, developing war plans, distributing food, developing and servicing communications networks, and a host of other proficiencies. The point is that skills and knowledge provided by the people permit governments, at all levels, to function.[42]

People can chose to withhold these skills—typically through a general strike—thereby disrupting business as usual and interrupting state operations.

The sixth way that citizens can nonviolently subvert a regime is by *undermining the state's sanctioning power*. When people resist, rulers often resort to repression to make non-cooperation costly. Yet rulers do not inflict punishments on their own. They rely on members of the armed services and police force to do so. Although soldiers and police officers work for the state and are paid to protect the regime, they can be persuaded to side with the citizenry. Civil resisters may appeal to security force members as individuals, demonstrating how their interests are congruent with movement goals or, conversely, how their interests are not being served by the regime. Oppositional activists may also reframe troops' responsibilities as defending the people rather than the state. If the movement succeeds in winning troops' sympathy, then police may refuse to carry out orders, and soldiers may defect. When this occurs, a ruler loses the capacity to impose sanctions.

The state's sanctioning power is further depleted when citizens refuse to be deterred by repression. Sanctions are designed to frighten the population into submission. Yet ultimately resisters are the ones who decide whether they will allow punishments to dissuade them or whether they will continue their resistance in the face of great danger. If citizens can overcome their fears and persist, the power of sanctions is diminished. Thus, it is citizens' response to sanctions that largely determines their effectiveness.

Since citizens have the capacity to undermine a regime in these six ways, a ruler's position is always tenuous. Political theorist Gene Sharp states:

> When people refuse their cooperation, withhold help, and persist in their disobedience and defiance, they are denying their opponent the basic human assistance and cooperation that any government or hierarchical system requires. . . . Subjects may disobey laws they reject. Workers may halt work, which may paralyze the economy. The bureaucracy

may refuse to carry out instructions. Soldiers and police may become lax in inflicting repression; they may even mutiny. If people and institutions do this in sufficient numbers for long enough, that government or hierarchical system will no longer have power. . . . Its power has dissolved.[43]

Thus nonviolent uprisings can defeat even ruthless dictators *if* people are willing to withdraw their support from the regime, regardless of the costs.

However, spontaneous defiance rarely topples authoritarian leaders. A successful revolt requires good strategists who can identify a ruler's weaknesses and devise effective methods of withdrawing popular support from the state. This type of nonviolent action can be more effective than armed revolt because it enables resisters to strike directly at the state's vulnerabilities.[44] For example, if a regime is highly dependent on foreign trade and assistance, then activists can target its economic base by persuading the international community to cut off aid and suspend trade until a ruler steps down. The Montgomery bus boycott in the U.S. Civil Rights movement illustrates this point clearly. The Montgomery bus company eventually conceded to the movement's demands for fair treatment of African American customers, not because of a moral conversion or bad publicity, but because the company—whose sole purpose is to make profit—was on the verge of financial ruin. Similarly, if a conflict is primarily about control of an occupied region, local residents can withhold their cooperation and skills, making it exceedingly difficult for occupiers to conduct daily operations and consolidate power.

The Electoral Model

In addition to the Gandhian approach, a second nonviolent revolutionary strategy is what Valerie Bunce and Sharon Wolchik call the electoral model. This strategy has generally been used in "electoral autocracies," where authoritarian leaders work with an elected legislature that has been put into office through fraudulent means. In this model, activists nonviolently organize "to transform rigged electoral rituals into fair elections," thereby facilitating a transition to genuine democracy.[45] In this strategy, emphasis is put primarily on the following actions. First, civil resisters build a cross-class opposition coalition. Second, the coalition concentrates on increasing voter registration, improving the quality and accuracy of registration lists, and expanding voter turnout. Third, organizers solicit the help of domestic and international election monitors and public opinion pollsters. Fourth, civil resisters implement plans for mass demonstrations if the election is stolen or rigged.[46] These protests are designed to expose the regime's fraudulent actions, stripping the proclaimed winner of any legitimacy. This nonviolent strategy has been successfully used in the recent "color revolutions" in Serbia, Georgia, Ukraine, and Kyrgyzstan.[47]

The electoral model inherently links civil resistance with democratization. Although we must remember that nonviolence can be used to establish other forms of government and that this study is concerned only with the overthrow of authoritarian states, the electoral model does makes an important contribution to our knowledge of democratization by focusing on human agency in a field dominated by structural models. For instance, one prominent approach, known as modernization theory, has argued that a nation's social, economic, and cultural characteristics are linked to its probability of democratizing. Specifically, wealthier nations with a high level of education and urbanization are more likely to democratize than less developed nations.[48] Yet modernization theory tells us very little about how democratization is actually achieved; in fact, critics note that economic development has more to do with democratic sustainability than with the formation of democratic polities.[49] Similarly, scholars who work within the so-called structural approach also overlook the role of citizen-based contentious action. Instead, this approach places primary emphasis on how changing class relations and the degree of inequality may encourage or inhibit democratization.[50]

Only the transition approach to democratization examines the role of human actors. But the focus in this model is on political elites who negotiate the transition to democracy and help consolidate it. In fact, the transition approach tends to view citizen revolts as an impediment to democratization instead of its driving force.[51] In short, democratization scholars have largely neglected an important part of the political transformation process. Hence, these scholars will find that the electoral model of nonviolent resistance adds a critical piece to our understanding of how authoritarian regimes or electoral autocracies are challenged, disrupted, and transformed.

Both models of nonviolent civil resistance will be evident in the cases that I explore in subsequent chapters. Some cases, such as China, East Germany, and Panama, reflect the Gandhian approach. Other cases, including Chile and Kenya, are more in line with the electoral model. In reality, however, most nonviolent revolutionary movements combine some elements of each approach. This is most evident in the Filipino case, where nonviolent activists initially used the electoral model. However, once Marcos stole the election, plans were developed to implement a Gandhian-style revolution.

Regardless of whether nonviolent revolutionaries take more of a Gandhian or electoral approach, the question remains: precisely which types of strategic action are most effective? Should movements focus on mobilizing large numbers of protesters to demonstrate the regime's lack of legitimacy? Or should they primarily concentrate on depleting a regime's finances through boycotts, general strikes, and tax resistance campaigns? Is a revolutionary movement more likely to win if it devotes most of its energy to persuading the international community to impose sanctions? Or should civil resisters place greatest emphasis on noncooperation in order to disrupt the regime's daily functions?

One recent study provides insight into these questions. In this study, social scientists Maria Stephan and Erica Chenoweth collected data on 323 violent and nonviolent resistance campaigns from 1900 to 2006. Only those campaigns that had a major disruptive political goal—such as the overthrow of a regime or the termination of a foreign occupation—were included.[52] Each campaign was determined to be a success (i.e., it met its stated objective), a limited success (i.e., the movement did not meet all its objectives but did make significant gains), or a failure (i.e., neither goals nor concessions were achieved). The authors then compared violent with nonviolent movements to discern which variables influenced whether a movement won or lost.[53] What they discovered is that violent and nonviolent movements exhibit distinctive dynamics, since the factors that strengthened one type of struggle did not have the same effect on the other. Three factors in particular had important but differential effects on armed versus unarmed struggles: (1) international support and sanctions, (2) security force defections, and (3) state-sponsored repression.

International Support and Sanctions

Movements often solicit the support of the international community.[54] Governments and nongovernmental organizations can offer financial assistance to resistance movements, strengthening their capacity to mobilize and sustain action.[55] But foreign support does not affect armed and unarmed revolutionary movements similarly. In Stephan and Chenoweth's study, international financial support had no measurable effect on the outcome of nonviolent insurrections. Yet this factor nearly tripled violent insurrectionary movements' chances for success.[56] Stephan and Chenoweth offer some possible reasons for this finding. They suggest that receiving direct financial assistance from an external group may delegitimize a local nonviolent movement as citizens question whether it is a front for foreign interests. If the broader population believes this to be true, it will be difficult for the movement to recruit participants. This may not be a serious problem for armed movements, which are not as dependent on widespread participation to achieve their goals. Another potential explanation is that nonviolent revolutionaries may rely too heavily on foreign contributions, neglecting efforts to build local support that can translate into mass mobilization.[57]

The international community may additionally fuel insurrectionary momentum by imposing sanctions on a regime. By weakening the state, sanctions can tip the odds in resisters' favor.[58] But empirical evidence indicates that sanctions do *not* always improve nonviolent movements' odds for victory.[59] Indeed, in some cases examined in this book, international sanctions harmed civil resistance movements. However, externally imposed sanctions double violent groups' changes of winning.[60] We need further research to understand why sanctions help armed movements but potentially hurt unarmed ones.

Security Force Defections and Unreliability

The different dynamics of violent and nonviolent revolutions are also evident in the impact of another factor: security force defections and refusals to repress. Stephan and Chenoweth found that unarmed insurrections were *46 times more likely to succeed* when security force defections occurred. Why? When police are unwilling to repress protesters, and when mutinous soldiers no longer protect rulers, even the most tyrannical leader is left vulnerable and powerless. But surprisingly, this factor is not critical to the success of armed insurrections. Stephan and Chenoweth's data reveal: "For violent campaigns . . . the effect of security force defections on campaign outcomes is insignificant."[61]

Although security force defections clearly have significant consequences for nonviolent revolutions, we know little about the causes of mutiny. Some may argue that troops defect when they sense that a movement is on the verge of victory and—fearing violent reprisals—they shift their loyalties to the winning side. Yet this assumes that mutiny is an effect of revolutionary success rather than the cause of it. Another perspective is that security officers have a transformation of consciousness, recognizing the merits of the movement or, at a minimum, recognizing that the corrupt regime must be jettisoned for the country to progress. But what factors lead to this shift in consciousness? That is, how do troops who have put their lives on the line for regime rulers suddenly decide to oppose them?

There is scant information about the motives, decision-making processes, and conditions that lead security officers to shift their allegiance from a regime to a revolutionary movement. We do know, however, that civil resisters often try to undermine troop loyalty through a combination of persuasive and deterrent techniques.[62] For instance, in the Ukraine's orange revolution (2004), activists provided incentives for defections by claiming that if the movement seized power, it would address officers' poor salaries and living conditions. Activists also worked with retired military leaders, who were uniquely positioned to win soldiers' trust. The retired officers convinced troops that there was widespread support for the movement's goals and that the regime's demise was inevitable. This led to a tacit agreement that officers would not crack down on civil resisters.[63]

Ukrainian activists also deterred security forces' attacks by raising the political and moral costs of repression. During the 2004 demonstrations in Kiev, civil resisters set up cameras to transmit video coverage 24 hours a day. If troops attacked the crowds, the repression would have been televised throughout the world, causing serious political repercussions. To raise the moral costs of repression, civil resisters maintained nonviolent discipline. They knew that officers would find it difficult to justify orders to repress if demonstrators were peaceful. Thus organizers trained participants to remain composed during tense confrontations. They also trained volunteers to diffuse any potential clashes between civil resisters and security forces.[64] These measures worked; security officers took no action against the demonstrators.

Repression

But not every movement is successful in deterring attacks and promoting mutiny. In many cases, police and soldiers do take repressive action.[65] Some authoritarian leaders may even try to annihilate a movement by killing leaders and massacring rank-and-file activists.[66]

But does repression have its intended effect? Sometimes. However, in the case of nonviolent movements, sanctions can actually backfire through a dynamic known as "political jiu-jitsu."[67] This term denotes the paradoxical consequences that occur when regimes use coercive measures against an unarmed population. Brutal sanctions expose the regime's viciousness, causing sympathy for the nonviolent resisters to increase and support for the ruler to decrease—both domestically and internationally.[68] In fact, traditional regime supporters, including business elites and security force members, may be so disturbed by these brutalities that they sever ties to the regime. Similarly, repression may mobilize new segments of the population who, in the face of such atrocities, become convinced that change is desperately needed.[69] Thus, state-sponsored repression can inadvertently strengthen an unarmed movement.

Armed revolutionary movements, however, are less likely to experience political jiu-jitsu or backfire during periods of repression. This is partly because rulers can depict revolutionaries as terrorists and the state as the defender of law and order, making it easier to justify repressive measures. Similarly, the international community is less likely to side with violent revolutionaries since nongovernmental organizations generally prefer to support unarmed groups.[70] Nations may be also be less likely to intervene when state repression is directed against violent revolutionaries since many countries are reluctant to get entangled in domestic conflicts, especially after debacles such as the U.S. involvement in Vietnam.

These claims about the differential effects of repression are substantiated by Stephan and Chenoweth's study. While they found that repression had no statistically significant effect on the outcomes of armed or unarmed struggles, they did find that nonviolent movements are more likely to achieve their goals in the face of repression. Specifically, they found that "in the face of regime crackdowns, nonviolent campaigns are more than six times likelier to achieve full success than violent campaigns that also faced regime repression."[71]

REMAINING QUESTIONS

This review of the literature reveals that the causes of violent and nonviolent revolutions are generally the same, but armed and unarmed struggles employ different strategies and have distinct dynamics. While Stephan and Chenoweth's research and other studies have significantly advanced our knowledge of strategic nonviolent struggles, there are still numerous issues that merit further investigation. In this book, I address the following questions to develop a more nuanced theory of how, when, and why civil resisters win.

The first question this book addresses is: *which types of nonviolent action have the greatest impact on authoritarian regimes?* To answer this, I focus on the six civilian resistance techniques identified by Gene Sharp: (1) refusing to acknowledge rulers' authority, (2) challenging ideologies of obedience to the state, (3) refusing to cooperate with laws and government expectations, (4) refusing to use citizens' skills to sustain state activities, (5) withholding material resources, and (6) undermining regimes' sanctioning power. I closely analyze which tactics were critical in turning the tide toward movement victory and which had more limited effects. In other words, by comparing the effects of each technique, I assess their relative strength.

The second question that I address is: *what strategies do rulers use to defeat nonviolent revolutions and preserve their power?* In this study, I explore how authoritarian leaders try to reestablish legitimacy and how they shore up the cultural and ideological influences that justify their rule. I analyze how they try to stop strikes and keep their economies afloat when boycotts or sanctions disrupt access to traditional revenue sources. I examine how rulers attempt to create divisions within oppositional movements and tarnish revolutionary leaders' credibility. To truly understand the strategies that help one side or another win, we must study the interactions of revolutionary movements *and* the rulers they seek to oust.[72]

Next, I address unanswered issues raised in Stephan and Chenoweth's study. Specifically, my third question is: *why don't international sanctions help nonviolent movements?* To complement Stephan and Chenoweth's quantitative study, I use a qualitative approach to see why external pressures may not benefit civil resisters. I also identify the pitfalls and problems that can arise when sanctions are put into effect. The fourth question I explore is: *why do some security force members defect while others remain loyal?* I examine the incentives and deterrents that movements use to induce mutiny, as well as rulers' efforts to keep their troops and police loyal.

In addition to these strategy-related questions, I seek to understand the other factors that can shape nonviolent revolutionary outcomes. Thus my fifth and final question is: *what factors can derail well-planned nonviolent revolts?* To address this question, I analyze movement dynamics and traits that can disrupt resisters' ability to act collectively. I also examine the constraints that leaders may face and the types of shifting conditions that may make it particularly difficult for movements to attain power. In general, studies of armed and unarmed revolutions have not given much attention to failed movements, and thus our knowledge in this area is particularly weak.

OVERVIEW OF THE BOOK

To get answers to these five questions, I compare successful and failed nonviolent insurrections that operated in parallel polities. In part I, I compare the 1989 Chinese uprising, which tragically ended in the Tiananmen Square standoff, with the 1989 East German revolt that overturned a long-standing socialist regime. In part II, I turn the focus to military dictatorships in Latin America. In this section, I analyze the failed movement to overthrow Panama's General Manuel Noriega (1987–1989) and the successful movement that ousted Chile's General Augusto Pinochet (1983–1988). Part III examines personal dictatorships in Kenya and the

Philippines. While dictators in both countries faced nonviolent uprisings in the 1980s, Kenyan President Daniel arap Moi retained power, but Philippine President Marcos was toppled.

By pairing movements that had different outcomes, I am able to shed light on the factors that contributed to the victory or failure of these non-violent revolutionary movements. I summarize my findings in the book's final chapter, where I conclude that, in these six cases, the factors that had the greatest influence on movement outcomes were (1) whether security forces defected or remained loyal and (2) whether international sanctions were involved. Regarding the first point, I move beyond merely confirming that security force defections are important to describe how they happen and what factors are linked to troops' decisions to shift allegiance. Regarding the second point, I find that international sanctions against the regime can actually hurt nonviolent movements rather than help them. I explain how external pressures may generate new support for a dictator if the sanctions are perceived as acts of foreign domination. International sanctions can also create problems by shifting the locus of power to international actors and undermining local resisters' power.

In the concluding chapter, I also highlight the effects of rulers' counter-strategies. We know authoritarian leaders often resort to repression to maintain control, but the cases in this book reveal that rulers' methods of holding onto power are often diverse and sophisticated. Any strategic struggle entails at least two parties, and thus we must explore not only the efforts of movements who challenge authoritarian regimes but also the rulers who seek to preserve them.

PART ONE

Nonviolent Revolts Against Socialist Regimes

CHAPTER 2

The Tiananmen Tragedy and the Failed Uprising in China

I n June 1989, troops encircled Tiananmen Square in Beijing, where several thousand workers and student protesters were huddled at the foot of the Monument to the People's Heroes. For weeks, students had non-violently struggled to transform the Chinese communist regime. They had boycotted university classes, mobilized mass demonstrations, staged hunger strikes, and occupied the square. Hundreds of thousands joined the students' call for political change. While they succeeded in capturing the world's attention, they did not usher in a new era of democracy. Instead, a brutal military crackdown caused the students to retreat and brought the movement to an abrupt halt.

Why did the students and their supporters fail? Was it a matter of poor timing, faulty strategy, or a weak organizational base? Was the state's repressive capacity simply overwhelming, eliminating any chance that David could overcome Goliath in this case? What role did structural factors play in the outcome of their struggle? To answer these questions, I begin with a brief overview of the movement's history.

DEMOCRATIC STIRRINGS

In the spring of 1988, Beijing University was celebrating its 90th anniversary. Administrators invited alumni to return for the event, and some departed from the official program by sponsoring a discussion on academic freedom and democracy. The conversation, held on a grassy spot near the university entrance, was so engaging that a group continued to hold these "lawn salons" on a weekly basis. By the following winter, "democracy salons" had spread to several other universities.[1]

Students had plenty to discuss at these meetings. Many were concerned about the economy, which was deteriorating because of flawed policies implemented by the Chinese Communist Party (CCP). Under Deng Xiaoping's leadership, the CCP had tried to stimulate economic development by permitting limited private enterprise and introducing modern technology. While this led to initial improvements, a financial crisis erupted in the late 1980s due to some critical mistakes. One mistake was that the government created a twofold structure that included (1) state-owned enterprises, equipped with skilled personnel and more advanced technology, and (2) private enterprises, mostly owned by rural residents with minimal education and limited technology. Government policies put state-owned industries at a disadvantage by taxing them at higher rates and rigidly controlling workers' wages. Thus state-owned enterprises declined, even though they had superior technology and intellectual capacity. This painted a grim picture for university students since crumbling state businesses did not offer enticing job prospects.[2]

This two-tiered enterprise system also generated rampant inflation and flourishing corruption. The government set quotas and fixed the price of state-manufactured products but allowed private companies to sell surplus goods on the free market for whatever price they could get. This caused inflation rates to rise to double-digit levels. It also enabled officials in the trading business to profit by accepting bribes to increase the quotas to state distributors. Those distributors could then sell the excess goods on the free market at exorbitant prices.[3] The general public was indignant. The government had promised that the reforms would improve people's financial lives; instead, most saw their purchasing power decline precipitously while food and other basic necessities were in seriously short supply. People were even more outraged by the stark contrast they observed between their own suffering and the huge profits that corrupt officials were reaping.[4]

In addition to the financial crisis, Chinese students were also growing frustrated that Deng's economic reforms were not accompanied by political reforms. Freedom of expression was extremely limited, and those who challenged the Chinese Communist Party's practices were often persecuted.[5] In the spring of 1988, one repressive episode was particularly on students' minds: the crackdown that had occurred nearly a decade earlier against "Democracy Wall" activists. The Democracy Wall movement started in 1978 when Deng released hundreds of political prisoners and, for the first time in decades, permitted popular action that was independent of state control. Taking advantage of this new freedom, citizens gathered for discussions along a brick wall near the Beijing bus depot. They covered the wall with hand-written posters addressing various social and political issues. After a while, those posters were transformed into magazines that were sold on location.[6]

Initially, Deng was not concerned about the Democracy Wall movement since it mostly engaged in magazine production of a limited scope. But everything changed in the spring of 1979, when some activists aimed their criticisms directly at party leadership. Activist Wei Jingsheng called on Deng to expand his goal of modernizing four areas—agriculture, industry, science, and technology—to include a fifth arena: politics. In a poster titled "The Fifth Modernization," Wei wrote:

> We want no more gods and emperors, no more saviors of any kind. We want to be masters of our own country, not modernized tools for the expansionist ambitions of dictators. . . . Democracy, freedom and happiness are the only goals of modernization. Without this fifth modernization, the other four are nothing more than a new-fangled lie.[7]

Not surprisingly, this outraged Deng, who subsequently imposed formal restrictions on Democracy Wall activities. In response, Wei denounced Deng as a "new dictator." Wei was quickly charged with the crime of producing counterrevolutionary propaganda and releasing state secrets. He was found guilty and sentenced to 15 years in prison.[8]

In 1988, there were new calls for Wei's release, which prompted discussions in the democracy salons. In February 1989, salon participants formed a working group to investigate the conditions of political detainees such as Wei. As a result of their investigation, students drafted a petition calling for democratization, freedom of speech, and the release of all political prisoners. They also developed plans to commemorate two events: the 10th anniversary of Wei's arrest and the 70th anniversary of the "May Fourth movement"—a movement of Chinese intellectuals and students who demanded democracy in the spring of 1929. Thus groups convened inside and outside the university, congregating in coffeehouses, restaurants, bookstores, and research centers. A culture of opposition was growing in these free spaces, and organizers recognized that the anniversary commemorations provided an opportunity to launch resistance activities.[9]

ACTION BEGINS

As it turned out, students did not have to wait for the anniversary events since protest erupted earlier than anticipated. It began with the unexpected death of Hu Yaobang on April 15, 1989. Hu had served as the Chinese

Communist Party's secretary general until January 1987, when he was dismissed for failing to crack down on student protests. This turned him into a hero for student activists, even though Hu had not advocated democratic rights.[10] But more important, Hu's death provided the pretext for students to mobilize. As one activist recalled, "Hu Yaobang himself wasn't that important. . . . But in China, a leader's death serves as an excuse for people to assemble. The party can't very well tell the people not to mourn a Party leader! Since a funeral is the only situation when people can assemble, you take advantage of the opportunity."[11]

Over the next days, thousands of student mourners marched to Tiananmen Square, where they placed a huge painted portrait of Hu at the Monument to the People's Heroes. By April 18, several hundred students staged a sit-in at the Great Hall of the People, located on the west side of Tiananmen Square, which houses the government's legislative and executive branches. The goal of their sit-in was to present a petition to Premier Li Peng. The petition called for an end to corruption and officials' privileges, increased funds for education, freedom of speech, and the right to dialogue with party officials, among other things. But Li Peng never came out to accept the petition; it was only after hours of waiting and kneeling that three members of the National People's Congress (NPC) finally received it. The next day, April 19, more than 100,000 gathered at the square in protest.[12]

Forming Movement Organizations

The sit-in and marches transformed student democracy salons into formal organizations. By April 24, Bejing students from 21 campuses came together to establish the Beijing Provisional Federation of Autonomous Students Association, which became the primary coordinating body for the movement. After electing Wang Dan and Wuer Kaixi as leaders, the federation's inaugural act was a boycott of classes. By the end of April, every university in Beijing was involved in the boycott except the People's University for Police Officers, the School for Diplomats, and the Public Security University.[13]

The government quickly condemned the students' activities in an editorial published on April 26 in the *People's Daily*. Aiming to discredit the students and tarnish their image, the editorial read:

> During the period of mourning . . . an extremely small number of people used the opportunity to fabricate rumors and attack leaders of the Party and state by name, and to deceive the masses. . . . Taking into consideration the broad masses' grief, the Party and government took a tolerant, restrained attitude to uncertain inappropriate words and actions of

emotionally excited young students. . . . But after the memorial was over, an extremely small number of people with ulterior motives continued to take advantage of the young students' mourning for Comrade Hu Yaobang. . . . In some universities and colleges, illegal organizations were established and tried to grab power from the student unions by force. Some even took over the schools' public address facilities by force. In some universities, students and teachers were encouraged to boycott classes; students were forcibly prevented from going to classes. . . .

If we take a lenient, permissive attitude toward this turmoil and just let it go, a situation of real chaos will emerge. . . . A China with a great hope and a great future would become a China wracked with turmoil, a China with no future. . . . Illegal demonstrations are forbidden. Going to factories, to the countryside, and to schools to link up with others is forbidden. Those who smash, loot, and burn must be punished according to the law. The normal right of students to attend classes must be guaranteed.[14]

Shortly thereafter, additional rumors spread, indicating that Deng was willing to use violence to stop the protests. "What do we have to fear?" he purportedly claimed. "They are only some 100,000 people; we have three million soldiers."[15]

Militarization

Indeed, Deng was in the process of militarizing the situation. During the first days of student protests, thousands of public security officers and members of the People's Armed Police were deployed. By the time Hu's official funeral ceremony was held, the People's Liberation Army was on full alert. Army commands within the Beijing Military Regime had been moved into "positions of readiness" around the city. And when class boycotts began, 20,000 troops from the 38th Group Army had moved into the Beijing area.[16]

But students had great hopes that they could win the troops' sympathy—especially since some soldiers had friends and family members in the movement. After one university group did research on the armed forces, they concluded that "new recruits were mainly peasants who benefited greatly from reforms. Having a personal investment in the new economy, they were unlikely to be brainwashed easily or to obey orders blindly. Another part of the Army was composed of young officers who had recently graduated from military schools. They were well educated and likely to be sympathetic to the Democracy Movement. . . . We felt that if we did not go too far, the Army would not present a real danger."[17]

Those feelings intensified when 150,000 students marched on April 27 to protest the *People's Daily* editorial. The line of police stationed outside

Beijing University did not stop the march. But when the students arrived at Tiananmen Square, they discovered hundreds of additional security officers, so they quickly changed their plans and marched past the square. As they continued on, the students encountered more police lines. But the police were unarmed, attempting to hold the crowd back merely by linking arms. The students were was able to break through police lines with relative ease, evoking cheers from the crowd. After that incident, the troops more or less stayed on the sidelines during the May 4 demonstrations.[18] This reinforced student beliefs that security forces would not engage in a crackdown.

Tactical Innovation

After sponsoring numerous marches that mobilized hundreds of thousands, students saw little in terms of concrete gains. Thus a few suggested embarking on a more radical form of action: hunger strikes. The action began on May 13 as students gathered at the Martyrs' Monument at Tiananmen Square. Within a few days, thousands of students were fasting. Since they refused both food and drink, it did not take long for them to collapse. Between May 14 and May 24, 32 hospitals in Beijing treated 9,158 cases of collapse; more than 8,200 of these individuals were hospitalized.[19]

The hunger strikes were remarkably effective at eliciting solidarity from the broader population, as more than a million people came to the square to show their support.[20] But the tactic also revealed a division within the movement. A militant faction was emerging, centered around Chai Ling, the leader of the hunger strikes. Other student leaders, who emphasized dialogue and negotiation, called for an end to the hunger strikes so that the movement could prepare for an upcoming meeting with the State Council spokesman.[21] When the meeting took place on May 14, it was disastrous. Craig Calhoun explains why:

> Ultimate blame for the breakdown of negotiations probably must rest with the government's failure to broadcast the dialogue [as it had earlier promised]—its refusal, in effect, to make it public—but the students' internal discord was also a problem. Some of the discord resulted from simple lack of organization and discipline—too many people tried to ask questions at once. More deeply, just as the government was split between those trying to find a way out of confrontation and those prepared to see it escalate (if only to justify repressing it), the students were split between those looking for a basis to withdraw from Tiananmen and build a long-term movement and those seeking to intensify the current confrontation.[22]

Since the negotiations failed, students chose to continue the hunger strikes and remain in Tiananmen Square during Soviet Premier Mikhail Gorbachev's highly anticipated visit, which was scheduled to begin the following day.[23] Gorbachev's visit was significant in that it marked the end of the Chinese-Soviet rift that developed in 1960 between Mao Zedong and Nikita Krushchev. Western journalists were present to cover the event, but protesters stole media attention away from formal diplomatic events. During Gorbachev's stay, Deng's hands were tied. He could not forcefully remove the students without tarnishing China's international image.[24]

Relations with Security Forces

As the movement gained global media coverage, students grew bolder. Their confidence was also related to their belief that the police and the military were increasingly sympathetic to their cause. Several police officials had marched to Tiananmen Square carrying a banner proclaiming, "The People's Police Love the People."[25] Staff members from the People's Liberation Army's General Logistics Department appeared during a march shouting, "We demand democracy!"[26] A soldier released an open letter to the students, proclaiming, "As soldiers, obeying orders, we cannot support you openly. But we are sons and brothers of the people, Chinese like yourselves. . . . You have suffered greatly, and we will not remain silent. Let this document support you. . . . I salute you with the greatest respect!"[27] And a bulletin was disseminated throughout the city that alleged: "The 38th Army has refused to enter Tiananmen Square and carry out clearing operations. . . . A young Beijing policeman in a letter to the students says, no matter what bureaucrat orders us to suppress you, we will not act."[28]

The troops' camaraderie was not completely surprising because students had made numerous appeals to security officers. To undermine troops' loyalty to the state, students repeatedly reminded them that their duty was to protect the people, not the Chinese Communist Party.[29] Similarly, open letters to soldiers were published, highlighting the discrepancy between corrupt officials' growing wealth and the declining purchasing power of soldiers' salaries.[30] The point was to show that soldiers and protesters shared similar economic hardships and frustrations. The following letter from student activists underscores these points:

> Greetings to all soldiers in the People's Liberation Army! Before everything else, please remember that you are the army of the people and the country, responsible for the

protection of their welfare. However, the people here believe in you, and ask you to look at the real nature of things.

> You will see that people are suffering, that the future of our nation lies in your support for the university students, some of whom have been on hunger strike for seven days.... We speak with the voice of the people, and want to replace economic manipulation and corruption by the bureaucracy with democracy and legality. What is wrong with that?... Soldiers! We love you, and your hands must not be stained with the people's blood. Facing you there are starving students supported by millions of people.... Soldiers and brothers, please think again, and do not violate the hopes of the people. Think carefully about your own families![31]

Finally, students emphasized the long-term moral consequences of repression: "If you dare to raise your hands against the people ... history will forsake you.... You will all remain condemned through the ages."[32]

Divisions within the Movement

By the middle of May, students were riding an emotional high from their successes: the restraint of security forces, an outpouring of support for hunger strikers, and successful international media coverage during Gorbachev's visit. But even during these elated moments, the movement's internal divisions and organizational challenges grew. The hunger strikers, led by Chai Ling, were fighting against student federation leaders Wang Dan and Wuer Kaixi for control of Tiananmen Square. Moreover, there was a huge influx of students from outside Beijing who were demanding a voice in decision-making processes. Frustrated that they were not fully included, they eventually formed their own associations. These divisions—between militant and dialogue-oriented Beijing students and between students from Beijing and those outside the city—led to escalating suspicion, distrust, and rumors. Such rumors were undoubtedly exacerbated by the fact that students in Tiananmen Square had little access to television or newspapers. While they were effective at getting their message out to the wider world, they were not very effective at communicating with one another.[33]

There were also escalating tensions between student protesters and workers who had come to the square to join the movement. Although workers had expressed support for the students early on and had raised funds for the hunger strikers, the students remained hostile and distant. In one report, a group of students linked arms to prevent workers from joining their ranks.[34] They also denied them access to loudspeakers and other equipment. And when the workers' leader, Han Dongfang, stood up to speak at the Monument to the People's Heroes, the students shouted him down, yelling: "Who is this guy? We are the vanguard! Get down, leave!"[35] Consequently, workers formed their own organization, the Beijing Workers Autonomous Federation, which drew in roughly 5,500 members.[36]

Divisions within the Government

As conflicts intensified among civil resisters, divisions were also growing among Chinese Communist Party elites, especially between Secretary General Zhao Ziyang and Premier Li Ping. Zhao and Li had been locking horns over policy issues for years. Zhao had pushed for increased reform and modernization in the military and economic sectors. In contrast, Li was a hard-liner who advocated slow and modest change. Zhao was losing stature as the nation's economic troubles grew, but the democracy movement drove an even deeper wedge between the two men. Zhao advocated leniency with the protesters while Li argued that the government should exercise its power to bring the situation under control.[37]

MARTIAL LAW

Deng, who served as chair of the Communist Party's Military Commission, sided with Li. This marked the end of Zhao's career and the party's turn toward a hard-line position. This hard-line approach became immediately evident as the party prepared to impose martial law. The news was leaked to the students on May 19; they decided to end the hunger strike so they could prepare for this next stage of confrontation.[38] The following day, May 20, Premier Li officially announced that martial law was in effect.

Students in Tiananmen Square prepared for a bloody confrontation that day. But it did not happen. As the People's Liberation Army headed for the city, tens of thousands of citizens built barricades to stop the tanks and trucks. Citizens offered soldiers food and drink and began pleading with them to not harm the protesters.[39] Student organizers had encouraged this, distributing leaflets that stated, "You must believe in the basic quality of the people's soldiers. Do careful ideological work with them. Don't just tell them to not come into the city: tell them to turn their guns and stand on the side of the people."[40] To nearly everyone's amazement, the soldiers did not push through the barricades or use the weapons they carried—from tear gas to handguns and missiles. Hence the troops remained at a standstill, unable to clear a path and unwilling to smash through the wall of people.

Within 45 hours, the troops were ordered to withdraw. But retreating proved to be nearly as difficult as advancing, since the masses did not allow them to move. Eventually, after being stuck in their trucks for five days, they were able to disengage. But the soldiers did not vacate the vicinity. They were stationed roughly one to two hours outside the city, where they set up logistics centers, implying that the confrontation was not over.

Although the students had temporarily won the battle to remain in the square, they were still divided over goals, strategies, and leadership. By this point, students from outside Beijing outnumbered local students.[41] The tensions between these groups boiled over on May 27, when Wang Dan of the Beijing Student Association announced the movement's 10-point program. In addition to the aims they had articulated earlier, the new program included a call to remove Premier Li Ping from office and to withdraw from Tiananmen Square after a mass rally on May 30. But students from outside provinces were determined to keep the occupation going until June 20, when the National People's Congress was scheduled to convene. Moreover, they wanted more direct confrontation with the government. Disillusioned with the lack of unity in the movement, several Beijing leaders, including Wang Dan, resigned.[42]

The conflicts took a toll on student resisters, who were quickly growing tired and discouraged. But the movement gained new momentum when the students heard that Shanghai demonstrators had carried a Statue of Liberty replica to City Hall. Students quickly contacted Beijing's Central Academy of Fine Arts, which agreed to make a similar statue dubbed the Goddess of Democracy. When the 37-foot-tall statue was unveiled at Tiananmen Square on May 30, the Goddess gave the movement a new confrontational edge. She was positioned to directly face the official portrait of Mao Zedong—a potentially defiant gesture.[43] Moreover, the sculptors had intentionally made her as large as possible so that it would be difficult to remove her. One sculptor stated, "If they decide to do this, they'll have to smash her into pieces, thereby exposing their antidemocratic faces."[44]

But the enthusiasm generated by the Goddess was short-lived, and the movement rapidly unraveled in the first days of June. Several factors contributed to this situation. First, the government began to stage its own counterdemonstrations; while those who attended readily admitted that they were paid by the government to participate, it still indicated that the support for the students was not universal. Second, on June 1, soldiers took control of the Beijing television and radio stations, along with telegraph and postal services. They used these media sources to warn residents to stay at home, emphasizing that soldiers and police officers had "the right to use all means to forcefully dispose of those who defy martial law regulations."[45] Third, the movement's internal tensions had escalated to the point that some provincial students attempted to kidnap Chai Ling, the hunger strike leader. The kidnappers were angry over allegations that Chai Ling had misappropriated movement funds. Obviously, movement leaders were not widely trusted or perceived as legitimate. Finally, a growing number of unemployed men had joined the protesters in Tiananmen Square. Some of these men had formed "dare to die" squads that roamed through the area, occasionally vandalizing government property. Their presence made the atmosphere in the square more aggressive and provocative.[46]

THE MILITARY CRACKDOWN

On June 3, the army made its fateful move into the city, entering from all directions. Once again, citizens surrounded the trucks, erected barricades, and obstructed the troops' movement. But the tone was different than it had been two weeks earlier, when the people forced the troops to retreat. With emotions running strong, protesters began to vent their anger at the security officers. When police at the Zhongnanhai compound used tear gas, the crowd began throwing rocks. In other areas, local residents spat on soldiers and kicked them. Protesters also captured military vehicles and then climbed onto tanks and trucks to display the helmets, clothing, and weapons confiscated from the soldiers. Behind the Great Hall of the People, demonstrators used tree branches to pound on the buses that carried the soldiers to the square. Near the Princess's Tomb, several miles west of downtown, protesters tried to jam iron rods into the tracks of armored personnel carriers and tossed Molotov cocktails to ignite the vehicles. And groups of men—mostly young and unemployed—roamed the streets, armed with hammers and wooden clubs, shouting at soldiers. In response, student leaders appealed for nonviolence, but others clearly did not share their commitment to peaceful means.[47]

Shortly thereafter, the troops start shooting. One young man described what he witnessed:

Without warning, the troops fired on us. People cursed, screamed, and ran. In no time, seventy or eighty people had collapsed around me. Blood spattered all over, staining my clothes. . . . We saw bodies scattered all along the road. I must have seen several hundred bodies, mostly young people, and including some children. As the army reached Liu-bukou, an angry crowd of over ten thousand surged forward to surround the troops. This time the soldiers turned on the people with even greater brutality. The fusillades from machine guns were loud and clear. Because some of the bullets used were the kind that explode within the body when they struck, the victims' intestines and brains spilled out. I saw four or five such bodies. They looked like disemboweled animal carcasses. I recall one scene clearly. A man with a Chinese journalist's identity badge on his shirt, waving a journalist's identity card covered with blood rushed toward the troops screaming, "Kill me! Kill me! You've already killed three of my colleagues!" Then I saw them shoot him and when he fell, several soldiers rushed over to kick him and to slash at him with their bayonets.[48]

All over the city, troops resorted to violence to clear the path to Tiananmen Square, killing thousands in the process.

When word of the massacre reached students and workers at Tiananmen Square, there were mixed reactions. Some found it hard to believe that the People's Army would turn against the people. Others prepared to fight as Beijing student leader Wuer Kaixi told the crowd of resisters, "The citizens have the right to defend themselves, and the only way to do so is with force."[49] Others appealed for consistent nonviolence. One individual from the Beijing Workers Autonomous Federation implored, "When the Dare-to-Die squads find themselves face-to-face with the soldiers, the first thing they must try is persuasion. With our songs, our truth, and our sense of justice—persuade, persuade, and persuade again." This call for nonviolence was echoed by Chai Ling, who called out: "Many students, workers, and ordinary citizens have asked the student command for permission to use weapons. We share their rage at the attack on the innocent. But we remain true to the . . . principle of peaceful demonstration."[50] As Chai spoke, some turned in guns and Molotov cocktails while others gathered whatever they could find to defend themselves against the troops.

The troops finally arrived at Tiananman Square around 1:30 A.M., armed with AK-47 automatic rifles. They broadcast a warning over loudspeakers, stating that the People's Liberation Army had shown restraint long enough and was now prepared to crack down on all those who were defying martial law. Students and workers were ordered to leave the Square or face the consequences. When soldiers fired warning shots, protesters huddled together at the foot of the Monument to the People's Heroes. Once again, students and workers were divided about their next move. Should they evacuate or defend the occupation at all costs? Chai Ling spoke, "There is a story . . . about a clan of a billion ants who lived on a mountain. One day there was a terrible fire on the mountain. The only way for them to escape was to hold each other tight into a ball and roll down the mountainside. But the ants on the outside of the ball would be burnt to death. . . . We are the ones who stand on the outside of our nation. Only our sacrifice can save it, only our blood can open the eyes of our people and the rest of the world." But a leader from the Beijing Workers Autonomous Federation countered, "We must all leave here immediately . . . for a terrible bloodbath is about to take place. There are troops surrounding us on all sides and the situation is now extraordinarily dangerous. To wish to die here is no more than immature fantasy."[51]

As the protesters debated, a couple of individuals—a rock singer and an intellectual who had just embarked on a new hunger strike—negotiated with the army. Two officers spoke with them, reiterating the warning: "There is only one way the troops will not, by mistake, do any harm to the students in the Square while carrying out our orders. The students and other people must leave unconditionally. You have until daybreak. The southeast corner of the Square has been left open."[52] When the two returned to report on their conversation with the officers, they told the crowd that they must evacuate since they had no remaining bargaining chips and too many lives had already been lost. Student leader Li Lu proposed a vote. Since it was still dark, they conducted a voice vote of either "Evacuate" or "Stand Firm." Although it was close, those wishing to evacuate won out. Within 25 minutes, all the students had left the square.[53] The occupation was over and so, too, was the movement.

Over the next few days, reports of casualties ranged wildly—from government claims of 300 killed to the Chinese Red Cross's estimate of 3,000 deaths.[54] One thing was clear: a massacre had happened. While some citizens spoke of revenge, many were simply trying to get news about current developments. This was difficult since rumors were rampant. These included stories that a young man shot Li Peng in retaliation for the death of his girlfriend. Another rumor was that the 38th Army, which had refused to repress citizens, was battling for power against the 27th Army that had been responsible for much of the slaughter. Still other stories spread that universities were under military occupation.[55]

By June 7, it was evident that no serious political or military battling was taking place and the country would not sink into civil war. The political hard-liners, led by Deng Xiaoping and Li Peng, had defeated the uprising, and protesters were no longer on the streets. To ensure that such insubordination did not occur again, the government arrested hundreds of people and court-martialed soldiers who refused orders to arrest. While the movement had been brought to an end, the memory of the uprising would live on.

FACTORS CONTRIBUTING TO THE UPRISING'S FAILURE

Why did the movement fail? In the beginning, student protesters appeared to have several factors in their favor.[56] First, the weak economy made the government vulnerable since escalating inflation and corruption angered a significant portion of the population. Second, there was a division within the Chinese Communist Party between those, such as Zhao Ziyang, who sought more wide-ranging reforms and party hard-liners, represented by Li

Peng. Third, an easing of political repression in the mid-1980s enabled free spaces to emerge in the form of democracy salons. This fostered a culture of opposition and provided the basis for initial mobilization. Finally, the historic visit of Soviet Premier Mikhail Gorbachev in the spring of 1989 provided an important political opportunity as a large number of foreign journalists traveled to Beijing. This increased students' chances of broadcasting their struggle to the wider world and potentially winning the support of international community members.

Students acted on these advantageous conditions, quickly forming movement organizations and mobilizing resistance. Protesters used multiple methods over the movement's seven-week life span, including sit-ins, boycott of classes, mass demonstrations, hunger strikes, negotiation, and nonviolent obstruction of troops. Thus the movement's downfall was not due to a lack of tactical diversity, as some nonviolent theorists suggest.[57] Rather, it was partly due to students' failure to withdraw key forms of support from the Chinese Communist Party.

Protesters were able to persuade a large number of Beijing residents to question the authority of the regime. This was evident as hundreds of thousands came out during demonstrations to denounce the government's failed policies and to call for the removal of Premier Li Peng. It was also apparent in the widespread disgust at the state's claim that only 300 individuals (100 troops and 200 civilians and students) had died during the June 4 crackdown. By June 9, an army general revised that estimate, claiming that no students had died. From firsthand experience, many Beijing residents knew that this was a blatant lie, deepening their conviction that Chinese Communist Party leaders lacked legitimacy.

Civil resisters also withdrew cooperation from the regime by refusing to comply with certain laws. Despite official prohibitions against demonstrating and congregating during the martial law period, people defied orders and remained in Tiananmen Square. Furthermore, this defiance indicates that protesters no longer held mentalities of obedience toward the Chinese Communist Party.

But the other three civil resistance techniques—withholding skills, withdrawing material resources, and undermining the state's sanctioning power—were not successfully used in the uprising. At one point, activists did propose a general strike, which could have weakened the government. But it never materialized.[58] This was partly because student activists alienated workers, pushing them to the margins of the movement. Despite the fact that tens of thousands of workers joined the demonstrations and one trade union donated $27,000 for medical aid to the hunger strikers, students still considered themselves the rightful vanguard of the uprising.[59] One sympathetic worker stated:

The workers could see that participation was being strictly restricted by the students themselves, as if the workers were not qualified to participate. . . . The issues that the students raised had nothing to do with the workers. For example, Wuer Kaixi in his speeches only talked about the students. If he had mentioned the workers as well, appealed to the workers . . . in a sincere manner, the workers might really have come out in a major way.[60]

If the workers had been welcomed and fully incorporated into the movement, the situation might have played out differently. When workers fail to show up at factories, industrial productivity drops, and the economy suffers. When employees refuse to pick up garbage or run transportation systems, the government finds it imperative to act. But when students do not attend classes, the regime does not become more vulnerable.

Another reason a general strike never happened was that managers of state enterprises threatened to fire anyone who participated.[61] But independent entrepreneurs could have gone on strike without fear of such sanctions since they operated autonomously. And many of them were highly sympathetic to the student movement. In fact, a group of entrepreneurs staged a sit-in in solidarity with the students, and many donated funds that enabled the student protesters to buy equipment such as megaphones and fax machines. Another group formed the "Flying Tiger Brigade" that navigated the city on motorbikes to deliver news of troop movements to protesters. Despite their support and assistance, the students held disparaging attitudes toward the commercial entrepreneurs, viewing them as amoral and untrustworthy.[62] When they refused to build a working coalition with them, they lost an opportunity to weaken the regime through the withdrawal of skills and material resources.

Student activists also failed to undermine the state's repressive capacity. This can be done in two ways: (1) by undermining the loyalty of troops and encouraging mutiny and (2) by refusing to be deterred by punishments, persisting through repression. The students did initially win sympathy from police officers and soldiers. When citizens blocked troops from advancing after martial law was declared on May 20, the soldiers did not resort to violence because of the connection they felt to the people. Several high-ranking military officers—including Defense Minister Qin Jiwei, former Defense Minister Zhang Aiping, former Higher Military Academy Director Xiao Ke, former Naval Chief Ye Fie—and 100 others publicly stated that they were sympathetic to the movement.[63]

Why, then, did soldiers shoot on June 3 and 4? There are several answers. One reason is that Chinese Communist Party leaders were aware of the troops' reluctance to take action against the people. So they mobilized vast numbers of additional soldiers—estimated between 150,000 and

350,000—mostly from units outside the area.[64] These newcomers had not been subjected to protesters' appeals over the previous weeks, and thus they were not as hesitant to follow orders. There were even reports that some troops were brought from Inner Mongolia and thus did not understand the Mandarin Chinese spoken in Beijing, making them relatively immune to protesters' pleas.[65] Furthermore, some of the new troops had little knowledge of what had transpired; state control of the media meant that news of Tiananmen Square activities did not reach every region. Thus, they had little reason to doubt the validity of the orders they received.

Another reason troops obeyed orders to use violence that night was that they faced hostile crowds. Unlike earlier events, when protesters generally had peaceful interactions with soldiers, the evening of June 3 was different. Nonviolent discipline was not maintained. People threw bricks and Molotov cocktails, damaged army vehicles, berated and cursed soldiers. Although such instances were not widespread, they were sufficient to heighten emotions of anger and frustration while changing the atmosphere to an aggressive one, which probably put the soldiers on the defensive. Moreover, while peaceful protests had made it difficult for troops to justify the use of force, this was no longer the case. Some soldiers truly felt that the situation was now out of control and only a heavy hand could save the nation from complete chaos—a line that senior party officials repeatedly iterated.

The aggressive turn among protesters was undoubtedly linked to fatigue from nearly two months of opposition, combined with the infiltration of government *agents provocateurs*.[66] But it additionally reflected weak movement leadership that had not sufficiently prepared people to remain peaceful. In fact, student leaders varied considerably in their commitment to nonviolence, and some argued that resisters had the right to use force against attacking troops. Thus all the divisions within the movement— between workers and students, between Beijing students and those from outside provinces, and between militant and dialogue-oriented protesters— meant that leaders were not able to develop an effective plan to deal with the outbursts of hostility and the looming repression. While the Chinese Communist Party overcame its divisions, with hard-liners gaining ascendancy over reformists, the students did not overcome theirs. This gave the government the upper hand. Soldiers no longer saw confusion from the top; they had clear orders to proceed. Protesters, on the other hand, did not have clear guidance, and subsequently people responded independently and, in some cases, aggressively.

In addition, leaders were unable to minimize the impact the repression had on the movement's future. To generate the backfire dynamic—whereby people are so outraged by a regime's brutality that they fight harder— movement leaders need to frame the situation in a manner that channels outrage into action. In other words, student leaders needed to interpret the crackdown as a temporary setback or even a sign of movement success since regimes typically resort to these measures when they fear their power is slipping away. Moreover, they needed to have provisions in place to enable survivors to persist. But none of the leaders offered these things, in part because the repression was so swift and comprehensive that the movement's leadership was decimated and incapable of responding. As a result, the repression did lead to the movement's demise.

Undoubtedly, other factors played a role as well. For example, protesters' geographical confinement in Tiananmen Square made it easier to physically control and repress the movement. Moreover, since the Chinese government was not highly dependent on other sources for financial support and military reinforcement—as many Eastern European countries were on the Soviet Union—they were less susceptible to any pressures from the international community.

But the CCP's countermoves were one of the most important factors that shaped the struggle's outcome. Initially, the Chinese government tried to undermine movement support by publishing an editorial that denounced student activists as disloyal malcontents driven by ulterior motives. The CCP also tried to amplify its own legitimacy by sponsoring counterdemonstrations. These moves had little effect, and support for the Tiananmen Square resisters continued to grow. But party leaders did find an effective way to reverse the waning commitment of security force members, thereby ensuring that they could carry out a crackdown. The government accomplished this through a twofold method. First, they brought in tens of thousands of outside troops who had not been subject to appeals over the previous weeks of protests. Second, the CCP allegedly promoted hostile actions among citizen supporters. This, coupled with the movement's lack of ability to maintain nonviolent discipline, meant that it was easier for troops to justify the use of repression. Furthermore, the crowd's hostility decreased the likelihood of defections. In fact, when one soldier did defect, angry citizens beat him to death.[67] As other soldiers witnessed this assault, any thoughts of defection were probably eliminated.

The outcome of this movement, therefore, reflects a combination of factors. The movement was unable to overcome internal divisions, facilitate troop defections, and maintain nonviolent discipline. But the Chinese Communist Party also contributed to this outcome by strategically shoring up its sanctioning powers.

CHAPTER 3

The Collapse of the East German State

At the beginning of 1989, numerous scholars and political commentators viewed the German Democratic Republic as a model of stability. Of all the Soviet-style states, it was considered the least likely to collapse.[1] Erich Honecker, head of the East German government, proclaimed that the Berlin Wall would be intact for at least 100 years.[2] Yuli Kvitsinky, Soviet Ambassador to Bonn, admitted that not a single Soviet leader anticipated that the East German state would soon disintegrate.[3] In fact, only 5 percent of East Germans said they had sensed a civil revolt was on the horizon, and 76 percent admitted that they were completely surprised by it.[4] But it happened. And when citizens stormed the Berlin Wall in November that year, they inspired others across Eastern Europe, who unleashed a wave of civil resistance that transformed the region.

HISTORICAL CONTEXT

Before exploring how the East German government was nonviolently dismantled, I begin with a brief historical overview. East Germany, formally known as the German Democratic Republic (GDR), was formed in the aftermath of World War II when Germany was partitioned into four zones, occupied by the militaries of Great Britain, the United States, France, and the Soviet Union. Although this arrangement was to be a temporary measure, it quickly became evident that the country would remain divided; the Western zones were allied with NATO nations while the Eastern zone implemented Soviet-Stalinist practices. By 1949, the East German zone became an independent state, headed by the Communist Party known as the SED (Sozialistische Einheitspartei Deutschlands or the Socialist Unity Party).[5]

The SED was intolerant of groups that hindered its socialist agenda. Religious organizations, in particular, suffered from state repression. In 1952 and 1953, numerous ministers and church leaders were arrested, incarcerated, or exiled. Three hundred members of church youth organizations were expelled from high school on false accusations of espionage.[6] Harsh measures were also taken against other "internal enemies." For instance, in Leipzig, two workers were convicted of belittling Stalin and were given four- and six-year prison sentences. The repression instigated a wave of emigration to West Germany. In 1951, nearly 166,000 people left the GDR; by 1952, the number increased to more than 182,000. The following year, over 331,000 citizens fled.[7]

Emigration also rose in response to the government's drastic economic policies. The SED collectivized private farms and set unrealistic productivity requirements, which alienated many farmers. Additionally, the government attempted to spur industrialization through burdensome work quotas and lower consumption levels. Basic goods were rationed, including meat, sugar, linens, electricity, and coal. These austerity measures led to occasional food riots, but the SED continued to increase work quotas. Industrial production accelerated, but the economy still struggled due to high postwar reparation costs and large military expenditures. Thus citizens put in long workdays but found their purchasing power decimated. Consequently, a number of strikes erupted throughout the country as workers called for immediate change.[8]

By the spring of 1953, Soviet leaders pressured the SED to alter their economic measures, fearing that citizen unrest and emigration would cause national destabilization. Hence the East German government conceded that it had implemented socialist policies too quickly. It introduced a "New Course" that included many reforms but kept the stringent work quotas intact.[9] Ironically, the new course did not appease the population; it actually inspired an uprising.

The June 1953 uprising began when shop stewards at a Berlin construction site launched a sit-down strike to protest work quotas. During the strike, they drafted a resolution, but they feared that whoever delivered it would be sanctioned. They decided to present it to the government collectively. On June 17, they marched down the streets of Berlin, holding a banner that read: "We demand a quota reduction." Others spontaneously joined them—from off-duty police officers to streetcar passengers. As they marched, they chanted: "We want free elections!" and "We want to be free human beings, not slaves!"[10] When the crowd arrived at the Council of Ministers, someone suggested a general strike. The next day, strikes and demonstrations erupted throughout East Germany. Years of pent-up anger surfaced as citizens stormed government offices, destroyed SED documents, tore socialist propaganda posters off walls, and mocked members of the secret police.[11] Official reports estimated that nearly half a million employees participated in the strikes and 418,000 participated in demonstrations that day.[12] Everyone was astonished that this uprising erupted in such a quick and spontaneous manner. Within a matter of hours, a construction worker strike turned into a nationwide revolt.[13]

The East German government tried to gain control of the situation. When demonstrators were not readily subdued, the Soviet military commander in Berlin declared martial law. He ordered Soviet troops to disperse demonstrations, secure borders, and occupy factories. Public gatherings of more than three people were prohibited under threats of severe punishment. But this did not stop the uprising. Despite the presence of tanks and troops, 44,000 people demonstrated in Berlin, while those forced back to the factories called in sick or engaged in work slowdowns and sabotage. In response, the Soviets cracked down ruthlessly. By the end of August, 13,000 people had been arrested. Of these, 1,400 received life sentences, and 200 were executed.[14]

Over the following years, security forces vigilantly kept a lid on any protest, and ordinary citizens had few avenues for challenging SED policies.[15] With little hope for reform, more and more people emigrated. By the beginning of the 1960s, more than 2.5 million had fled,[16] causing the SED to tighten its borders. In August 1961, barbed wire and wooden barricades sealed off the border between East and West Berlin; soon, concrete blocks made the border even less penetrable.

In addition to restricting movement, the East German government increased its surveillance of citizens, primarily through the Ministry of State Security, also known as the Stasi. After the June 1953 uprising, Stasi ranks grew steadily. Full-time staff climbed from 1,100 in 1950 to more than 19,000 by 1961. By the late 1980s, the number of Stasi staff had exploded to 91,104. The number of secret informers also expanded, culminating in the 1980s at 176,000 citizens who served as the eyes and ears of the Stasi by reporting the activities of friends and neighbors.[17] Another 1 to 2 million informers worked on a free-lance basis with the government.[18] Once people were identified as enemies of the state, the Stasi spread false information about them and—with the aid of secret informers who were present in every official organization in the country—orchestrated career and personal failures.[19] This omnipresent surveillance created a climate of suspicion and apprehension, minimizing any overt opposition to the SED.[20] One pastor commented, "This was an ever present fear somehow; it permeated all walks of life, this haunting fear that you could be arrested anytime, right off the street. The Stasi heard everything, knew everything, were everywhere, and everybody knew that."[21]

Although the Stasi largely silenced civic organizations, it did not completely eliminate critical voices. But in an authoritarian regime, oppositional cultures and ideologies will grow only in areas that are not directly controlled by the state. In East Germany, there was only one real free space: the Protestant Church.[22]

In many regards, the Protestant Church was an unlikely spot for an insurrectionary movement to emerge because East Germany was a largely secular society. In the 1980s, only 15 percent of East German children were baptized and only 10 percent of the population reported an active religious faith.[23] Despite low participation rates, the Union of Lutheran Churches[24] became a convening point for civic groups concerned about peace, human rights, and environmental issues. Those interested in peace were drawn to the church-sponsored Peace Decade—a 10-day program held each November that entailed prayer services, workshops, and dialogue about nuclear weapons, militarism, and peace.[25] And after SED leaders signed the Helsinki Declaration of Human Rights, some congregations sponsored human rights groups. For example, an East Berlin congregation permitted activists to use church facilities to produce reports on international human rights standards and SED violations, which were then distributed with a cover page designating "For Internal Church Use Only." Although the Stasi were aware of this information network, they were unable to suppress it because of the church's protective coverage.[26] Other churches established environmental libraries. The first was formed in 1987 at East Berlin's Zion Church, where activists reported on the state's environmental abuses. Within two years, the number of church-based environmental libraries had grown to more than 20.[27]

Why was the church permitted to sponsor such activities while other civic groups were repressed? In 1978, church leaders struck a deal with the East German government. Socialist Party chief Erich Honecker agreed to make churches a protected domain—perhaps because the church's dwindling membership numbers indicated that this institution posed no real threat to the state.[28] In exchange, religious leaders consented to operating as "church within socialism," conducting their ministries within the system rather than against it.[29] As a result of this agreement, the police were not permitted to interfere with any church-sponsored activities. There were some violations, such as the raid on Berlin's Zion Church in the fall of 1987, where police destroyed the environmental library and arrested seven activists on charges of producing illegal publications.[30] Despite such periodic transgressions, it was far safer for activists to organize inside the church than outside its semiprotected boundaries. Thus Protestant congregations were the only free spaces available for oppositional organizing. As one scholar observed, "It is beyond question that the churches offered a haven, a shelter for the growing number of oppositional groups. Within this haven the church buildings and parish houses opened opportunities for not only religious inspiration, but for sharing uncensored information and for airing opinions and criticisms."[31]

But how did the church transform itself from a free space to the central mobilizing force in this nonviolent revolt? A closer look at the Leipzig churches, which were at the forefront of the movement, sheds light on this question. Leipzig was home to a larger-than-average number of activist pastors. Two of these pastors were Christian Führer, who took over St. Nicholas Church in downtown Leipzig in 1980, and Wolfgang Groeger, who assumed responsibility for Leipzig's youth parish office in 1981. Under Führer and Groeger's leadership, roughly 20 to 25 groups emerged at St. Nicholas, focusing on peace, justice, human rights, and environmental concerns. One of these was the Working Group in the Service of Peace (Arbeitsgruppe Friedensdienst), largely comprised of former "Bausoldaten"—conscientious objectors who worked in army-controlled construction projects as an alternative to military service.[32] When Dresden pastor Christoph Wonneberger proposed the idea of peace prayer services, this working group immediately responded, holding the first service on September 13, 1981. Pastor Führer agreed to make this a weekly event, and thus peace prayers were held at St. Nicholas church each Monday at 5:00 P.M.[33]

While attendance was initially quite limited, the peace prayer services gained momentum when Pastor Wonneberger was transferred from Dresden to St. Luke's church in Leipzig in 1985. Within a short time, Wonneberger assumed responsibility for the services, which followed a format of Bible readings, hymns, prayer requests, exchange of information, meditation, and free time for presentations and discussion.[34] This format provided plenty of room for activists to promote their agenda, and thus by 1988, peace prayer services were drawing in approximately 700 people a week.[35] This growth was partly fueled by concern over the number of medium-range nuclear missiles stationed on German soil. But it also reflected Pastor Führer's effort to reach out to nonreligious individuals. He had placed a sign in front of St. Nicholas Church that read, "Open for all." He also called a meeting for individuals seeking to emigrate; he was startled when he sent out invitations to 50 people and 800 showed up.[36] Many of these people began attending the peace prayer services. As one scholar observed, "The message had obviously reached beyond religious circles: if you want to voice your grievances, St. Nicholas on Monday evening is the assembly point."[37]

But as participation expanded, Pastors Führer and Wonneberger realized that they were tapping into citizens' deep resentment toward the state. They knew that this anger could easily erupt into political resistance, and when it did, they wanted it to take a nonviolent form. Thus they established the Initiative Group for Life (IGL), which offered workshops and training in nonviolent direct action.[38]

The Initiative Group for Life soon decided to move from training to action. Around midnight on January 12, 1989, IGL activists quietly distributed thousands of leaflets calling for a demonstration at Leipzig's City Hall. The date was chosen to coincide with a commemoration for Rosa Luxemburg and Karl Liebknecht, who 70 years earlier proclaimed: "Freedom means always the freedom of those who disagree."[39] Within hours, police got word of the demonstration and arrested a dozen activist leaders. That did not deter a crowd of 800 people from gathering at City Hall on January 17 for a silent march. Police attacked with nightsticks and jailed nearly 100 participants. Although the marchers never reached their destination, this action marked an important turning point: Leipzig had become the national center for opposition, and resistance was now taking place outside church parameters.[40]

REVOLUTIONARY CONDITIONS

Leipzig's churches provided fertile ground for oppositional activities, but we must also examine the other elements that generated revolutionary conditions in the late 1980s. One important factor was the East German government's vulnerability to external influences and changes. From its inception, the nation was inextricably linked to the Soviet Union in terms of economic subsidies, military reinforcement, and political policies. Thus when Soviet leader Mikhail Gorbachev came to power in 1985, his "new thinking" reforms had repercussions that emanated to the German Democratic Republic. Gorbachev proposed a dual program of economic reconstruction (*perestroika*) and greater political openness (*glasnost*). Confronted by an ailing Soviet economy, he also pushed for détente with Western nations in hopes of reducing exorbitant military expenditures that had been propelled by the arms race.[41]

Soviet reforms did not initially evoke much reaction from East German officials, but SED leaders became deeply concerned when Gorbachev announced that Eastern Europe's communist regimes would be granted greater autonomy and Soviet forces in the region would be dramatically reduced. Despite assurances that the Soviet Union was not abandoning the GDR, SED leaders knew that they could no longer rely on the type of military intervention that the Kremlin provided during the 1953 uprising. Thus

Soviet withdrawal of economic and military support decreased the regime's power and increased the opposition movements' leverage.[42]

A second factor that made the East German regime vulnerable was its deteriorating economy. Once ranked as the 10th leading industrial power in the world, the German Democratic Republic had slipped to the 26th spot by 1988.[43] There were a number of reasons for this: the nation's inability to keep pace with technological developments, the high cost of repairing infrastructural decay, and declining demand for East German products. Moreover, by 1989, the nation had accumulated a foreign debt of $26.5 billion.[44] While party officials were able to hide the country's economic problems from the world by manipulating statistics, its own citizens were acutely aware of the state's financial troubles by the lack of consumer goods and the substandard quality of services. For instance, even in East Berlin, the nation's prize metropolitan area, mail delivery within the city took a solid week, and customers seeking to install a phone line faced a 10-year wait. Throughout the entire country, basic goods such as clothing, furniture, and shoes were difficult to come by. Thus the implicit agreement—that political quiescence could be bought through financial well-being—no longer held true.[45]

NONVIOLENT ACTION UNFOLDS

Emigration: The "Exit" Tactic

By the spring of 1989, conditions were ripe for an uprising. Opposition had sprouted under the church's protection while an economic downturn and Gorbachev's new policies undercut the East German government's capacity to subdue an uprising. But the triggering event that launched the movement occurred in May, when Budapest's reformist government dismantled some guard posts and barbed-wire fences at the Austro-Hungarian border. Already that year, 46,000 people had received exit visas to leave East Germany legally.[46] But when Western media groups broadcast news of a weak spot in the iron curtain, thousands of East Germans slipped through illegally over the course of the summer. Unlawful emigration grew exponentially after September 11, when Hungarian officials chose to fully open their border to Austria and to unilaterally terminate their agreement with the SED to return all East Germans caught in escape attempts. Within three days of the Hungarian policy change, 15,000 people fled through Hungary to Austria and on to various Western destinations. Over the next couple of months, the number would rise to roughly 100,000.[47]

This mass exodus through Hungary inspired a second exit strategy. Thousands occupied West German diplomatic offices in Prague, Budapest,

Warsaw, and other cities, where they filed for refugee status. By the end of September, the two German states made provisions to transport these individuals by train to the West. When news of this plan was broadcast, thousands more attempted to board the trains. In all, approximately 15,000 people left the German Democratic Republic through office occupations.[48] Media coverage of crowded diplomatic offices and trains packed full of people eager to leave East Germany undermined the SED's reputation for being a model socialist state.

But how does emigration—the tactic referred to as *exiting*—constitute part of a nonviolent strategy? The mass departure of young East Germans had devastating social and economic consequences for the state. More than 80 percent of those who fled were under the age of 40, and most were professionals or semiskilled laborers; in fact, 90 percent had completed an apprenticeship or some type of formal training.[49] One study estimated that the loss in working potential was around 10 billion German marks for every 10,000 emigrants.[50] Not only did this constitute an unintentional withdrawal of material resources that the state desperately needed but also it meant that skills and labor were withheld. Roland Bleiker aptly described the situation:

> [T]he human drain created chaotic situations throughout the country. Many spheres, such as industry, the service sector, public transportation, and hospitals either totally collapsed or functioned with great difficulty. The employment of army units in some of the affected sectors was not sufficient to replace the lacking civilian work force. "Exit" had torn holes in the East German society to the extent that even the senile and anachronistic leadership had to stop pretending that the country was still on a straight and glorious path to Communist utopia.[51]

East German leaders recognized the severity of the problem, referring to it as a massive bloodletting. But they were divided over how the situation should be handled. In the fall of 1989, after several weeks of deliberation, the government finally announced that it was suspending travel to Czechoslovakia, which was the sole country that East Germans could visit without a visa. Since this was the central route to Hungary (and on to the West), they hoped this would stop the outflow.

Demonstrations: The "Voice" Tactic

The massive exiting, combined with news about citizen movements in Poland and Czechoslovakia, emboldened opposition groups to express their dissent on the streets, not just within the church. Leipzig activists decided to hold a demonstration outside St. Nicholas Church right after the peace prayer services that, after a summer break, were scheduled to resume on September 4. More than a thousand people attended the prayer service and demonstration that evening. The following week, September 11, police cordoned off St. Nicholas square. When a thousand prayer service participants exited and joined another thousand demonstrators, security officers ordered them to immediately disperse. As the crowd hesitated, police aggressively arrested 100 people. In response, churches throughout East Germany held vigils to pray for the release of the prisoners. During the September 25 peace prayer service, Pastor Führer read aloud a letter denouncing the police actions and the 2,000 people in attendance applauded loudly. Then Pastor Wonneberger emphasized the necessity of remaining strong but nonviolent. As he concluded the service, the people exited singing, "We Shall Overcome." Outside, the crowd grew to 4,000. But for unknown reasons, few arrests were made that night.[52]

East German officials met during the last week in September to devise plans to stop the demonstrations. Their strategy had four components. First, they would mobilize the SED militia to occupy downtown Leipzig. Second, they pressured church officials to remove activist pastors and keep the prayer services focused exclusively on spiritual matters, not political issues. But Bishop Hempel refused, replying that the SED ought to deal with the nation's problems, not the symptoms. Third, the state would undertake a propaganda campaign to depict demonstrators as malcontents. Fourth, they would detain a few key leaders and some theology students to deter others from joining the movement. In short, "the party could think of no new approaches, no creative remedies, and certainly never considered dialogue with any dissidents. The pen of propaganda and the sword of repression . . . would simply be wielded more energetically!"[53]

The regime's counterstrategies had little impact as civil resistance continued to grow. On October 2, the St. Nicholas peace prayer service drew 10,000. Demonstrators were met with water cannons, attack dogs, and police clubs. Then, seemingly overnight, a variety of organizations emerged including New Forum (Neues Forum), Democracy Now (Demokratie Jetzt) and Democratic Awakening (Demokratischer Aufbruch). New Forum received the greatest media attention as 200,000 signed the organization's founding manifesto in the days leading up to the East German state's anniversary celebration on October 7.[54] On that day, the SED held a parade and reception for 80 foreign delegates who were attending the celebration. Roughly 10,000 demonstrated in Berlin, and police arrested nearly 1,000 individuals. Similar protests occurred in cities throughout the country.[55]

However, the real showdown between demonstrators and the regime happened during Leipzig's October 9 peace prayer service. Before the service,

SED leader Honecker announced that he was prepared to declare a state of emergency, and it was rumored that he had issued shoot-to-kill orders.[56] A militia group leader published a letter in the Leipzig newspaper that warned, "We are willing and able . . . to stop these counter-revolutionary actions once and for all—If necessary with weapons in hand."[57] Nearly everyone feared a violent confrontation—a sentiment that was underscored by reports that hospitals were stocking blood supplies, clearing space in emergency rooms, and calling in doctors with expertise in gunshot wounds. As 8,000 to 10,000 troops encircled St. Nicholas church, many believed that the situation might play out like the Tiananmen Square tragedy.[58] In fact, one survey found that nearly 70 percent of Leipzig protesters antici- pated that East German security forces would take more drastic measures than the Chinese took.[59] Their fears were justified. Political officers briefed the troops before the demonstrations by stating: "Comrades, from today on it's class war. . . . Today it will be decided, either them or us. So be class watchful. If sticks aren't good enough, use firearms. [If children are in the crowd, then] too bad for them. We have pistols, and we don't have them for nothing!"[60]

In the hours leading up to the prayer service, church leaders and oppo- sition organizers searched for ways to avoid bloodshed. Theology profes- sors and students gathered to pray. New Forum leaders distributed leaflets calling demonstrators to strictly adhere to nonviolence: "Violence pro- duces violence. Violence cannot solve any problem. Violence is inhuman. Violence cannot be a sign of a new, better society. . . . Abstain from vio- lence!"[61] And six prominent individuals—including world-renowned symphony conductor Kurt Masur, three district party officials, a theology professor, and a well-known cabaret entertainer—issued an appeal, urgently asking the SED to initiate dialogue and for citizens to remain calm and levelheaded. This "Appeal of the Leipzig Six," which was repeat- edly broadcast on local radio stations, marked the first time that party offi- cials collaborated with the opposition and endorsed the appeal without their superiors' consent.[62]

Despite the very real potential for violent confrontation, an estimated 70,000 people gathered at St. Nicholas church on October 9.[63] When the service began and the pastors spoke, the crowd listened intently to their call for courage in the face of repression, the need for a united front, and peace- ful, disciplined behavior. Bishop Hempel beseeched the crowd to "maintain a cool head, be reasonable, and absolutely nonviolent." Another pastor implored: "The spirit of peace must go forth from these walls. See to it that the men in uniform are not antagonized. Make sure that no songs or slogans are shouted that would provoke the authorities. Snatch away the stones that have found their way into the balled fists of your neighbors." And Pastor

Hans-Jürgen Sievers recounted stories of the U.S. Civil Rights movement to illustrate how police, faced with peaceful protesters, can lose the will to repress. Sievers claimed that if the protesters remained adamantly nonviolent, the "men in uniform" would become reluctant to carry out orders and might even side with the crowd.[64]

Those appeals were taken to heart. Despite the palpable tension and fear, the peace prayer demonstrators remained nonviolent. Protesters also spoke with the troops, calling, "Brothers, join us!" and "We don't want violence."[65] The crowd's peaceful demeanor meant that security forces had no grounds for using force. Moreover, personal contact with soldiers had some impact on troops' attitudes. One member of the workers' militia recalled:

> I must say that at the beginning of the demonstration we were really called names. Expressions came out like "dirty pigs," "communist pigs," "betrayers of the workers." . . . Relaxation of tension began only with the announcement of the appeal [for nonviolence]. . . . Many honest comrades actually thought that this was the mob. Then we saw they were entirely normal people shouting *Wir sind das Volk* (we are the people), and we belong to them too.[66]

Thus, to nearly everyone's astonishment, the October 9 demonstration concluded without bloodshed.

The Unreliability of Security Forces

The demonstrators' peaceful behavior that night undoubtedly made it difficult to justify any type of violent crackdown. But there are other reasons why security forces did not resort to a "Tiananmen solution." One possibility is that party officials wanted to avoid international sanctions that might result if Western media groups, who had been following the protests, televised footage of SED soldiers attacking unarmed citizens. A second explanation is that the troops were unprepared for the massive turnout and feared for their own safety—especially since they could no longer count on reinforcement from Soviet troops.[67] A third explanation is that the SED leaders were divided about how to handle the demonstrations. In Leipzig, local SED leader Helmut Hackenberg was prepared to give orders to shoot, but three other local officials were opposed to it. Due to the divided opinions, Hackenberg waited for orders from his superiors in Berlin. But the orders never came, making Hackenberg reluctant to act independently.[68]

Another factor was also at play. Evidence shows that militia members were increasingly unwilling to fight for the state. Steven Pfaff observed:

As the state prepared for the showdown on October 9, militia personnel were on the verge of mass insubordination. One militia commander reported to the district leadership that he and his men were unwilling and unable to fight. A report by the Leipzig PKK in the days following the events of October 9 explained that some militiamen simply failed to muster for action. Others refused to be deployed against protestors and resigned from their units. Some wondered why the state wanted them to terrorize ordinary citizens instead of having them simply round up the "hard core of the opposition." Many explained that they were ready to defend property but otherwise the demonstrations should be allowed to proceed and they were not willing to go against the demonstrators. Although mutinous members risked severe disciplinary measures, internal reports reveal that militia units were already seriously compromised by defection and disobedience in the weeks leading up to October 9.[69]

Moreover, many militia members who might have used force had a change of heart due to their experiences on October 9. One commander stated, "I can tell you that this deployment was a turning point in my life. What we experienced there . . . was a real disillusionment. We said to ourselves, we will never allow ourselves to be used like this by the party leadership again."[70]

This sentiment was also prevalent among police officers. Most of these individuals were not career policemen but rather reservists and conscripts. In early October, some had refused mobilization orders on account of their sympathy with the opposition movement. Others became less reliable and insubordinate, resentful that they were forced to carry out the SED's dirty work. As one high-ranking police officer told a Western journalist, "I am sick of this, these people are peaceful. Now our image is completely ruined."[71]

Despite the prospect of being court-martialed and imprisoned, many police officers and militia members were withdrawing their loyalty, and the regime knew it. As early as August 1989, the Stasi cautioned the state against using the military against civilians because of troop unreliability. Leipzig officials were aware that if they gave orders to shoot, the troops were unlikely to cooperate. Even Military State Attorney Köcher admitted that security force leaders expected that rank-and-file troops would disobey orders. He stated, "When these units were gathered together, there came resistance, especially from the soldiers. They came out and said directly: 'We're not going to attack.'"[72] Thus the reason that East German officials did not use a Tiananmen solution was because the regime no longer had the ability to impose ruthless sanctions. This is a critical point because it reveals that the decision to repress or not lay with the soldiers, not the rulers. It was not simply the case that SED leaders were more humane than their Chinese counterparts. In fact, on that fateful day of October 9, SED chief Erich

Honecker was hosting Chinese Deputy Premier Yao Yilin in East Berlin so that he could learn how to subdue civilian uprisings such as the Beijing student movement.[73]

So what led to troops' disintegrating loyalty? First, they could see that demonstrators were not contemptible enemies of the state, as the SED claimed. Second, many troops identified more with the people than with the party. As one former Politburo member claimed, "The members of the militia were prepared to defend the GDR and their factories, but the very thought of having to beat up *their buddies* evoked dismay" (italics mine).[74] While preexisting friendships and family ties fostered this solidarity, it also developed as demonstrators talked with soldiers in an attempt to undermine their loyalty. One woman recalled:

> I left the house at 2:30 P.M., conscious that I was becoming a participant in a bloody confrontation. . . . I had to go through an army camp of police and state security. The [St. Nicholas] church was really besieged. . . . [I went inside.] From outside, the mighty chorus [of protesters] penetrated through to us: besides whistles and boos and clapping, "Out with the Stasi!" "Gorby, Gorby!" and . . . the wonderful "Wir sind das Volk!" But loudest the shout [was], "No violence!" The atmosphere in the church was tense to the bursting point. . . . Then regional Bishop Hempel came . . . and said he prayed that this night might pass without the worst happening. None of us wanted to say the word civil war or bloodletting aloud, but it seemed tangibly near to everyone. [Afterward we went outside.] Now the fear in me was so great that I thought I must do something against it. So I went up to the people from the workers' militia that stood at the Opera Park. Other demonstrators did this too. We spoke with them and asked them if we looked like "chaotics" or enemies of the state and if they then would really hit us.[75]

Naturally, others claimed credit for the tranquil outcome in Leipzig. Egon Krenz, the Politburo member in charge of security, claimed that he had made a call to Leipzig leaders, ordering them to refrain from violence. But this was quickly discredited as local leaders countered that they had been waiting for direction from him but that he failed to call until after the demonstration subsided. Similarly, Party Chief Honecker stated that he was responsible for the troops' restrained demeanor, but it is well documented that his call for restraint came five days after the October 9 showdown. Others argue that Soviet military leaders demanded a no-shoot policy, but party insiders and East German generals deny this. In short, there is no reliable, documented explanation for the troops' restraint that night except their own statements that they were unwilling to carry out unjust orders.

Elite Division

When the October 9 peace prayer service revealed that the state had lost its power to repress, the movement gained greater momentum. Activists were further empowered by news that a serious rift had developed within the Politburo—the committee of high-ranking SED leaders. Due to Party Chief Honecker's poor handling of the emigration crisis and the deteriorating economy, Politburo members Egon Krenz and Günther Schabowski decided that it was time for new leadership. After some contentious debate, on October 18 the Politburo dismissed Honecker and appointed Krenz as the head of the SED. Krenz promptly announced that he would dialogue with opposition groups about needed reforms.[76]

The Fall of the Berlin Wall

Yet this change in old guard leadership and Krenz's promise of dialogue did not appease civil resisters. During the first week of November, an estimated 500,000 people in East Berlin and 500,000 in Leipzig demonstrated.[77] Opposition also spread from the streets to the workplace, where small waves of strikes occurred.[78] The people's demands became stronger and clearer: an end to SED dominance, genuinely free elections, and unrestricted travel rights.

On the last issue, Krenz proposed a modest change: citizens would be allowed to travel abroad up to one month per year but only with governmental permission. In response, a demonstration was held in Leipzig demanding the right to travel without visas and the dismantling of the Berlin Wall. Under growing pressure, the Politburo made provisions on November 3 for the immediate distribution of exit visas that allowed retention of East German citizenship and the right to return without sanction. But things really began unraveling when the Volkskammer (House of Representatives) failed to endorse Krenz's proposed travel reforms. Recognizing that they no longer had support inside the system, the SED's Council of Ministers resigned on November 7. A few days later, the entire Politburo resigned. The new Politburo members encouraged Krenz to adopt a more liberal travel policy that would enable any East German with a passport to cross borders freely. Krenz capitulated, and the new policy was announced on national television on the evening of November 9. When people heard that the policy was effective immediately, roughly 20,000 gathered at the Berlin Wall. By 11:00 P.M., they were shouting for the crossing gate to be opened. Within an hour, all crossing points in Berlin were open, causing young people to dance jubilantly on the wall, joined by West Berliners who came to celebrate.[79]

By this point, it had become painfully evident to SED leaders that their control was gone. Citizens traveled freely, soldiers would not reliably carry out orders, and mass emigration had depleted the nation's skill and knowledge base, ravaging the country's economy. Throughout the next weeks, the SED government disintegrated. On November 24, the article that granted the SED the sole power to rule was removed from East Germany's constitution. Four days later, the Ministry of State Security (i.e., the Stasi) was dismantled. By December 4, all members of the Politburo and Central Committee resigned. The next day, Erich Honecker and several other leaders from the old regime were arrested. Finally, Krenz resigned on December 6. The newly appointed leader declared that elections would be held on March 16, 1990. On that day, 93.4 percent of the voting population turned out to elect a new government that eventually agreed to unification with West Germany.

REASONS FOR MOVEMENT SUCCESS

What does this case reveal about the conditions needed for a successful nonviolent revolution? Undeniably, the movement was aided by new political opportunities—namely, the reformist spirit initiated by Gorbachev, a new Soviet policy of not militarily intervening in the internal affairs of fraternal nations, the opening of Hungary's border, and inspiration from resistance movements in neighboring Poland and Czechoslovakia.

But these changing structural conditions were not the only factors that contributed to the regime's demise; we must also examine the strategic actions of civil resisters. The opposition movement used few tactics, relying mostly on emigration (exit) and demonstrations (voice). But those tactics enabled civil resisters to withhold all six forms of popular support from the regime. Mass emigration constituted a withdrawal of *cooperation and obedience*, since citizens were prohibited from leaving the country unless the government granted them exit visas. By leaving, citizens merely disregarded laws that they considered unjust. Emigration also entailed the withholding of *skills*, as many talented workers left their jobs. This practically paralyzed the industrial, transportation, and service sectors, undercutting the amount of *material resources* that the state could access through business revenues. Thus human action was largely responsible for the government's economic vulnerability. Although the country had fiscal problems before, the withdrawal of these forms of citizen support turned a problematic situation into a highly precarious one, forcing regime leaders to make concessions. Moreover, these economic and emigration problems created divisions among party leaders, who could not agree on the best way to address the crisis.

Thus changing structural conditions were actually in part *caused by* nonviolent actors.

The second tactic—demonstrations—enabled citizens to withdraw the three remaining forms of citizen support. First, *attitudes of submission* were transformed as more citizens joined the Monday prayer service demonstrations. The Protestant Church's role in the movement indicates that religion was not functioning as an opiate, encouraging people to accept their lot in life in exchange for heavenly rewards. Although some pastors opposed the movement,[80] activist pastors such as Führer and Wonneberger—along with those involved in church-based peace and justice groups—successfully challenged ideological and religious beliefs about obeying the government. Second, the demonstrations revealed that many East Germans no longer viewed the SED party as legitimate and thus they were refusing to acknowledge its *authority*. Third, demonstrators' nonviolent demeanor and their appeals to troops helped undermine the regime's *sanctioning power*.

Movement leaders also avoided the problems that derailed the Chinese uprising. Specifically, Pastor Führer recognized the potential for movement fragmentation since there were tensions between church-based activist groups and those applying to emigrate. Church-based activists were committed to staying and building a more humane socialist system in East Germany; hence they viewed would-be emigrants as self-interested opportunists who had given up on their nation and simply sought better lives for themselves. Additionally, those seeking to emigrate were often more confrontational and unruly. Some created disturbances in St. Nicholas Square in hopes of being expelled from East Germany. To address these problems, Führer took two actions. First, he gave would-be emigrants a sympathetic hearing and, as the pastor of St. Nicholas Church, invited them to participate in the peace prayer services. This turned out to be a very wise move since "emigrant applicants ... more than any other element, deserve responsibility for the large increase in attendees."[81] Although there continued to be some strains between the two groups, Führer emphasized that the church was open to all, and eventually the two groups worked together to increase attendance at the prayer services and demonstrations. The second action that Pastors Führer and Wonneberger took was to charge the church-based groups "Initiative for Life" and the "Working Group in Service of Peace" with the task of training those drawn to St. Nicholas in nonviolent techniques. Thus, even if the SED had planted provocateurs in the crowd to instigate a violent confrontation, demonstrators were prepared to identify these situations and quickly diffuse them.

But how can we account for this church emphasis on nonviolence? Undoubtedly, much of this came from pastors and church activists who were personally committed to nonviolence. Wonneberger, for instance, had worked for the rights of military conscientious objectors, and Führer had been convinced of the power of the nonviolent techniques by studying Martin Luther King and Gandhi.[82] Moreover, the Working Group in Service of Peace, which had started the peace prayer services, was initially comprised of conscientious objectors who had, as Bausoldaten, done alternative service in lieu of military service. Hence, in contrast to the Chinese movement leaders, the core leaders in the East German uprising were in agreement that exclusively nonviolent methods would be used. This does not mean that everyone involved in the uprising was a principled pacifist; in fact, most were not. But as pastors repeatedly called for nonviolence during the October 9 standoff, people listened. While they may have done so for strategic reasons—recognizing that violent attacks on police could have been suicidal—the church leaders are to be at least partially credited for the lack of rioting.

The activist pastors' emphasis on nonviolence was also important in the transition to a new government since they arranged, moderated, and hosted round table discussions between opposition forces and the crumbling regime. Church leaders also set an important tone of reconciliation that deterred violent reprisals against Stasi informers and party leaders. For example, one Protestant pastor invited deposed party chief Erich Honecker into his own home when the government could not find a suitable place for the ousted leader to live, even though Honecker's anti-church policies had prevented the pastor's 10 children from attending college.[83]

In short, movement organizers used effective tactics and successfully addressed problems that could have derailed the uprising. In contrast, the SED succumbed to internal divisions and devised an ineffectual counterstrategy. Regime leaders relied on their standard methods of social control: repression and propaganda to discredit dissidents. This time, however, repression did not work because security officers would not reliably carry out orders. Unlike Chinese Communist Party leaders who overcame this problem, the SED did not find mechanisms to keep security forces loyal. In addition, their propaganda efforts fell flat, primarily because troops and the broader public could readily see that demonstrators were not the punkish brutes that the government claimed they were. In short, SED leaders were unable to generate new, innovative counterinsurgency measures. As Pastor Führer recalled, "The authorities later said they were ready for riots, violence, almost anything but prayer meetings and candles!"[84]

To summarize, a variety of factors contributed to the successful overthrow of the authoritarian socialist regime in East Germany. Changes in the international arena meant that conditions were ripe for action. But favorable conditions alone did not bring down the regime. A good strategy was critical to this task, and here the movement was exemplary, acting in the face of potentially severe repression and using all the sources of power that the population possessed. Their actions created further economic instability and elite divisions, but the turning point came when troops were no longer reliable. Once the party could no longer threaten the people or use force to dominate, the revolution was over. The people won.

PART TWO

Nonviolent Revolts Against Military Regimes

CHAPTER 4
Panama's Struggle for Democracy

hile the East German case reveals how strategic nonviolence can
work quickly and effectively, an unarmed uprising in Panama shows
how international influences and a ruler's counterstrategies can undermine
revolutionary potential. Starting in 1987, civil resisters challenged Panama's ruling military leader, General Manuel Antonio Noriega. Calling
themselves the National Civic Crusade, activists used various tactics to
withdraw their support from Noriega's regime, creating a national crisis.
But Noriega managed to counter these moves, retaining power until the
United States intervened militarily in December 1989.

HISTORICAL CONTEXT

One cannot understand the failed uprising in Panama without taking into
account the role of international influences. In Panama's case, the strongest
foreign influence came from United States, whose involvement dates back
to the mid-19th century, when Panama was still a province of Colombia.
Numerous countries were vying for control of Panama, due to its potential
as a canal site. One of those nations, Great Britain, announced in 1846 that
it was willing to use force to establish a territorial claim. The United States
seized this opportunity to broker a deal with Colombia's president: in
exchange for transit rights through Panama, the United States would ensure
Colombia's sovereignty over the region. Known as the Bidlack-Mallarino
Treaty, this agreement was ratified by the U.S. Congress in 1848. But the
treaty included a clause that permitted U.S. military intervention in Panama,
setting a contentious tone that would continue for another 140 years.[1]

Shortly after the Bidlack-Mallarino Treaty was signed, U.S. entrepreneurs built a railroad system across Panama, and many U.S citizens moved into the region.[2] But they did not treat locals well, and tensions boiled over in 1856, when a U.S. citizen took a melon from a black Panamanian vendor but refused to pay for it. When the vendor demanded compensation, the American drew his gun, provoking others to brandish their weapons. The confrontation left 16 people dead. When the incident was reported to Washington, U.S. officials recommended a military occupation of the region because of the "colored population's hatred of Americans."[3] Six months later, this recommendation was fulfilled. But this was only the beginning. Over the next 50 years, there would be 13 more interventions.

Despite the conflict that the U.S.-operated railroad system generated, Panamanian officials eventually gave the United States rights to build and operate a canal since the United States had helped Panama gain independence from Colombia in 1903. To protect this lucrative business, the United States established the Canal Zone and increased its military presence. By the end of World War I, there were 14 U.S. bases in the Canal Zone and 7,400 U.S. soldiers.[4]

Popular resentment over U.S. control of the canal expanded through World Wars I and II, erupting in the spring of 1958, when local students entered the Canal Zone to plant Panamanian flags. Although they intended to conduct a peaceful demonstration, the National Guard and U.S. soldiers assaulted the students, killing one and injuring 120. This scene was repeated, in a much bloodier manner, in 1964, when University of Panama students attempted to fly a Panamanian flag at the U.S. Canal Zone high school and were confronted by U.S. students, their parents, and Canal Zone police. When a fight broke out, U.S. troops opened fire on the university students. Outraged by the attack, roughly 30,000 Panamanian citizens rioted. When the fighting ended several days later, 28 people were dead and hundreds wounded. An estimated 250,000 mourners attended a funeral for the martyred students. This event caused U.S. policy makers to rethink the viability of maintaining control of the canal in perpetuity. Subsequently, President Lyndon Johnson proposed a new canal treaty that included a turnover to Panamanian authorities in 1999.[5]

Not surprisingly, canal issues and U.S. relations played prominently in Panama's presidential election of 1968. When Arnulfo Arias won—a former president who was twice deposed by Panama's National Guard—many citizens hoped he could change these contentious dynamics. But their hope was short-lived. Once Arias was sworn into office, he fired two senior National Guard officers and appointed others to foreign posts. This was partly motivated by revenge for being ousted in 1941 and 1951, but it was also done to secure his position by replacing these individuals with loyal supporters. However, many officers were not willing to accept these changes. Eleven days into his term, President Arias was overthrown by the National Guard for the third time.

THE RISE OF PANAMA'S MILITARY DICTATORSHIP

After Arias was deposed, Panama's era of military dictatorships began, as Colonel José María Pinilla declared himself the interim president. He established a ruling council that included both military and civilian members and announced that elections would be held soon. But a few months later, in January 1969, two National Guard officers—Colonel Boris Martinez and Lieutenant Colonel Omar Torrijos—staged a coup. Civilian politicians resigned en masse to protest the National Guard's increasingly dictatorial tendencies. Those tendencies were clearly evident as the National Guard dismantled the national assembly, closed the University of Panama, banned opposition parties, and exiled prominent critics. By spring of 1969, Colonel Martinez was deposed, leaving Torrijos with the reins of political power.[6]

Once Torrijos was in command, he enacted labor, agricultural, and banking reforms. He altered regulations and implemented tax exemptions to establish offshore banking. This turned Panama into an international finance center, as funds flowed into the country from legitimate and illegitimate sources. Yet Torrijos was not only interested in expanding commerce but also committed to improving the living conditions of the poor. Under his leadership, funding for social programs increased 700 percent, literacy increased by 20 percent, and social security was provided to 60 percent of the population, compared with just 12 percent before the Torrijos era. Torrijos also built health clinics, made rural infrastructural improvements, and enacted land redistribution policies.[7] But these programs were costly, and the Panamanian government took out loans to sustain their payrolls. By 1976, Panama had a debt of $1.3 billion.[8]

To alleviate this debt, Torrijos focused on winning canal rights. The situation looked promising in 1974, when U.S. National Security Adviser Henry Kissinger consented to negotiations. But when Kissinger admitted in a press conference that the United States intended to maintain the right to defend the canal, Torrijos became convinced that the United States would never relent. Hence he created a special military unit to prepare for guerrilla warfare in the Canal Zone.[9] The battle never materialized since negotiations resumed when Jimmy Carter took office. In 1977, Torrijos and Carter signed a treaty stipulating that a U.S.-Panamanian commission would run the canal until 1999, at which point Panama would gain exclusive control. It also increased the amount of revenue that Panama received from canal profits during the treaty period.[10]

The canal treaty was a major accomplishment for Torrijos, who decided the following year to repeal the 10-year-old ban on political parties. Although Torrijos's own party—the Democratic Revolutionary Party (PRD)—remained dominant, he promised to fully democratize Panama by 1984. That never happened. Torrijos's 13-year rule ended in 1981, when he died in a plane crash.

After Torrijos's death, General Manuel Noriega seized power. As leader of the Panamanian G-2 intelligence unit, Noriega had been a paid informant for the U.S. Central Intelligence Agency (CIA) since 1967. The Reagan administration initially supported Noriega's new role, mainly because it believed he would be useful for Washington's anticommunist battle in Central America. But it became increasingly difficult for the United States to support Noriega. Not only was he was involved in drug trafficking and weapons dealing but also he made a sham out of the 1984 presidential election. Representing the PRD party was Noriega's appointed candidate, Nicolas Ardito Barletta. Opposing him was thrice-deposed former president Arnulfo Arias. When the election took place, the count was prolonged for days due to 2,000 charges of vote manipulation and vote buying. In the end, Noriega bribed Panama's Supreme Court judges, who declared Barletta the winner.[11]

The stolen election angered the population, and opposition to Noriega's rule quickly expanded. But Noriega believed that repression would stop any opposition and thus he used it liberally. One of his most notorious acts was the assassination of former Minister of Health Hugo Spadafora, a vocal critic of the regime. To silence him, Noriega ordered G-2 intelligence agents to abduct, torture, and decapitate Spadafora.[12] Instead of deterring opposition, Spadafora's murder actually increased it, as many outraged Panamanians felt that this act signaled a new era of barbarism.[13] Puppet President Barletta promised to conduct an investigation into the murder, but before he could do so, the military forced him to resign. He was replaced by Vice President Eric Delvalle, the first "Kleenex president"—a term Panamanians coined to denote political leaders' disposability.[14]

These actions severely strained General Noriega's relationship with the Reagan administration. To improve Noriega's image, the White House pressured Noriega to reinstate President Barletta. He refused. He also rejected Reagan's request for Panama to provide sanctuary to deposed Philippine dictator Ferdinand Marcos. The Reagan administration had previously tolerated Noriega's corruption, money-laundering practices, and ties to Colombia's Medellín drug cartel.[15] But when he no longer cooperated with Washington's efforts to oust the revolutionary Sandinista government in Nicaragua, they turned against Noriega.[16]

THE NONVIOLENT UPRISING BEGINS: THE NATIONAL CIVIC CRUSADE

Civilian opposition to Noriega had been growing throughout the 1980s, but widespread popular resistance first erupted in June 1987. The triggering event occurred when Noriega, fearing a military coup, forced the military chief of staff, Roberto Díaz Herrera, into retirement. Indignant, Díaz sought revenge by doing a radio interview on Sunday, June 7, in which he publicly accused Noriega of electoral fraud, of killing General Torrijos by planting a bomb on his plane, and ordering Spadafora's assassination.[17]

After the interview, acts of opposition unfolded quickly. On Monday, June 8, numerous politicians walked out of the Legislative Assembly when they were not permitted to address the allegations.[18] Mayin Correa, the radio host who had interviewed Díaz, went on the air that day to call all those angered by the allegations to demonstrate in the banking district. Thousands showed up, chanting "Down with Noriega."[19] In response, Noriega sent out riot police, known as Dobermans, to disperse the crowds with tear gas, water cannon, and shotgun pellets.[20] This did not deter the protesters, who continued demonstrating over the next three days.[21]

The demonstrations gave Chamber of Commerce President Aurelio Barria great hope that Panama's citizens could overthrow Noriega. Barria had recently returned from a trip to the Philippines, where he had been profoundly impressed by the nonviolent revolution that had ousted Ferdinand Marcos. Barria was determined to emulate this feat, toppling Noriega through civil resistance.[22] To achieve this, Barria invited business elites and civic leaders to a meeting on Tuesday, June 9.[23] That night, they formed the National Civic Crusade (NCC), which released a communiqué calling for a campaign of civil disobedience and the immediate removal of all those implicated in Colonel Díaz's allegations.[24] Eventually 200 professional, business, church, union, and civic groups joined the NCC.[25]

On the morning of Wednesday, June 10, an opposition leader got on the radio to ask Panamanians to express their resistance to Noriega each day at noon and 6:00 P.M. by banging pots and honking horns. At 6:00 that evening, groups all over Panama City responded loudly. Spontaneously, many also waved white handkerchiefs. Soon, others adopted the practice, and white became the color of the uprising. Again the Dobermans attacked, wounding more than 70 demonstrators.[26] Outraged by the repression, the

National Civic Crusade—also known as *civilistas*—called for a general strike the following day.

The demonstrations and proposed general strike prompted Noriega to declare a state of emergency in the early hours of Thursday, June 11. He immediately suspended eight constitutional guarantees, including the right of habeas corpus and freedom of movement, expression, and assembly. He rescinded the state's obligation to inform detainees of the charges against them or to permit them legal council. Censorship rules were imposed on newspapers. Moreover, Noriega ordered troops to occupy the capital and detain NCC leader Aurelio Barría. The troops took Barría to a local police station, stripped him naked, placed a hood over his head, and threatened to rape and murder him. After five hours, Barría was released, more determined than ever to overthrow the military regime.[27] Similarly, other Panamanians were not intimidated by the state of emergency; they continued to beat pots, honk horns, and wave white handkerchiefs at noon and 6:00 P.M., leading some journalists to name it the "clock-watching revolution."[28]

In response to the state of emergency, National Civic Crusade leaders asked the Catholic Church to hold a special Mass at noon on Friday, June 12. Although they had historically been reluctant to get involved in politics, Panama's Roman Catholic leaders readily agreed and scheduled a Mass at the Church of El Carmen.[29] When 2,000 people gathered for the service, they were confronted by troops armed with automatic weapons and hand grenades. The troops teargassed the crowd and fired off shots while military helicopters, equipped with M-60 machine guns, flew low over the church.[30] This began the regime's self-declared 10-day "state of siege" that culminated in more than 1,000 arrests, more than 100 injured, and several deaths.[31] The siege prompted Panama's Catholic leaders to condemn the government's actions as "beyond all limits of proportion and justice."[32] It also caused one of Noriega's former allies, Gabriel Lewis, to flee Panama and set up a Washington, D.C., branch of the National Civic Crusade, which became the center for anti-Noriega lobbying.[33]

When the siege failed to stop the protests, Noriega turned to other means. Since many of the National Civic Crusade's organizers were prominent business leaders, they soon became targets. Many found that the loans they had secured from state banks were now being denied, that their import licenses were being revoked, and that they were subject to surprise visits from government inspectors. Some of their businesses were destroyed through arson and fire bombings.[34] And the president of the Rotary Club, who was one of the founding members of the National Civic Crusade, was murdered.[35]

Nonetheless, the National Civic Crusade gained momentum. Since direct repression proved to be an ineffective counterstrategy, Noriega attempted to divide the movement internally by arguing that movement leaders were wealthy professionals seeking to advance their own material interests and that he was the only true champion of the poor.[36] But little support could be found for Noriega, even in Panama City's most indigent neighborhoods. Additionally, he tried to exploit Panama's traditional racial tensions by claiming that National Civic Crusade leaders were racist.[37] Noriega also appealed to Panamanians' nationalism, claiming that the U.S. Embassy had organized the uprising to maintain control of the canal. Perhaps for the first time in Panama's history, it did not work; even anti-American Panamanians wanted Noriega out.[38]

Undaunted by Noriega's slanderous accusations, the National Civic Crusade scheduled a mass demonstration for Friday, July 10. Marches would begin in five different parts of Panama City, ultimately converging at the Church of El Carmen. The date of the demonstration infuriated Noriega because his daughter's extravagant wedding was to be held on July 11 in the plushest downtown hotel. He was forced to reschedule the wedding to July 8, and the ceremony was held in a much more modest setting. Perhaps to retaliate, Noriega planned a particularly brutal crackdown for demonstrators. When July 10 arrived, more than 100,000 people—all dressed in white—filled Panama City streets. Along all five routes, people hung white towels and bed sheets from their windowsills to express their support for the marchers.[39] One observer described what happened next:

> Under a brilliant white sky, on an afternoon refreshed by pleasant sea breezes, Panamanians [were] attempting to exercise their . . . rights to public assembly and freedom of transit, offering no violence, merely receiving it. . . . The Dobermans went crazy. They rushed forward shooting, hosing, arresting people. They fired at windows that showed white. They fired gas grenades into buildings and shot people as they fled out. A large number of marchers took refuge in the National Sanctuary Church. . . . The Dobermans fired tear gas in through the windows and shot-gunned people point blank as they tried to get out. . . . Then [they] charged into the church, shot-gunning and hosing left and right . . . grabbed people and dragged them out . . . flung them into patrol trucks and took them to prison, beating them along the way.[40]

The Dobermans' rampage was the single worst incident of repression in Panamanian history, causing the event to be quickly dubbed *Viernes Negro* (Black Friday). Between 500 and 1,000 people suffered gunshot wounds, and an estimated 1,500 demonstrators were arrested.[41] After this incident, a poll indicated that 75 percent of Panamanians wanted Noriega to resign.[42] Thus the violence of Black Friday did not thwart the movement; it actually deepened people's convictions that regime change was imperative, and thus demonstrations and noise riots continued over the next weeks while more and more people brandished white handkerchiefs.

Encouraged by people's determination to bring Noriega down, the National Civic Crusade intensified resistance in late July. They called another general strike for July 27 and 28. Despite appeals from the president to conduct business as usual, people did not report to work. Commercial activity stopped, and banks remained locked. The bank closures raised serious concerns for the government since Panama's 130 financial institutions held more than $30 billion in assets. As news of the country's political turmoil was reported, foreign investors withdrew an estimated $3 to $4 billion in just a few days.[43] The regime's financial situation was further decimated when local business leaders began a fiscal disobedience campaign whereby they refused to pay taxes.[44] This depleted the national treasury, and thus there were insufficient funds to pay Panama's foreign debt, which had ballooned to $6 billion—roughly half of the national budget.[45]

In addition to economic trouble, Noriega also had to contend with mutinous appeals to the Panama Defense Forces (PDF). The U.S. Senate passed a resolution that eliminated all U.S. aid to the PDF and called upon Noriega to resign, and U.S. Assistant Secretary of State Elliot Abrams publicly asked the PDF to overthrow Noriega, suggesting that their aid would be reinstated if they did so.[46] Retired Panamanian General Rubén Parades made a radio appeal, calling on PDF officers to remove Noriega from office. Many Panamanians took Parades's call as a sign that the tide was turning among the troops and that Noriega's downfall was imminent.[47] Consequently, the National Civic Crusade began urging PDF soldiers to revolt against Noriega,[48] and soon many *civilistas* wore lapel pins that read, "I ♥ sedition."[49]

But the PDF refused to turn against Noriega for a couple of reasons. First and foremost, PDF troops had grown wealthy under Noriega's rule. Not only had they embezzled funds from government agencies but also they demanded hefty bribes from Cubans who traveled to Panama as a launching point for emigration to the United States. The PDF troops routinely sold visas for $3,500 to $10,000 a piece.[50] Thus, in Koster and Sánchez's words, "Noriega's colleagues [PDF troops], though thieves, had already stolen a great deal of money and were more concerned about living to enjoy it than about stealing more. . . . Suppose they risked [a coup] and were successful. Where would they find a leader as ruthless as he to keep the PDF in power and thus save them from paying for their crimes?"[51] The second reason that the PDF remained loyal is that the enticement of renewed U.S. aid had little impact. The PDF had grown from a rather small paramilitary force of 5,500 in the 1960s to a professional and financially independent force of 16,000 in the mid-1980s. Although the country was in an economic crisis, the military was always paid first, and thus the PDF's economic autonomy made it less suscepti-ble to U.S. pressure.[52]

Although Noriega was not ousted by his troops, he was feeling the effects of civilian resistance. Thus he sought to definitively silence his critics—especially Colonel Díaz, who had stoked popular anger through his accusa-tions. On July 26, Noriega ordered PDF troops to shut down opposition newspapers and radio stations. Then, in the early morning hours of July 27, troops lobbed tear gas grenades through the windows of Colonel Díaz's house while helicopters strafed the grounds. Antiterrorist commandos blew open the doors of the Díaz home, forcing everyone outside where they were promptly arrested.[53]

The movement swiftly responded to the attack on Díaz. National Civic Crusade lawyers began investigating the legality of these arrests while 200 to 300 students staged antigovernment demonstrations and obstructed traffic near Panama's National University.[54] Next, the National Civic Cru-sade called for the "Second White Demonstration for Democracy" on August 5. Tens of thousands attended, expressing their opposition to Nori-ega through the traditional Civic Crusade methods: motorists honking horns, residents clanking pots and pans, pedestrians waving white flags, and white ticker tape falling from high-rise office buildings.[55]

But after this August demonstration, the National Civic Crusade's mo-mentum began to subside. In an attempt to save their businesses, some com-panies negotiated with the government in early August to lift fines and warrants in exchange for the cessation of their fiscal disobedience campaign.[56] When the National Civic Crusade subsequently called for a general strike on August 17, it generated only half the response of the July strike. By late Sep-tember, only 5,000 participated in a NCC-sponsored demonstration.[57]

MOUNTING INTERNATIONAL SANCTIONS

Even as the National Civic Crusade's actions decreased in the fall of 1987, U.S. pressure increased. The U.S. Congress eliminated all economic and military aid to Panama, which totaled more than $80 million,[58] and U.S. leaders pressured multilateral agencies in the international community to do the same. Thus the World Bank canceled a $50 million loan to Panama.[59] Next, the United States canceled its sugar quotas from Panama, forcing one-third of the nation's sugar mills to close. By the end of 1987, the coun-try's economy was suffering severely from the combination of domestic strikes and international sanctions.

The country's financial situation declined further in February 1988 as grand juries in Miami and Tampa indicted Noriega on drug-trafficking charges. The indictments enabled the Reagan administration to freeze $296 million of Panamanian assets held in U.S. banks and to suspend $115 million in tax payments from U.S. companies operating in Panama.[60] In an attempt to stop the escalating financial crisis, President Delvalle made a televised appearance on February 26 to announce that he was firing Noriega. But Noriega turned the tables, convincing the military-dominated National Assembly to impeach Delvalle and appoint Manuel Solis Palma as acting president.[61] Solis, of course, was nothing more than a puppet president who allowed Noriega to call the shots.

As Noriega clung to power, the United States kept the economic pressure on. By March 3, 1988, the U.S. Senate introduced legislation that would ban imports from and exports to Panama and prohibit the transfer of funds to Panamanian banks. Next, deposed President Delvalle froze all National Bank of Panama assets held in U.S. financial institutions—entailing roughly $50 million—thanks to the assistance of acting U.S. Secretary of State John Whitehead. This meant that Panama's local banks had no access to currency, and thus the nation's banking commission announced that domestic and international banking operations would be suspended indefinitely.[62] No one was able to cash checks or make deposits or withdrawals. Within a couple of weeks, Noriega was out of funds and unable to pay the 150,000 people on the government payroll—with the exception of his troops.

When paychecks were not delivered on March 15, roughly 10,000 civil servants and pensioners rallied in Panama City, and in some cases, the rally digressed to rioting. Meanwhile, 2,000 port workers went on strike, claiming that they would return to work only when they got paid. They also placed large cargo containers in port entrances, obstructing deliveries.[63] In an attempt to appease workers, the government sold sacks of food staples called "dignity bags" for $15 to $16.[64] But this did not stop the riots. The next day, March 16, state hospital workers learned that they were not getting paid. They also took to the streets, chanting, "We want money, not bags of food." They battled police for six hours.[65]

The economic pressures generated tension within the Panamanian Defense Forces. A few officers, who felt that Noriega was bringing the country to ruin, plotted to overthrow him. They tried to carry out their plans on March 16, but Noriega loyalists quickly defeated the poorly planned rebellion. The attempted coup led Noriega to restructure his leadership system. He created the Strategic Military Council—comprised only of his most faithful supporters—which functioned as Panama's de facto parliament. Then, to discourage other attempts to oust him, Noriega imprisoned more than a dozen officers involved in the coup. They were given 20-year sentences and held in underground cells without lights or toilets. This led some, like former General Ruben Paredes, to conclude that another military uprising was not likely to occur for some time.[66] But others, including the leaders of the National Civic Crusade, gained new hope from this split in the PDF and thus called for a new general strike on March 21, 1988.[67]

COUNTERING SANCTIONS WITH SUPPORT
FROM INTERNATIONAL ALLIES

With a new general strike on his hands, Noriega sought assistance from allies to alleviate the nation's financial troubles. He found support from various sources—mostly from countries, such as Cuba and Nicaragua, who ardently opposed U.S. policies. The first nation to provide financial help was Libya; Libyan leader Muammar Qaddafi granted Noriega an emergency $24 million loan.[68] Taiwan offered $40 million in loans, followed by $1 billion in funding for various projects. Cuba sent advisers to help with propaganda, psychological warfare, and independent currency printing. In addition to these direct forms of assistance, Japan indirectly helped Noriega by refusing to join U.S. sanctions.[69]

All of this assistance enabled Noriega's regime to stay afloat for a while, albeit barely. Then, on April 1, the Reagan administration relented a bit when U.S. companies operating in Panama appealed for the right to pay their taxes to the Panamanian government; they feared that their licenses to operate in the country would be revoked if they did not make their payments. The result: Noriega received $19 million in tax revenue.[70]

Throughout these tumultuous economic times, Noriega's personal financial situation remained strong. He was still on Cuban, Nicaraguan, and Libyan intelligence payrolls[71] and continued to make a lucrative living through his ties to Colombian drug cartels. Thus as the economic crisis continued throughout 1988—with unemployment more than 20 percent, industrial production off 60 percent, and $7 billion drained from Panama's banks[72]—the nation's citizens suffered terribly, but the personal fortunes of Noriega and his comrades were largely unaffected.

LAST DOMESTIC EFFORTS TO OUST NORIEGA

When it became evident that Panama's economic crisis was not going to cause Noriega's downfall, the National Civic Crusade shifted its focus to the elections scheduled for May 7, 1989. Newly inaugurated President George H. W. Bush secretly channeled $10 million to the political opposition parties to help them defeat Noriega.[73] But few believed that elections were a viable method of social change; one survey indicated that 80 percent of the population felt that it would be impossible to hold fair elections while Noriega was in power.[74] They were right. On election day, exit polls showed that the opposition coalition had received 73 percent of the vote while Noriega's party got only 26 percent.[75] International election observers confirmed this outcome. But Noriega insisted that his party had won.[76]

The stolen election led to an outburst in the streets of Panama City. By May 10, Noriega nullified the election, claiming that "the normal electoral process was altered by the obstructionist actions of a number of foreigners."[77] As protests continued throughout the summer and into the fall, cracks in the Panama Defense Forces surfaced again on October 3, 1989, when officer Moisés Giraldi attempted to overthrow Noriega. Giraldi and his comrades surprised Noriega at his office, took him captive, and tried to persuade him to resign. Giraldi had tipped off the U.S. Southern Command troops, who blocked roads to prevent Noriega's loyal troops from reaching him. But troops from the Machos del Monte infantry boarded a plane and landed at the airport. They seized private cars and drove in on the only access route that the Southern Command had not blocked. When they arrived at Noriega's office, some shots were exchanged before Giraldi surrendered. Noriega immediately ordered his troops to execute him. At least 10 more officers were murdered that day, and Noriega went on a rampage in subsequent weeks to purge the PFD of traitors.[78] Human rights groups estimate that between 100 and 233 junior officers involved in the coup, along with their supporters, were killed.[79]

THE U.S. INVASION

For some time, U.S. Secretary of Defense Dick Cheney and General Colin Powell had contemplated invading Panama and removing Noriega. But the planning became more serious in December 1989. On December 15, Panama's puppet government bestowed on Noriega the title of chief executive officer of the government; Noriega used the occasion to declare that Panama was in a state of war with the United States. Things heated up further on December 16, when two conflicts occurred between U.S. troops and the PDF. By December 17, President Bush issued the order to invade, dubbing the action "Operation Just Cause."[80]

Just a few days later, on December 20, the United States sent 24,000 troops into Panama. They came with the most sophisticated military equipment—from new Stealth fighters and Apache helicopter gunships to

2,000-pound bombs. The PDF was no match for them, both in terms of equipment and size, and thus they were easily defeated as U.S. forces attacked 27 different targets throughout Panama. One of the key targets was PDF headquarters, located in an impoverished neighborhood called El Chorillo. Within hours, entire city blocks of El Chorillo were bombed and burned to the ground. While PDF troops gave up after about 12 hours of fighting, Noriega was not found for several days. He was eventually located at the Vatican nunciature, where he had sought refuge. After several days of negotiations, Noriega surrendered on January 3, 1990. He was immediately arrested and flown to Miami, where he was prosecuted for drug trafficking and money laundering.[81]

While the U.S. government considered Operation Just Cause a great success, the rest of the world did not react so favorably. Many Latin American countries denounced the action as a blatant act of aggression that may have been motivated by U.S. interest in preserving canal rights.[82] The United Nations condemned the invasion as a violation of international law. And nongovernmental agencies noted that significant losses had been incurred. The Central American Human Rights Commission and the International Red Cross estimated that at least 3,000 civilians had been killed during the invasion, 20,000 people had lost their homes, and $2 billion in damages had occurred. In fact, the indigent neighborhood of El Chorilla, which had taken the brunt of the fighting, was quickly dubbed "little Hiroshima." Rebuilding the nation was not going to be easy, especially since the U.S. military imposed martial law and arrested 7,000 Panamanian opposition leaders—many of whom were held for months without charge.[83]

Thus, in the post-Noriega period, the process of establishing Panama's democracy was not smooth. The inducted civilian president formed a new Legislative Assembly that restored basic freedoms. He also worked to revive Panama's ailing economy that had been battered from years of sanctions. The new government pledged to reform the Panamanian military and keep it under civilian control. Eventually, the nation solidified its democratic transition and formally assumed control of the canal in December 1999. While Noriega's ouster was the final outcome of this struggle, it was achieved by military intervention from an outside state—not the nonviolent uprising led by the National Civic Crusade.[84]

WHY THE NATIONAL CIVIC CRUSADE FAILED TO OUST NORIEGA

Why did the National Civic Crusade fail to nonviolently overthrow Panama's military regime? As it mobilized, the movement benefited from favorable conditions that ought to have strengthened its efforts. For example, Panama's economy had been weak for nearly a decade. High unemployment, declining wages, and cuts in social security programs generated widespread frustration among members of the working class, professionals, and government employees.[85] Moreover, blatant political corruption, PDF involvement in international drug trafficking, and brutal crackdowns caused many of Noriega's traditional supporters to cut their ties to the regime. Additionally, the Catholic Church functioned as a free space where opposition groups could gather when public assembly was banned.[86] Finally, the attempted coups indicated divisions within the Panamanian Defense Forces. These are the conditions that scholars argue are essential for revolutionary success.

Favorable structural conditions were complemented by the National Civic Crusade's nonviolent strategy. The *civilistas* won the backing of powerful international supporters while employing multiple tactics (demonstrations, strikes, noncooperation) that withdrew many forms of support from the regime. Specifically, the NCC was able to withdraw *authority* from the military regime by mobilizing an estimated 750,000 people for demonstrations, out of a total population of 2 million.[87] Many of these demonstrations were directly linked to events that revealed Noriega's lack of legitimacy in the public eye—such as the revelations that he was behind Spadafora's murder and the rigged elections in 1984 and 1989. These demonstrations also constituted the withdrawal of *cooperation and compliance with laws*, since marchers were defying the ban on public gatherings. Additionally, the general strikes reflected the withdrawal of *skills* and *material resources*, as profits were not being generated that could benefit the regime. Material resources were also withheld from the regime in other ways: through business owners' refusal to pay taxes; through the cancellation of international aid, loans, and imports; through the divestment of foreign capital; and through the freezing of Panamanian assets in U.S. banks. Finally, when the Catholic Church denounced the regime and sided with the National Civic Crusade, it challenged any traditional *religious mentalities of submission to the regime*.[88] Even appeals to nationalism and Panamanians' historical opposition to U.S. involvement did not shore up support for the military regime. In short, the National Civic Crusade used five of the six civil resistance techniques, but Noriega still held on.

So why couldn't the National Civic Crusade depose this military dictator? Some argue that the movement never established sufficient credibility among the labor sector.[89] Certainly, the media emphasized the elite character of many NCC leaders. One observer commented, "Despite the presence of blacks, Indians, and women from all classes, the most visible Crusade members were fancy-pants male Yuppies. They got noticed a lot by the international press ... [who commented that there were] so many BMWs, Hondas, and Mercedes ... at the opposition rallies that they resembled pregame traffic at the Yale Bowl."[90] But evidence shows that people from all backgrounds participated in NCC demonstrations and strikes, and hence this cannot fully explain the movement's failure. Nonetheless, race and class factors may have limited the National Civic Crusade's strength. As Richard Millett noted, "Despite the deep race and class divisions in Panamanian society, the constant identification of the opposition with white elite families has won few supporters for [Noriega]. Still, it may have kept some Panamanians on the sidelines, alienated and apathetic."[91]

I argue that the primary reason the National Civic Crusade failed was that it never prompted widespread unreliability or mutiny among PDF troops. In fact, Noriega was quite effective at ensuring that the majority of his troops remained loyal. He accomplished this in four ways. First, Noriega repeatedly reminded PDF troops that assaults on him were tantamount to assaults on the military institution as a whole. While many officers may have held unfavorable views of Noriega, few wanted to see the demise of a system that had made them wealthy. Second, Noriega removed soldiers whose loyalty was questionable. Those whom Noriega did not trust were transferred to overseas posts or forced into early retirement; those officers who pledged total support were promoted. Third, Noriega kept close tabs on all his officers. He fired the bodyguards of several high-ranking officers and had the new guards report directly to him about the officers' activities. This made it virtually impossible to conspire without Noriega's knowledge, minimizing officers' ability to engage in seditious acts. Fourth, his ruthless treatment of those who turned against him may have deterred others from following suit.[92] In short, by keeping control of the military, Noriega was able to keep control of the regime.

Noriega was also able to maintain power because he countered international economic sanctions with new aid from allied nations. Many policy makers felt that the impact of general strikes, frozen assets, and canceled aid would cause Noriega's regime to crumble. It nearly did. But the financial assistance from Libya and Taiwan kept Noriega solvent a little longer. If international sanctions had been universally applied, Panama's military regime might have collapsed under the weight of the nation's economic troubles. Yet in this Cold War era, when U.S. foreign policies had created numerous enemies, it was unlikely that the United States could get comprehensive trade and aid bans placed on Noriega. Ultimately, then, the sanctions harmed the Panamanian people more than Noriega himself—especially since much of his personal wealth was derived from illicit sources.

This last point raises an additional question: why did Noriega cling to power to the very end? Why did he not take the path of other dictators who preserved their lives and fortunes by fleeing into exile? Noriega certainly had this opportunity, as numerous countries offered enticing deals that would persuade many tyrants to step down. Even the United States offered to drop the drug-trafficking charges against him in exchange for his resignation. According to some, his tenacious grip on power is a reflection of the fact that he was no ordinary military dictator; he headed the world's first "narco-military regime." Roberto Eisenmann, editor of the Panamanian newspaper *La Prensa*, commented:

> Noriega has put Panama's military forces at the service of a multinational criminal enterprise. He must not be viewed as just another military ruler, but as a member of an international brotherhood of crime.... The mafia and criminal groups like it are held together by a code which says that once you join, you cannot retire and continue breathing. This is the basic covenant of these organizations, and the key reason why Noriega resists any deal that would require him to give up power. Noriega has no options.... If he leaves, he is a dead man. The real threat to him is not the United States or other countries that oppose him. It is not the indictments. It is the Medellín drug cartel.[93]

Similarly, Kevin Buckley argued, "Noriega could not have retired; he would have been murdered by the Medellín Cartel. In power, Noriega was useful to them. Out of power, he was dangerous; he knew too much. Staying in power and staying alive were the same for Noriega."[94]

Eisenmann notes that the narco-military nature of the regime also explains why the economic sanctions were not as effective as people anticipated.

> Another unique feature of the narco-military regime is that it has its own separate economy, wholly disconnected from the national economy. The Panamanian economy is going down the drain, but the economy of Panama's narco-mafia—with Noriega as its head—is doing better than ever.... Hence the kinds of economic sanctions that are usually applied to put pressure on dictatorships are of virtually no use against Noriega. As long as his drug economy continues to thrive, Noriega will not be concerned about what befalls the economy at large.[95]

In conclusion, this case reveals that theories of civil resistance need to account for the counterstrategies of opponents—especially those that can strengthen troops' loyalty and minimize the impact of international sanctions. Strategy and political opportunity are not the only factors that matter. As this case shows, the dictator's own maneuvers must be examined to have a full picture of how tyrants fall or how they remain in power.

CHAPTER 5
Ousting General Pinochet

Although Chile had a nearly 150-year-old legacy of democracy,[1] this tradition was abruptly interrupted in 1973, when a bloody coup d'état put in place a military regime. At the regime's helm was General Augusto Pinochet, who served both as president and commander in chief. Upon assuming power, Pinochet dissolved the Congress and the Constitutional Tribunal, destroyed the electoral register, outlawed all political parties, and detained opponents in internal exile camps. Within a couple of months of the coup, Pinochet's regime was responsible for thousands of civilian deaths; additionally, tens of thousands were arrested and held without due process of law.[2] Chileans braced for a dark period—one that seemed unlikely to end nonviolently. Yet despite Pinochet's brutality, megalomania, and determined efforts to cling to power, he was eventually deposed through civil resistance.

PINOCHET'S RISE TO POWER

The events that brought Pinochet to power began in the 1960s, when Chilean political attitudes increasingly shifted toward the left. This was partly due to growing dissatisfaction with conservative President Jorge Alessandri's policies that promoted foreign investment and free enterprise but failed to address the country's problems of unemployment, unequal distribution of wealth, and severe housing shortages.[3] One of the most vocal presidential critics was Salvador Allende, a physician who had represented the Socialist Party in Chile's Senate since 1945. In an attempt to change Alessandri's policies, Allende ran for the presidency in 1964 but lost to the centrist candidate Eduardo Frei.[4] The U.S. government had supported

Frei's bid for office, sending $20 million in covert funds to ensure Allende's defeat.[5] But Allende remained a potent political force. By 1966, he became Senate president and helped forge the Popular Unity coalition that linked Socialists, Communists, Radicals, Social Democrats, and other small political parties.[6]

The strength of the Popular Unity coalition expanded throughout President Frei's term. Although Frei made laudable gains—such as modest agrarian reform and winning partial ownership of U.S. copper companies operating in Chile—his policies did not notably improve the lives of common citizens. Moreover, he was unable to manage the country's escalating economic troubles.[7] Hence many were open to Allende's message during the 1970 presidential election as he promised to strengthen Chile's economy by taking control of its natural resources and industries. He also vowed to address the inequality that plagued Chile, where the wealthiest 2 percent of the population took in nearly 46 percent of the national income.[8] Therefore, the Chilean people elected him as president, albeit by a narrow margin.[9]

Once he was sworn into office, Allende quickly took action on Chile's economic and social problems. He froze prices on basic commodities and raised wages. With the unanimous backing of Chile's Senate, he nationalized the nation's copper companies[10] and expropriated 80 other industries. He reformed labor, educational, and health care policies to benefit the poor and working-class sectors. But these changes generated opposition from Chile's business leaders, who embarked on a strike. Shops closed, and large landowners refused to cultivate their fields, causing a food shortage. Transportation companies ceased operations, and industrial production slowed. The strike infuriated peasants and members of the working class, who were determined to keep their newly acquired gains. Thus workers took over factories, and peasants seized plantations in an effort to produce essential commodities. The elites responded with violence, sponsoring groups that destroyed railroads, bridges, highways, gas lines, and power plants.[11]

The country was on the brink of chaos when the 1973 election took place. Many thought that Allende's coalition would lose ground because of the strikes and commodity shortages. Moreover, the economy had worsened as the consumer inflation rate rose 508.1 percent from the previous year.[12] But to the surprise of many, the Popular Unity coalition actually gained votes, up from 36.3 percent in 1970 to 43.4 percent in the 1973 election.[13] Discouraged by the election outcome and their inability to dislodge Allende, conservative forces immediately began to contemplate other methods of removing him from office.[14]

Elite civilians were not the only ones conspiring against Allende. So, too, were members of the Chilean armed forces, who believed that a military intervention was the only way to prevent civil war. Some officers were opposed to a coup, arguing that the military must uphold the constitution and retain its tradition of political neutrality,[15] but the pro-intervention forces won out, eventually carrying out their plans on September 11, 1973.

The Coup

The coup began early in the morning. President Allende received a phone call that the military had rebelled; troops had blocked Santiago's major streets, taken control of the radio and television networks, and ordered tanks to encircle the presidential palace. Allende, however, refused to flee. At 9:15 that morning, he made the following statement on the socialist radio station, Radio Magallanes:

> Surely, this will be the last time I will be able to speak to you. . . . My words do not reflect bitterness, but disappointment. . . . I say to the workers: I will not resign! Placed on this historic crossroad, I will pay for the people's loyalty with my life. And I say to you that I am certain that the seeds planted in the worthy conscience of thousands upon thousands of Chileans will not be mowed down forever. . . . I speak to the worker, the peasant, the intellectual, and to those who will be persecuted, because in our country fascism has been present for a long time in the form of terrorist attacks, blowing up bridges, cutting off railroads, destroying oil and gas pipelines, in the face of the silence of those who had the duty to take action. History will judge them.
>
> Surely, Radio Magallanes will be silenced and the calm metal of my voice will no longer reach you. It does not matter. You will continue to hear me. I will always be with you. . . . Workers of my homeland: I have faith in Chile and its future. Other men will overcome this dark and bitter moment when treason is attempting to prevail. You must continue to believe that, sooner rather than later, the grand avenues will open again through which free men will pass to build a better society. Long live Chile, long live the people, and long live the workers![16]

Even as Allende was delivering his message, troops were advancing on the palace. The president gathered his cabinet members and advisers together, urging them to depart before the fighting began. When they pledged to remain with him to the end, he insisted that they leave, stating: "Someone has to relate what has happened here, and only you can do that."[17] Shortly thereafter, two fighter jets bombed the palace while planes strafed the building. Allende's guards were defeated within 90 minutes. When the soldiers finally reached the president's office, they found Allende dead from a gunshot wound to the head—an apparent suicide.[18]

By late afternoon, the military had gained control of the nation. By nightfall, a four-person junta held the reins of power. The junta was comprised of

Army General Augusto Pinochet, Air Force General Gustavo Leigh, Navy Admiral José Torinio Merino, and General César Mendoza of the national military police. Pinochet was appointed to head the new military regime, but he told the press that leadership would rotate among the junta's four members. That never happened. Within a year, Pinochet consolidated his power to become the sole ruling general—a role he would not relinquish for 16 years.[19]

The Onset of State Repression

Immediately after the coup, Pinochet began a search-and-destroy mission to root out leftists in shantytowns, factories, and universities throughout Santiago. Troops rounded up Popular Unity supporters and brought them to the National Stadium, which had been transformed into a detention center. There suspects were interrogated, tortured, and often executed. An estimated 50,000 people were held as prisoners in the weeks that followed the coup.[20] But the repression was not limited to the capital. A special military commission traveled throughout the country, punishing those who had resisted the coup. By mid-October, the commission had been dubbed the "Caravan of Death" because it had executed 75 people.[21] By the end of 1973, the death count was astonishingly high. While the Chilean military claimed that 1,260 citizens had died, a U.S. State Department report estimated that 10,800 were killed within a three-month span.[22]

The post-coup repression was not a brief stage. It became a long-term state of affairs when Pinochet created the Directorate for National Intelligence (DINA) to eliminate so-called subversives. From the time of the coup until 1978, DINA terrorized the population, primarily targeting political leftists, those involved in social movements and church organizations, and officers whose loyalty was questionable.[23] Its activities even extended beyond Chile's borders. One year after Pinochet took power, DINA agents killed General Prats, who had been living in Argentina since he was forced into exile after the coup. Because Prats was still widely respected by members of the armed forces, Pinochet wanted to eliminate the possibility that he could organize a counter-coup. It also took action against Orlando Letelier—Allende's defense minister who had fled to the United States. Living in Washington, D.C., Letelier became a vocal critic of the military junta and launched a campaign to suspend all international aid to Chile. In 1976, DINA operatives planted a car bomb that killed Letelier, just a few blocks from the White House.[24] The message was clear: Pinochet's opponents were never safe, no matter where they were.

In addition to the widespread use of repression, Pinochet reinforced his rule by enacting major political changes. He dissolved the Congress and Constitutional Tribunal, declared that all political parties were in recess, and banned the Popular Unity coalition. In June 1974, Pinochet implemented Legislative Decree 527, which granted the military junta constitutional and legislative powers, and he gave himself executive power and the title of "Supreme Chief of the Nation." By the end of 1974, he convinced the junta to name him president of the Republic of Chile.[25] This gave Pinochet the capacity to issue decrees without the approval of his colleagues. Using his newly acquired executive powers, Pinochet shut down 75 percent of the nation's newspapers, ordered military control of universities, and prohibited public singing and guitars.[26]

Pinochet's next political move was to reverse Allende's policies and improve the country's ailing economy. To achieve this, he hired Chilean economists known as the "Chicago Boys" because they had studied with Milton Friedman at the University of Chicago. Friedman himself traveled to Chile in 1975 to offer consultation; he encouraged the regime to take drastic action, starting with the privatization of banks and the creation of free market enterprises.[27] As these policies were implemented, there were some signs of an economic turnaround: the economy grew 6.8 percent in 1978, 6.5 percent in 1979, and 5 percent in 1980.[28] Pinochet was applauded for this "economic miracle," even though it was short-lived.[29]

THE CHILEAN CHURCH AND THE EMERGENCE OF OPPOSITION GROUPS

As Pinochet transformed Chile from a civilian-controlled socialist democracy into a free market military dictatorship, the population did not passively accept these changes. Despite DINA's repressive actions, groups soon started to organize against the regime, and churches were at the forefront of these efforts. Initially, the most active opposition group was the Comité de Cooperación para la Paz en Chile (COPACHI), or simply the Committee for Peace. Under the Santiago archdiocese's domain, the Committee for Peace offered legal aid and material assistance to those suffering political persecution. It was quickly flooded with requests, and within six months of the coup, Committee for Peace lawyers responded to 1,300 petitions. Based on evidence from these clients, the committee released details of 134 torture cases. In response, Chile's bishops publicly expressed their concern over interrogation abuses and detentions without charges.

Although this marked the Catholic Church's first overt criticism of the Pinochet regime, the critique was tempered by ambivalence about the situation. Some bishops had opposed Allende and thus felt a degree of gratitude toward the junta for removing him from office. Others feared that a strong condemnation might put the Committee for Peace at risk. But this ambivalence quickly evaporated. By March 1975, the organization had taken on more than 18,000 cases;[30] these cases revealed a consistent pattern of human rights abuses, compelling Chile's Catholic hierarchy to release the following statement:

> The acts [of repression] that we denounce and condemn are not isolated incidents.... By constant appeal to national security, a model of society is being consolidated that takes away basic liberties, runs roughshod over the most fundamental rights and subjugates citizens to a dreaded and omnipotent police state.... The Church cannot remain passive or neutral in the face of such a situation. The legacy which she has received from Christ demands that she speak out in favor of human dignity and for the effective protection of the liberty and rights of the person.[31]

As it exposed the regime's abusive practices, the Committee for Peace infuriated Pinochet. But the dictator did not dare to directly attack this church-sponsored organization since 80 percent of Chileans were Catholic. Therefore, he searched for ways to eliminate the committee, and he got the opportunity when a shootout occurred between DINA forces and members of the armed Movement of the Revolutionary Left (MIR). One MIR member was killed in the fight, but several were wounded and sought refuge in a church. The local priest ensured that they received medical attention and then helped them flee the country. This gave Pinochet the ammunition to shut down the Committee for Peace at the end of 1975, claiming that it was a front for the armed guerrilla movement. But just as COPACHI was disbanded, Cardinal Silva formed a new organization in January 1976—the Vicariate of Solidarity.[32] According to Brian Smith:

> While there were some changes in personnel, the new organization continued the same services of COPACHI and was made an integral part of the juridical structures of the Archdiocese of Santiago. While the Church had lost a tactical skirmish with the government, the strategy of the cardinal was shrewd and foresighted. The new Vicariate of Solidarity was more closely tied to the official Church than its predecessor, making it both easier for the bishops to control and harder for the government to smash without directly attacking the core of the Church itself.[33]

But the Chilean Catholic Church did not stop with the formation of the Vicariate. It sponsored numerous other opposition organizations. These included research institutes such as the Academia de Humanismo Cristiano that housed professors who had been fired for their political views; the institute became an important source of alternative information during the period of government censorship.[34] The church also established the Association for Families of Those Executed for Political Reasons and the Association of Families of the Detained-Disappeared. Since most of those detained or killed were men, these associations were predominantly filled with their surviving wives, mothers, and grandmothers. In an ironic twist, these women—who had traditionally been viewed as weak and unthreatening—became a menace to Pinochet's regime. As they stood in front of government buildings holding signs asking, "Where are they?" the national police were reluctant to carry out orders to hurt these women.[35]

In addition to providing free space for these oppositional groups to organize, the Chilean church also offered monetary support. From 1974 to 1979, the worst years of repression, the Chilean Catholic Church received more than $67 million in financial and material donations from Catholic groups in Europe and North America. It received another $20 million from the Inter-American Foundation and $10 million from the World Council of Churches.[36] Not surprisingly, Pinochet tried to stop this influx of resources, but he eventually capitulated under mounting international pressure from the Roman Catholic Church, the World Council of Churches, members of the U.S. Congress, and representatives from the Inter-American Development Bank.[37] Without this critical funding, oppositional activities and human rights work would have been difficult, if not impossible, to sustain.

TURN OF EVENTS IN THE 1980S

During the 1970s, church-sponsored groups documented human rights abuses and offered legal aid to detainees. They did not try to oust Pinochet. But by 1980, the military junta developed a new constitution that made it nearly impossible to make political changes through institutional mechanisms since all proposed legislation would now have to be unanimously approved by the four-man junta. The new constitution also granted Pinochet discretionary powers to restrict freedom of information, to limit rights of assembly, to expel anyone espousing Marxist doctrines, and to arrest people without charges and detain them for up to five days. Although the regime had already taken these measures, such actions now had constitutional legitimacy.[38] Finally, the new constitution added eight more years to Pinochet's term, after which the junta would nominate a single candidate that the population could approve or reject in a plebiscite vote. Since only the junta could nominate candidates, Chileans had no chance of electing an oppositional leader.

To give the appearance of legitimacy, the junta allowed Chileans to vote on whether to ratify the new constitution. Unfortunately, no mechanisms were in place to ensure a fair process. Not surprisingly, the regime declared a victory, claiming there was popular support for the new constitution. Pinochet and his colleagues were able to get away with this dubious process for a number of reasons: the economy had begun to turn around, Jimmy Carter was leaving office and incoming President Reagan was more likely to support their ardent anti-communist position, and new atrocities in El Salvador, Cambodia, and other places were preoccupying the international community.[39] Thus at the beginning of the 1980s, opposition groups were not optimistic about their chances of restoring democracy.

Mass Mobilizations and Strikes Begin

Yet within a few years, the demand for change re-emerged when Chile's economy took a sharp downturn. The nation's unemployment rate rose to 20.8 percent, people's purchasing power declined to 1971 levels, and the country's debt ballooned to almost $1.5 billion. In the first half of 1982, 363 Chilean companies went bankrupt, causing the collapse of numerous banks.[40] This led the Copper Workers' Confederation to call for national demonstrations. Tens of thousands participated in rallies, work slowdowns, strikes, boycotts, and "noise riots" with honking horns and clanking pots. The regime responded quickly, detaining 300 people, injuring 50, and killing 2.[41] Despite the crackdown, organizers were inspired by the turnout and thus called for monthly national demonstrations. The success of these demonstrations led political leaders from the right, left, and center to join forces, forming a coalition called the Democratic Alliance.

As opposition grew, so too did Pinochet's brutality. Before an August 1983 demonstration, he ordered a 6:00 P.M. curfew and stationed 18,000 soldiers around the capital. Troops attacked protesters, killing 25 in the process. During the September marches, nine protesters were killed. At every monthly demonstration that followed, a handful of citizens paid for their resistance with their lives.[42] Finally, in an attempt to bring the demonstrations to a definitive end, Pinochet invoked his constitutional power and declared a state of siege in November 1984. *Siege* is the only appropriate word for what happened next. According to an Americas Watch report, during the next 17 months, nearly 39,500 citizens were arrested, and 621 were sentenced to "internal exile."[43]

The Effects of the Siege

The purpose of the siege was to demonstrate the regime's power and frighten citizens into submission. But it backfired. Instead of strengthening the regime, the repression produced divisions within Pinochet's cabinet. In February 1985, the finance minister and interior minister resigned in protest.[44] Then, in August 1985, the national police director resigned over concerns that state-sponsored violence would justify attacks on his officers. To rectify these internal divisions, Pinochet replaced his cabinet members with far more compliant individuals who would not question his policies.[45]

The siege also generated tension between Pinochet and some of his traditional supporters, including U.S. politicians. Although there was an initial honeymoon period between Pinochet and the Reagan administration, the White House began pressuring Pinochet to end the siege.[46] Tensions escalated during U.S. Assistant Secretary of State Langhorne Motley's visit to Chile in 1985. While Langhorne publicly stated that Chile was in good hands,[47] he later described a different type of encounter to a *New York Times* reporter. Motley stated:

> [Pinochet] was the toughest nut I've ever seen. He makes [Nicaraguan dictator] Somoza and the rest of those guys look like a bunch of patsies.... He put his finger under my nose and said, "We're not a colony of the United States. Relations have not been very good between us for a long time. We almost went to war in the last century, and I don't take advice." I told him I was not there to lecture but that I wanted to tell him what the reactions were outside, in Europe and the United States.... I told him that . . . he was helping the leftists in places like Washington and Paris and that he ought to do something to let the air out of the balloon.[48]

Pinochet made it clear: he was willing to fight his battle without American support.

Divisions within the Opposition Movement

Even as Pinochet was suffering from internal divisions and loss of international support, the opposition had its own problems. The movement experienced a rift between moderates, who supported the Democratic Alliance, and communists who had formed their own group, the Popular Democratic Movement. Although they were united by their interest in removing Pinochet from power, they were divided over strategy. Moderates wanted to pressure the regime into negotiating a democratic transition. Communists rejected any form of dialogue, convinced that "the only way to efficiently confront and bring down the regime is by making use of all forms of combat, including armed struggle."[49] The communists had already launched a guerrilla movement in early 1984 that was destroying transportation systems, assassinating police officers, and sabotaging electrical towers. This outraged Democratic Alliance members, who stated: "Our party does not wish to be, nor will it be, the civil arbiter of a dirty war between armed groups."[50] As a result of these divisions, plans for additional actions—including a general strike—quickly died out. The movement stagnated in early 1985.

The New Accord and the Emergence of the Civic Assembly

By August 1985, a new effort was underway. Despite the failures of the Democratic Alliance, organizers were aware that shifting political conditions offered a favorable opportunity to act. Specifically, three key changes had occurred. First, due to the siege, right-wing political groups were breaking ties with the regime and distancing themselves from Pinochet.[51] Second, the Chilean Catholic Church—under the new leadership of Cardinal Fresno—was willing to not only challenge human rights abuses but also take a leading role in negotiating a solution to the nation's political situation. As a respected institution with moral authority, this heightened the opposition's credibility—something it needed after the guerrilla attacks of 1984.[52] Third, the Reagan administration was increasingly turning against Pinochet. At home, Reagan faced mounting pressure to stop supporting abusive Third World autocrats. Moreover, as revolutionary movements throughout Latin America gained momentum, presidential advisers warned that continued support for Pinochet was likely to strengthen the Chilean communist movement; it would be wiser to negotiate a transition to democracy.[53]

Under these new conditions—where Pinochet lost his traditional support base while his opposition gained new allies—Cardinal Fresno asked his advisers to draft a "National Accord for the Transition to Democracy." The accord called for an immediate end to the state of emergency and proposed that the scheduled 1988 plebiscite be replaced by free and fair elections. Parties from all ends of the political spectrum signed the accord, although radical communists were excluded since they continued to advocate armed struggle. Eventually, 800,000 individuals endorsed the document, but Pinochet still refused to budge. Unable to provoke a response from the regime, this initiative withered.[54]

As it became clear that Pinochet would not negotiate a transition, many concluded that they would have to force him out of office through nonviolent resistance. This led to the April 1986 formation of the Civic Assembly. This coalition of labor and civic groups went into action immediately, calling for demonstrations and a general strike in July. Although the actions drew thousands of participants, it also led the regime to new levels of brutality. On July 2, 1986, several teenagers were headed to a demonstration. One of these teenagers was Rodrigo Rojas, a 19-year-old freelance journalist who was raised in Washington, D.C., by Chilean parents. When an army truck turned onto the street where the teenagers were walking, the others fled, but soldiers managed to catch Rojas and his acquaintance, Carmen Quintana. After interrogating them, the soldiers doused the teenagers with gasoline and set them on fire. Eventually, they wrapped the charred bodies in blankets and tossed them into a ditch. Rojas and Quintana managed to crawl to a road, where a passing motorist brought them to a hospital. Rojas died two days later. Quintana was given a 6 percent chance of survival, but after outraged citizens offered skin graft donations and funds for her treatment, she eventually recovered and testified against the army.[55]

Opposition Setbacks

The international community condemned the immolations, and the resistance movement gained greater strength. But soon after this incident, two events marked a serious setback for the opposition. The first was the August 1986 discovery of arms caches containing more than a thousand M-16 assault rifles and Soviet rocket-propelled grenade launchers. According to U.S. intelligence sources, the weapons had been transported from Cuban vessels to various locations in Chile.[56] Pinochet used the discovery to his full advantage, playing up Cold War fears to win back support and justify harsh anticommunist policies. Then, in September 1986, a communist guerrilla group attempted to kill Pinochet during a presidential motorcade. Pinochet's car was riddled with bullets, and a rocket had blown the roof off. But Pinochet and all of the car's occupants escaped without harm.[57]

The attempted assassination deepened Pinochet's sense of destiny and invincibility. He believed he would handily win the 1988 plebiscite vote. Chileans, however, were not ready to acquiesce. In fact, despite the setbacks in 1986, one survey showed that 85 percent of the population was willing to take action to remove Pinochet from power.[58] But demonstrations and strikes had failed to rattle the regime. While some doubted whether nonviolent methods would work, the arms cache discovery and the assassination debacle made it clear that they had no other choice. Organizers decided to make Pinochet play by his own rules, and they began focusing their efforts on the upcoming plebiscite.

The plebiscite can hardly be considered a political election since it entailed two options: voting yes to keep Pinochet in power for another eight years or no to denote the desire for free elections. Free elections would be difficult to achieve since they would require changing the 1980 constitution. But when a few military leaders indicated that they would support such constitutional changes, opposition leaders took hope. Hence organizers formed a new coalition, the Concertación Partidos por el No (Coalition of Parties for NO).

To ensure a fair plebiscite vote, Concertación organizers secured the services of neutral election observers and independent pollsters. Their efforts were supported by the Reagan administration, which sent $1.2 million and convinced Congress to appropriate another million to finance a parallel vote count.[59] But organizers faced another major challenge: convincing people that voting was worthwhile. One survey revealed that apathy and skepticism were strong; up to 80 percent of the population believed that Pinochet would find a way to maintain power.[60] Eventually, the momentum of the campaign gave people hope and a vision of what could happen if the no vote was victorious. Even the communists, who had grown more isolated after the attempted assassination, eventually put aside their armed struggle and joined in. Next, the NO movement launched a voter registration campaign, since less than half of eligible voters were registered. Opposition leaders reminded people that Pinochet had burned the electoral registers in 1973 and this was their chance to restore them. The campaign was a tremendous success, with nearly 92 percent of eligible citizens signing up.[61]

But Pinochet was a formidable opponent, and he channeled massive resources into his campaign. He used $200 million in international loans to build homes for the poor in an attempt to win their support. He also barred his opponents from television, while the networks continuously aired ads depicting Pinochet as Chile's savior, defending the nation from communist evils. His ads additionally gave Pinochet credit for the economy—which was now on an upward trajectory—and warned that a NO victory would lead to anarchy and civil war. Pinochet even sent out nocturnal brigades of police to paint proregime slogans on public walls and curbs. His wife got into the action, too, mobilizing right-wing women's groups to promote the YES vote.[62] Naturally, Pinochet also relied on his traditional tactics of repression. Opposition offices were firebombed, campaign organizers were beaten and harassed, and nearly 1,800 people were arrested.[63]

When the plebiscite was held on October 5, 1988, hundreds of thousands were already in line when the polls opened at 8:00 A.M. Troops were stationed throughout Santiago, and Pinochet told reporters that 25,000 soldiers were ready to take action if necessary. Election observers dutifully carried out their functions, and North American pollsters carefully monitored the results. By 9:00 P.M., the independent polls showed that the NO count was well ahead. But an hour later, Pinochet ordered the state television network to announce that the YES campaign was victorious. He also ordered police to lift the security cordon downtown so his supporters could celebrate. The police commander, however, refused to do so.

Outraged, Pinochet called in his advisers and cabinet members, blaming them for his loss and firing them. Next, he summoned the other junta leaders—the commanders of the navy, air force, and military police. Presuming their unwavering support, he announced that he would declare martial law and annul the vote. But each of the commanders refused to go along with the plan. Indignant, Pinochet presented them with documents that broadened his powers to "deal with the post-plebiscite political situation."[64] The generals, however, knew that the end had come; instead of signing off on the proposed decree, they tore up the documents and left. Pinochet's closest supporters were no longer willing to carry out his orders, and they refused to allow their troops to overturn the plebiscite. With no one to enforce his will, Pinochet had no option but to concede defeat.[65] The following day, official tallies indicated that 54.7 percent of voters had cast their ballots for NO, compared to 43 percent who voted YES to Pinochet.[66]

The junta's break from Pinochet marked the end of the military regime. Constitutional amendments were soon passed that enabled free elections to be held, and a civilian president was elected in 1989. Pinochet was not immediately out of the picture, though, since he remained commander in chief until 1998, at which point he assumed his position as senator—a role that, as former president, he was legally entitled to until he died. As a senator, he was immune from prosecution, and thus it appeared that he would live out his years with impunity. Yet the situation changed when Pinochet traveled to Great Britain for medical treatment. While he was there, a Spanish judge tried to extradite him to stand trial on charges of torture, murder, illegal detentions, and forced disappearances. Eventually, Pinochet returned to Chile and argued that his medical condition made him unfit to stand trial. The judge ruled against him, and soon he faced roughly 300 charges of torture, embezzlement, and tax fraud. But the trials were never completed. Pinochet died from a heart attack in 2006 before any verdict was reached.[67]

FACTORS FACILITATING PINOCHET'S FALL

The effort to oust Pinochet occurred over several years, including some failed campaigns before the ultimately successful plebiscite approach. During this time, structural conditions fluctuated, sometimes favoring the opposition movement and in other instances favoring the regime. For example, it was the economic crisis in the early 1980s that precipitated the Copper Union Workers' strike and subsequent demonstrations. Dramatic economic changes—such as interest rates rising to 39 percent in 1981, gross domestic product declining by 14.1 percent in 1982, and unemployment rates reaching 30 percent by 1983[68]—brought a prime opportunity to mobilize since more people were struggling financially and even the wealthy began to suffer and distance themselves from Pinochet. But then the economy began to improve. Interest rates fell from 39 percent down to a more manageable 11.4 percent in 1984; that same year, Chile's economy grew by 6.3 percent.[69] It continued to expand throughout the late 1980s, strengthening support for Pinochet as the plebiscite approached.

International influence constituted another shifting variable. On the one hand, the resistance movement had strong external support—primarily through the solidarity networks built by Chilean exiles and the financial contributions from international church groups. The United Nations also weighed in on the situation, officially condemning Chile's human rights abuses but not imposing any sanctions. Moreover, by the mid-1980s, the opposition movement gained a surprising new ally in the White House. However, even as international pressures were mounting against Pinochet, the political landscape changed when Cuban-delivered arms were discovered in Chile, reviving Cold War fears and bringing the regime new support. Moreover, international pressures were muted by the developed world's financial interests. For instance, by mid-1986, some U.S. politicians were threatening to vote against ongoing loans to Chile. Chile had borrowed $3.1 billion from multilateral banks to deal with its economic crisis; given its economic vulnerability, the cessation of funds could have seriously destabilized the Pinochet regime. But the banks continued to make loans throughout Pinochet's reign since it was considered a sound investment.[70]

If structural conditions alone do not account for Pinochet's eventual demise, then we must examine how strategic factors shaped the struggle's outcome. Civil resisters withdrew their support from the regime in several ways. The mass demonstrations, noise riots, and plebiscite vote indicated that tens of thousands of citizens no longer considered Pinochet's rule *legitimate*. The Chilean church's denunciation of the regime, coupled with its support for the opposition movement, indicated that it was altering traditional *religious mentalities* that encourage submission to the government. And citizen *cooperation* was withheld, albeit often in symbolic ways—such as holding a rock concert during voter registration drives when Pinochet had banned guitars and public singing.[71]

Civil resisters also engaged in strikes, which temporary withheld *skills*. These general strikes had the potential to undercut the regime's *material resources* and paralyze the country, bringing industry and services to a standstill. But in the Chilean case, this tactic had a very limited effect. Government policies permitted strikes but allowed employers to hire new workers after 30 days. After 60 days, all employees were required to return to work; failure to do so could legally be interpreted as a resignation.[72] In Chile's crumbling economy, with record levels of unemployment, many workers were unwilling to strike long enough to undermine the regime's capacity to function. Hence, the opposition movement only managed to use three civil resistance techniques: the refusal to recognize Pinochet's authority, the refusal to cooperate and comply with laws, and challenging mentalities of obedience. The movement did not fully withhold civilian skills or material resources from the regime since international loans continued to flow into Chile.

In examining strategic factors, we must also take a closer look at Pinochet's counterstrategy, which primarily entailed two components. First and foremost, he used repression to terrorize people into submission. Second, he tried to conduct election fraud by declaring that the YES vote had won. When that effort was no longer viable due to the public's knowledge of the NO campaign victory, he planned to annul the vote. But neither of those strategies worked. Chileans refused to back down in the face of regime violence, and Pinochet could not pull off the planned electoral fraud.

Ultimately, the critical factor that brought Pinochet down was the defection of his top military leaders. By all appearances, Pinochet would have continued to rule if he had been able to annul or rig the plebiscite. But the other junta leaders refused to cooperate. This loss of his sanctioning power was not primarily due to the opposition movement's efforts since civil resisters made few attempts to undermine armed forces' loyalty. In fact, there was very little contact between civilians and troops. As one analyst noted, "The powerful socialization experience of military service in Chile made it difficult for civilians to build bridges to military leaders. . . . Indeed, excessive social contact of officers with civilians was severely sanctioned by military authorities."[73] Moreover, one survey indicated that 73 percent of civilians distrusted the armed forces. Since the military had already demonstrated its willingness to repress, trying to undermine troops' loyalty may have seemed a far-fetched prospect.[74] Finally, civilians and soldiers did not share a collective identity that would have made mutinous appeals resonate. Chilean military culture encouraged soldiers to see themselves as part of a professional government institution more than as a protective force for the people (as in China and East Germany). Hence their loyalty was to the government above all else.

In addition, Pinochet had worked hard to ensure loyalty. It started immediately after the 1973 coup, when the military junta gave Pinochet exclusive power over the promotion and retirement of officers. He used this authority to remove any potential rivals. He also promoted many young officers, increasing the number of generals from 25 in 1973 to 52 by 1985. But these officers were keenly aware that their careers depended on their ongoing devotion to Pinochet, who had required that they all submit a letter of resignation that was kept on file, should anyone begin to challenge his authority. If they remained loyal, Pinochet granted them numerous benefits, including ambassadorial appointments or other lucrative positions. This cemented commanders' commitment to the regime and to Pinochet.[75]

So why, then, did these commanders finally turn on Pinochet in 1988? There are three main reasons. First, resentment had grown as Pinochet subordinated the other military branches to the army, which had executive powers.[76] This angered the military police, who felt that the army was interfering in police responsibilities. Air force officers also resented how Pinochet had previously taken over their branch when their commander challenged his policies.[77] And the navy commander was at odds with the army high command over how to handle a territorial dispute with Argentina.[78] There is even evidence that some army officers wanted Pinochet removed because his favoritism toward the army was destroying the historic unity that had existed within the military.[79]

A second reason that military commanders turned against Pinochet is that they did not believe they could convince the population that the YES vote had won since numerous polls had verified a NO victory. News of the opposition's success had already leaked from several sources. Former Interior Minister Sergio Jarpa mentioned the plebiscite results on the Catholic University's televised talk show while air force commander General Fernando Matthei told reporters that the NO vote had won, just minutes before he attended the emergency meeting called by Pinochet. Matthei's statement was quickly broadcast on Santiago's Radio Cooperativa, an opposition-sponsored station. Although Pinochet was furious at the junta's admission of defeat, his military advisers feared that any attempt to alter or annul the outcome would create a national state of chaos.[80]

The third reason the commanders were willing to break from Pinochet was because the constitution ensured that the military would retain considerable power, even if Pinochet were no longer president.[81] Gregory Weeks argues:

> The military had constructed a firm legal and constitutional base of power before the transition began in 1988.... The constitution reflected a greatly enhanced military influence over the president, especially in times of emergency, as well as a strong voice in Congress. Since military budgets were largely protected, officers did not have to worry about significant financial erosion. Finally, since the constitution required large majorities for reform, none of this would change in the near future. In short, as the junta made

way for civilians to govern Chile once again, the armed forces were in a privileged and influential position.[82]

Based on these three reasons, the junta commanders were united in their opposition to Pinochet's plan to void the election. That made the difference in the outcome of this struggle. Structural conditions that favored the movement—including divided elites, international pressure, and finally a unified opposition—were not enough to bring down Pinochet. The nonviolent withholding of authority, cultural attitudes of submission, and cooperation did not cause the regime to crumble. Protesters had not persuaded troops on the street to refuse orders or desert. Rather, the definitive moment came when ruling military leaders sided with the population and refused to support an unjust leader any longer. The undermining of a state's repressive capacity and sanctioning powers—initiated by high-ranking officers or low-ranking troops—is what ultimately incapacitates any ruler.

PART THREE

Nonviolent Revolts Against Personal Dictators

CHAPTER 6
Kenya's Struggle against the Moi Dictatorship

Just as Chileans were resisting the Pinochet regime, Kenyans embarked on a similar struggle. They had watched their country turn into an autocracy, headed by President Daniel arap Moi. Like Pinochet, Moi resorted to deceit, fraud, repression, and violence to hold onto power. While he claimed that Kenya was a "one-party democracy," Kenyan citizens demanded genuine democracy, along with basic freedoms and an end to human rights abuses. Using an array of nonviolent tactics, the movement brought international pressure on Moi, forcing him to make concessions. But it was never able to force him out of office, and thus Moi ruled Kenya for 24 years. What explains this tyrant's political longevity? What enabled Moi to retain power while other dictators, such as Pinochet, were eventually deposed?

FORMATION OF THE MODERN KENYAN STATE

To understand Kenyan politics, one must consider its colonial history, which began when Great Britain took control of the region in the late 19th century. Kenyans resisted foreign rule and fought the discriminatory treatment that British settlers and European companies commonly practiced. Colonial rulers tried to strengthen their control by cultivating divisions among Kenya's ethnic groups, in hopes that they would fight each other rather than the British. They also gave tribal chiefs a role in assisting colonial leaders in local governance. But this gave Kenyans only limited political influence, and thus nationalist groups quickly emerged to fight for full independence.[1]

One of the leading nationalist groups was the Kenya African Union (KAU) headed by Jomo Kenyatta. Kenyatta realized that they would never win independence until they overcame ethnic rivalries, but this was a significant challenge since Kenya has more than 40 ethnic groups. The largest are the Kikuyu (21 percent), the Luhya (14 percent), and the Luo (14 percent); smaller groups include the Kalenjin (11 percent), the Kamba (11 percent), and small European, Arab, and Indian communities.[2] Kenyatta was Kikuyu, but he collaborated closely with other groups, especially the Luo. As a result, KAU membership quickly expanded to 150,000, and this multiethnic coalition continually pressured Britain to grant independence.[3]

A second nationalist group, the Mau Mau, used a different type of pressure. From 1952 to 1956, the Mau Mau waged guerrilla warfare, mainly against European settlers who had appropriated vast segments of Kenya's highlands. They also attacked colonial police stations and assassinated Kenyans who assisted the British government. In response to this violence, British leaders declared martial law in 1952. Shortly thereafter, they detained and interrogated thousands of Kikuyu, who filled the ranks of Mau Mau fighters.[4] Then, in 1953 the British banned the KAU and imprisoned its leader, Jomo Kenyatta.[5]

But British repression only strengthened Kenyan resistance. Thus, colonial leaders eventually convened a conference in London in 1960 to plan the transition to independence, create a new constitution, and fashion a Kenyan government around the Westminster parliamentary model. Two main political groups came to the forefront in this new Kenyan government: (1) the Kenyan African National Union (KANU), a Kikuyu-Luo coalition headed by Jomo Kenyatta, who had recently been released from prison, and (2) the Kenyan African Democratic Union (KADU), a coalition of smaller ethnic groups. When elections were held in May 1963, KANU triumphed. Independence was granted in December 1963, and Kenya, led by President Kenyatta, officially became a republic in 1964.[6]

The Kenyatta Years: 1963–1978

After assuming office, Kenyatta undercut any potential challenges to his presidency. He eliminated his primary political rival, the Kenyan African Democratic Union (KADU), by incorporating it into his own political party (KANU). The ethnic minorities that KADU represented agreed to this move partly because Kenyatta appointed KADU leader Daniel arap

Moi, an ethnic Kalenjin, as vice president.[7] Then, to remove his other major political opponent, Kenyatta banned the socialist-oriented Kenya People's Union (KPU) in 1969.[8] Kenyatta also strengthened his position by granting business leaders lucrative government contracts in exchange for their support. Moreover, he informed aspiring politicians that they could become parliamentarians only if they demonstrated unequivocal loyalty to him; all other candidates could expect that elections would be rigged against them.[9]

Through these strategic maneuvers, Kenyatta ruled with relative ease for nearly 15 years. But during his last years in office, he allowed corruption to expand, he increasingly used his political office for personal enrichment, he grew more intolerant of internal party dissent, and he demonstrated a greater willingness to use repressive measures.[10] This concerned Kikuyu elites, who feared that Kenyatta was alienating ethnic minorities who might try to gain political power and then overturn long-standing Kikuyu privileges. Therefore, as Kenyatta's health deteriorated in the mid-1970s, some Kikuyu leaders attempted to remove the constitutional provision that would grant power to Vice President Daniel arap Moi in the event of Kenyatta's death. But the proposed constitutional change was not approved before Kenyatta passed away in 1978. At that moment, Moi became Kenya's new president.[11]

The Moi Regime

Initially, newly inaugurated President Moi won praise as he released political prisoners and established social programs such as free milk for school children.[12] Amnesty International even proclaimed that "a new era of tolerance" had been ushered in.[13] But Moi was in a precarious situation: he was an ethnic minority president surrounded by politicians, military officers, civil servants, and business leaders whose interests and loyalties differed from his own. Thus Moi quickly began to de-Kikiyunize the government. He removed existing Kikuyu leaders by intentionally compromising their integrity and then forcing them to resign for moral violations. Then he moved ethnic minorities into these newly vacated positions.[14] Moreover, he tightened his control over Kenya's security forces by replacing high-ranking officers and the police commissioner. Moi also rushed a bill through parliament that enabled him to increase surveillance of opposition groups, restrict rights of assembly, and enact emergency powers during peacetime.[15] By 1982, Moi had additionally eliminated regional and ethnic welfare societies—since they had become a forum for political organizing—and he passed a constitutional amendment establishing KANU as the only legal polit-ical party.[16] Hence Kenya moved "from being a de facto one party regime to a de jure one."[17]

All these changes generated resistance, especially among the Kikuyu and Luo. Opposition to Moi increased further when the Kenyan economy declined in the early 1980s. Although Kenya had been one of the most financially stable African states, it now faced growing inflation and budget deficits. Consequently, a group of air force officers tried to overthrow the president in August 1982. But rather than weakening Moi, the failed coup caused him to consolidate his power more thoroughly.[18] He brought in new military and police leaders, who—as ethnic minorities—pledged loyalty to Moi. He removed more political rivals from office. He escalated the use of repressive tactics, including torture.[19] He limited negative information about the government by harassing journalists and interrogating profes-sors. And he eliminated dissent within his political party by forming a dis-ciplinary committee in 1985 that expelled any member who deviated from KANU positions or criticized Moi's leadership.[20]

THE EMERGENCE OF OPPOSITION

As Moi became increasingly dictatorial, those who sought change could not organize against him through institutional means since opposition parties were prohibited. Therefore, they had to find a free space where they could cultivate resistance and mobilize action. They found this space in uni-versities and churches.

Nairobi University

Some of the first actions against Moi came in February 1985, when Univer-sity of Nairobi students boycotted classes to protest the expulsion of several students accused of "activities similar to those which led to the disturbances [coup attempt] of 1982."[21] When government officials ordered the students to return to the classroom, they refused. Instead, several thousand gathered for demonstrations in downtown Nairobi and for an opposition meeting on the university's athletic grounds. Riot police broke up these events, killing one student in the process. Hundreds were charged with refusing to obey police orders and partaking in an illegal meeting.[22] The crackdown contin-ued into 1986, when dozens of university lecturers were arrested on charges of sedition. Although some were released, many received prison sentences ranging from 15 months to 5 years.[23]

Churches

As repression against students and faculty increased, it became more difficult to organize on campuses. Hence the churches offered the last remaining free space since congregational members still had the right to assemble freely, and as sacred institutions, churches had a degree of protection. As a result, Kenya's church leaders soon became the most vocal government critics. As press censorship and harassment of journalists grew, pastors provided an alternative method of airing grievances: the sermon. One analyst noted:

> The sermon was of course a long-standing vehicle of protest in Kenya. . . . Since the Anglican Church had always permitted its clerics to express their views freely, both in colonial times and under Kenyatta, churchmen who so wished had used their pulpits to criticize government action. Under Moi, the sermon became increasingly important. . . . These leaders were powerful speakers, who made skillful use of a long-established oral tradition, which aimed not only at arousing the interest of the congregation but also at stirring them up emotionally and engaging them intellectually. These Church leaders had huge congregations, which flocked to hear their sermons on political issues. The churches, which could seat over a thousand people, were generally overflowing when they preached, and loudspeakers were often placed outside to carry their message to the crowds. Sermons were also geared to the media, whose power they consciously enlisted. In the early and middle 1980s . . . they made sure that reporters knew when and where they were scheduled to preach. By the end of the decade, both local and international reporters followed them around of their own accord, knowing that there would be something to report.[24]

In 1986, church leaders moved from criticism to action when Moi announced an end to secret ballots. Instead of private voting, the new electoral process would entail a queuing system: voters would publicly line up behind photographs of their candidate of choice.[25] The National Council of Churches of Kenya (NCCK) immediately drafted a statement that denounced the queuing system and called for a national referendum on the proposed change. Roughly 1,200 ministers signed the document. When it became clear that the president was ignoring their concerns—and, in fact, was further limiting voting rights by permitting only KANU members who had paid their annual dues to cast ballots—the pastors asked their congregations to boycott the upcoming elections.[26]

Moi was outraged by the ministers' proposed boycott. However, since he portrayed himself as a deeply religious man and a devout member of the fundamentalist Africa Inland Church, he could not tarnish this image by directly attacking these churches or punishing religious leaders. Instead, he had his minister of state order the pastors to stay out of politics.[27] He also relied on Kenya's evangelical and fundamentalist churches, who denounced the National Council of Churches of Kenya and argued that churches should focus on personal salvation and leave political matters to their Christian president.[28]

But this did not stop Catholic, Anglican, and other mainline Protestant church leaders who opposed Moi. In fact, they were keenly aware that their religious positions gave them a degree of protection, and they took advantage of this. Presbyterian minister Timothy Njoya commented: "We are very consciously using President Moi's Christianity as our protection. . . . That's our secret as pastors in Kenya. As long as our politicians go to church, they are at the mercy of the Christian tide they are creating. Any time the president is seen on TV going to church, he is giving me advantages which he cannot calculate. . . . If he is not seen going to church, I lose."[29] With this protection, many pastors began to circulate copies of their sermons through their ministerial networks. Alexander Kipsang Muge, an Anglican bishop, disseminated his politically searing sermons to Anglican and Episcopalian leaders globally. The international Anglican community responded, persuading the British Broadcasting Company to air footage of Muge's sermons.[30] Soon international church networks were shining a spotlight on Moi.

RESISTANCE AND REPRESSION EXPAND

Despite the international attention that churches brought, Moi continued his repressive practices throughout 1987. As more dissidents were arrested, accounts of torture surfaced. Many detainees claimed that they had been beaten, deprived of food, held in tanks of cold water for days, and forced to sign confession statements.[31] As a result, Amnesty International denounced Kenya's deteriorating human rights record in a widely publicized report, "Torture, Political Detention, and Unfair Trials." The report was released just as the U.S. Congress was scheduled to vote on the renewal of Kenyan aid, which totaled $53 million.[32] Yet the negative publicity and the prospect of losing aid did not make Moi repentant. He told Amnesty International to "go to hell" and threatened to arrest anyone from the organization who stepped foot on Kenyan soil.[33]

But the international clamor over Amnesty International's report inspired Kenyans to greater acts of resistance. Despite an official government ban on strikes, 10,000 textile factory workers went on strike in August 1987. This was not the first time that citizens withheld their skills and labor from the regime; more than 100 strikes involving 33,588 workers had resulted in nearly 170,000 lost workdays in the preceding 12 months.[34] Then, in October 1987, 4,000 Muslims in the town of Mombasa rallied for the right to organize.[35] And in November, the government arrested seven student leaders on charges of sedition. Upon their arrest, 3,000 students held a demonstration. The police responded by teargassing and clubbing the protesters and closing the university.[36] But this act backfired as parents increasingly condemned the government's harsh treatment and the disruption of their children's education.[37]

Resistance accelerated in 1988 after a suspected political dissident, Peter Karanja, died in police custody. According to Kenyan law, Karanja should have either been released or brought before a magistrate within 24 hours of his arrest. Instead, he was detained for 24 days and then brought to a hospital, where he died from massive internal injuries incurred from police beatings.[38] No one was ever prosecuted for Karanja's death or for violating his right to have his case processed within 24 hours. Instead, Moi "remedied" the situation by passing a new law that granted police the right to detain suspects for up to 14 days.[39] He also passed a constitutional amendment that granted the president power to dismiss judges and state attorneys. Consequently, many High Court judges—who were interested in maintaining their positions—became hostile to human rights cases and often dismissed political trials on technicalities.[40]

In light of the government's repressive acts, Kenyans knew that the March 1988 elections for KANU parliament members (the only political party in parliament) would yield little change. Moreover, given that the new queuing system would be enforced, 87 percent of registered voters heeded church leaders' call for an election boycott.[41] Those who did show up at the polls encountered intimidation by KANU Youth Wingers, bribery and vote buying, defacing of ballot papers, vote count skewing, and so forth. In fact, the extent of voter fraud turned comical as people who had been declared winners announced to the press that they had never been candidates.[42]

1990: The Height of Resistance

Political tensions continued to escalate throughout 1989, but the conflict reached new heights in 1990. In January, Pastor Njoya called on Kenyans to emulate East Germany's recent nonviolent revolution.[43] In February, Foreign Minister Robert Ouko's body was found in a field near his family's farm. He had been shot in the head, and Kenyans quickly suspected that the government was responsible.[44] Some speculated that Ouko's increasing popularity posed a threat to Moi. Others argued that Ouko had stirred Moi's wrath when he traveled to the United States to negotiate aid arrangements but was received unfavorably. Whatever the reason behind his assassination, the population was outraged, and riots broke out for several days.

Soon songs about the murder—such as "Who Killed Dr. Ouko?"—were being distributed on cassette throughout the country. Dozens of people who listened to the music were arrested for distributing and possessing subversive materials.[45]

In August 1990, Anglican bishop Alexander Muge was killed in a mysterious car accident. Muge had become a menace to Moi by systematically documenting cases of fraud in the 1988 elections. He also collected evidence of government land seizures in which Moi evicted tenants from valuable agricultural lands and then transferred the deeds to KANU politicians in exchange for their loyal support.[46] The president also ordered the eviction of 30,000 urban shantytown dwellers to make the plots available for business leaders who wished to develop the area.[47] Muge released his evidence to the press, drawing international attention to Moi's corruption. In retaliation, Minister of Labor Peter Okondo ordered Muge to stay out of his home region of Busia, where he was scheduled to hold services. If Muge dared to enter the district, Okondo warned that he would "see fire and may not leave alive." The automobile crash happened just after Muge left an open-air service in Busia. He knew that his defiance was risky, but he told those gathered at the service to "Let Okondo know that my innocent blood will haunt him forever."[48] Muge's death made it clear that now not even church leaders were immune to state-sponsored violence.

Elite Divisions

The other important development of 1990 was that some elites broke ties with Moi. One of these was Charles Rubia, a former cabinet minister. Although Rubia had long been a government insider, he had taken a stance against Moi on several occasions, including the electoral queuing system and the constitutional amendments that permitted Moi to fire judges. As a result of his disloyalty, Rubia found that his bid for reelection in 1988 was rigged against him, and he was removed from the Commercial Development Corporation's board. By 1989, he was expelled, along with 13 others, from the Nairobi KANU branch under accusations of participating in opposition demonstrations. At that point, he began working with Kenneth Matiba, a wealthy businessman who had held positions as minister of education, minister of home affairs, and minister of commerce. Matiba had resigned from Moi's cabinet in late 1988 to protest widespread election fraud.

When Rubia and Matiba joined forces, they held a press conference in May 1990 to call for the legalization of opposition parties, the implementation of a multiparty political system, and an end to corruption. They also announced that an opposition rally would be held on July 7.[49] But just days before the scheduled demonstration, police detained Rubia, Matiba, and nine other elites who opposed Kenya's one-party state.[50] Thousands of protesters gathered for the demonstration nonetheless, and the situation quickly became violent as paramilitary forces moved in, throwing tear gas and opening fire.[51] The crowd fought back, resulting in 28 protesters killed and more than 1,000 arrested.[52]

Increased International Pressure

Throughout 1990, the international community increasingly sided with the opposition's call for human rights and multiparty elections. Moreover, the end of the Cold War meant that the United States was now willing to put some power behind its demand for civil liberties and democratization.[53] Since Kenya was no longer needed as a strategic ally in the struggle against communism, U.S. politicians were making aid donations contingent on measurable democratic progress. And the United States was not alone. In November 1991, major donor nations announced that they were suspending $350 million in fast-dispersing aid to Kenya, pending political and economic reforms.[54] This was devastating to Moi, who had become heavily dependent on international aid that collectively amounted to more than $940 million annually.[55] Moi was faced with a choice: make political concessions or face a downward-spiraling economy and mounting resistance.

The president decided that he was more likely to hold onto power if he kept the economy afloat, and thus he made changes to satisfy aid conditions. Moi released political prisoners. He responded to Scotland Yard's report on Dr. Ouko's murder, arresting the former energy minister who was implicated in the investigation. And most significantly, in December 1991, the president announced that he would legalize oppositional parties and hold multiparty elections in 1992.[56]

THE 1992 ELECTION

As soon as political parties were legalized, political dissident Jaramogi Oginga Odinga joined with others, including the newly freed Rubia and Matiba, to form the Forum for the Restoration of Democracy (FORD). They called a rally in January 1992 that drew more than 100,000 participants. Since FORD reflected an alliance of various ethnic and regional groups, business professionals, and academics, it initially appeared to have a viable chance of defeating Moi's KANU party. But FORD's chances for winning quickly evaporated as internal divisions emerged. Soon, the Forum for the Restoration of Democracy had two branches: (1) FORD-Kenya, a multiethnic coalition headed by Luo leader Odinga, and (2) FORD-Asilia, a predominantly Kikuyu group led by Matiba. To add to the oppositional fragmentation, Kikuyu business elites from the northern part of Kenya decided to form their own group, the Democratic Party (DP).[57]

As the opposition began organizing in this splintered fashion, Moi developed a strategy to win the election. First, he stirred up ethnic tensions. In the first few months of 1992, "tribal clashes" exploded in Western Kenya's Rift Valley Region, where various ethnic groups had settled on the border of ethnic Kalenjin lands. These ethnic confrontations cost the lives of more than 1,500 people and left roughly 300,000 homeless.[58] Moi's government refused to intervene, and evidence indicates that the regime actually fueled the conflict by supplying weapons and paying cash to the attackers based on the number of houses burned and the number of people killed.[59] As news of the clashes spread, Moi used this information to his advantage, warning that the return of multiparty democracy would breed such ethnic hostilities that the country would be destroyed by violence. Moreover, the displacement of hundreds of thousands of citizens meant that this area was "ethnically cleansed," allowing pro-Moi Kalenjin votes to dominate in the region.[60]

Moi's second strategy was to "pass muster with Kenya's donors by staging a 'C-minus' election that would be reasonably clean on election day, but fraught with obstacles for the opposition in the period leading up to the balloting."[61] Moi obstructed the opposition's pre-election campaign efforts by denying FORD groups' requests for rally permits or by issuing permits after the event was scheduled. In some regions, FORD leaders were also refused entry by district administrators, limiting their ability to reach potential voters in key areas. Moreover, Moi stacked the electoral commission in his favor, appointing those who supported his candidacy. The commission was highly criticized for its refusal to register 1.2 million young voters who had not received their government-issued identity cards and for turning a blind eye to opposition party harassment. It also did not permit groups, such as the National Election Monitoring Unit, to serve as election observers. Additionally, opposition parties were not granted access to state-owned media sources until days before the election. And 45 opposition party candidates were physically prevented from filing their nomination papers, which meant that a number of KANU candidates ran unopposed for parliament seats.[62]

Moi's third strategic maneuver was to enact legislation that strengthened KANU's chances for retaining power. Specifically, Moi passed a constitutional amendment that required the winning presidential candidate to receive a minimum of 25 percent of the popular vote in five or more of Kenya's eight provinces. Since the opposition was dividing along ethnic and regional lines, Moi was the only candidate who could meet this standard, thereby ensuring that an opposition candidate could not assume office even if he or she received the largest number of votes. This amendment also prohibited the formation of coalition governments—which was the only viable way for opposition groups to succeed—and allowed the president to appoint all cabinet members from his own party.[63] Thus, before the election ever took place, this amendment made it impossible to remove KANU from power.

On account of these strategies, Moi did not have to resort to widespread fraud on election day. He had done enough pre-election maneuvering to virtually guarantee his victory, even without a majority of votes. Still, there were numerous irregularities, including voter turnout rates that exceeded 100 percent of the voting population and eyewitness accounts of rigging. But mostly, his fraudulent activities were not highly visible to observers. For example, KANU had spent an estimated $60 million of state funds and private donations to purchase votes in favor of Moi.[64] For those whose votes were not bought, Moi used threats: civil servants who supported opposition candidates were told that their disloyalty would cost them their jobs.[65] But these bribes and threats were not evident at the polling stations, where observers perceived people casting their ballots with few disturbances.

When the ballots were counted, no one was surprised by the results. The opposition had won roughly two-thirds of the popular vote, but those votes were divided among three parties—FORD-Asili, FORD-Kenya, and the Democratic Party—and thus Moi was returned to office with only one-third of the vote. Numerous analysts blamed the opposition for their loss, arguing that they had succumbed to inter-ethnic rivalries and had failed to employ the necessary measures to ensure a fair election. As a result, the opposition lost the opportunity to usher in a new era, as their Chilean counterparts had done in the 1988 plebiscite against Pinochet.[66] But others maintain that this case could not be compared to Chile since Kenya's electoral playing field was never a level one; even a united opposition stood little chance of winning since Moi had stacked the odds so definitively in his favor.[67] But because his fraudulent activities were subtle and predominantly took place before election day, Moi was able to convince international donors that the vote was fair enough to justify the restoration of aid. While election observers acknowledged that there were many problems, the overall verdict was that the election day procedures earned the C-minus that Moi had aimed for, and thus most (but not all) endorsed the results.

Moi held onto the presidency for another decade, employing similar practices to secure a victory in the 1997 elections. Like his first 14 years in office, the remainder of his rule was filled with violence and corruption. By the 2002 election, Moi was 71 years old and had decided to retire. He appointed a successor, Uhru Kenyatta, the son of Jomo Kenyatta, to run as the KANU candidate. But the opposition had learned its lesson from the failed elections of 1992 and 1997. It brought international pressure to bear to ensure an impartial election commission, and it solicited the support of 28,000 observers to ensure a fair vote. It paid off. The opposition beat Kenyatta, who was not nearly as crafty at rigging elections.[68] But as the new president took office, he found it difficult to make progress since the only thing that oppositional coalition members had in common was their shared interest in ousting Moi. That was something they never achieved. Moi had successfully clung to power for nearly a quarter-century. When he left office, it was on his terms; he chose to retire and was never forced to step down.

REASONS FOR THE MOI DICTATORSHIP'S LONGEVITY

What does this failed case reveal about the conditions needed to oust a dictator? If we look at the strategy employed by the opposition movement, we can see that it involved several civil resistance techniques. The demonstrations against Moi constituted a withdrawal of legitimacy, revealing that many citizens did not believe that the president had the right to rule. People also withdrew their cooperation and compliance with laws, such as when students held a gathering that was legally prohibited and then refused to obey police orders to disperse. Additionally, the churches' outspoken criticism of the KANU regime, and its call for Kenyan Christians to resist Moi's injustices, meant that mentalities of obedience were challenged. The movement also managed to undermine the regime's material resources by persuading donor nations to withhold $350 million in aid. Since Kenya was highly dependent on such foreign aid, this was certainly the precipitating factor that led Moi to legalize alternative political parties and schedule multiparty elections.

But the opposition movement did not use two other techniques of nonviolent resistance. While there were some sporadic strikes in the 1980s, the movement did not withhold essential skills to the extent that the regime's ability to function was impaired. One analyst argued that the opposition lost an important opportunity in this regard by failing to link up with the transportation sector. The bus company had already demonstrated its ability to successfully resist Moi when he enforced a rule in 1986 that prohibited passengers from standing in the aisles. The bus company responded to the no-standing rule by eliminating all services in Nairobi. The ensuing chaos led the government to quickly repeal the rule. That same year, *matatu* drivers, who offered low-cost transportation in private pickup trucks, showed their power when Moi raised safety standards that forced many vehicles off the road. In response, the Matatu Vehicle Owners Association (MVOA) launched a work slowdown that left many employees stranded or unable to reach their jobs on time. Under mounting pressure from business leaders, the government capitulated. When Moi's regime tried to increase *matatu* safety standards again in 1988, the MVOA embarked on a strike that generated such public outcry that the government again backed off. If the opposition could have harnessed this power source for political purposes, it would have increased its leverage against Moi.[69]

Similarly, Moi's power to sanction remained intact as members of the military and the police largely followed orders without question.[70] This was probably because Moi had replaced Kikuyu officers with Kalenjin appointees who were loyal to the president since he protected their interests as ethnic minorities.[71] And in moments of heated conflict, when minority troops faced protesters who were largely from dominant groups, long-standing ethnic hostilities contributed to troops' willingness to carry out orders. In other words, the troops identified more with Moi's ethnic minority regime than with ethnic majority resisters. Finally, when police resorted to violence, such as in the July 1990 demonstrations, protesters fought back instead of remaining nonviolent. Hence many soldiers likely felt that the unruly and chaotic situation justified the use of force.

While the loyalty of Moi's security forces helped him retain power, we must also examine the role that structural factors played. Each side in this struggle had certain structural advantages and disadvantages. The opposition benefited from elite divisions, as some politicians and business leaders, such as Rubia and Matiba, broke from Moi. The end of the Cold War also constituted an important political opportunity since international donors were more willing to withhold aid from Kenya, which was no longer a critical ally in the fight against communism. But Moi's regime benefited from the long-standing ethnic divisions that critically weakened opposition mobilizing efforts. This meant that any effort to organize behind a single figure—whether it was a business leader, political dissident, or church figure—ended up in failure.[72] Moi also benefited from a relatively stable economy. Inflation had declined to 12 percent by 1984, and the growth of Kenya's gross domestic product improved in the late 1980s.[73] While Kenya did have some economic challenges—such as an inability to create new jobs to keep pace with the exploding population and droughts that affected food production—the country's economy overall was much stronger than other African nations.[74] Consequently, many business elites remained Moi supporters.

So which factor best explains Moi's longevity and the opposition's failure to dislodge him? I argue the main reason that Moi was able to maintain power was his savvy counterstrategy. This strategy entailed holding multiparty elections in order to restore Kenyan aid. But he found a way to give the appearance of a free election, which appeased donor nations, while still controlling the outcome. By making his fraudulent election activities less visible to international observers, by limiting his obstructionist actions to the pre-election period, and by keeping vote balloting and counting relatively clean on election day, Moi was able to "reap the benefits of electoral legitimacy without running the risks of democratic uncertainty."[75] In short, he rigged the election but convinced the international community that it was fair enough so that they repealed the sanctions.

Here is the irony. By accepting a flawed vote, these donor nations—who are often credited with forcing Moi into multiparty elections—actually ended up undermining domestic efforts to promote genuine democratization. Many international donors were aware that Moi had taken measures to ensure his own victory; nine donor representatives had sent Moi a letter expressing their concerns about the unfair process. But when opposition leaders called for election boycotts on three separate occasions—hoping this would force Moi to level the playing field—donors pressured the opposition to rescind the boycott. They reluctantly agreed. Donors put similar pressure on the leaders of FORD-Kenya, FORD-Asili, and the Democratic Party when they declared the election results fraudulent. Donor representatives persuaded opposition leaders to accept the outcome, to take the seats in parliament that their parties had won, and try to reform the government from within.[76]

Why would donor nations do this? Why would they promote and endorse an election that was clearly flawed? Some argue that key leaders in the Northern Hemisphere feared that civil war would break out if a Kikuyu leader took office.[77] By accepting the election and its results, they hoped to avoid another Rwanda-like conflict.[78] Another explanation is that donor nations and election observers placed too much emphasis on the fairness of election day voting while largely ignoring the serious problems in the pre-election campaign period. Joel Barkan argues,

> [J]udgments of elections, particularly transitional elections, cannot be limited to the election itself. The credibility of both international and domestic observers turns on their ability to grade accurately each stage of the process. In the case of Kenya, most observers gave the government and its Electoral Commission failing or near-failing grades on each of the many steps leading up to casting of ballots, but accorded them relatively high marks on election day itself. In the final analysis, the government achieved its objective of conducting a "C-minus" election.[79]

Future civil resisters who use an electoral model of nonviolent revolt can learn from this situation, insisting that observers judge an election by the overall degree of fairness throughout the campaign period, not merely the fairness of election day.

Other analysts argue that donor nations accepted the results of this C-minus vote because they were mostly interested in the establishment of multiparty elections, not the quality or outcome of those elections. Stephen Brown explains:

> Donors had spent a total of about $2.1 million on the 1992 elections and were determined to see them take place, even under grossly sub-optimal conditions. . . . They were not necessarily seeking Moi's defeat; most would have been content for Moi to remain in power, as long as it was through free-and-fair multiparty elections. . . . International observers and donors endorsed the poll, whose procedural "success," they felt, outweighed the blatant unfairness of the campaign. . . . After the 1992 elections, donors greatly reduced their pressure for political change . . . and against the opposition's wishes, most donors resumed balance-of-payment support and new aid.[80]

Whatever the rationale behind the donors' decision, one thing is clear: by endorsing the vote, they gave Moi new credibility in the eyes of the international community, and they gave him new financial stability by reinstating Kenya's aid. This enabled Moi to prolong his repressive reign. After the election, he continued harassing opposition leaders, censoring the press, and detaining activists on charges of sedition. Little had changed.[81]

This whole scene played out again in the 1997 elections, when the International Monetary Fund suspended loans to Kenya, citing widespread corruption and poor governance. This prompted the World Bank, the European Union, and various bilateral donors to freeze aid. Thus donor nations withheld $400 million until Moi improved the situation. Just as he had done several years earlier, Moi made minor changes to appease donors, but the electoral process was once again less than fair. KANU claimed victory, Moi retained the presidency, and donors reinstated aid, even though reports from election observers state that widespread irregularities had invalidated the election results.[82]

Some international actors have since admitted that it was a mistake to accept the election results. Smith Hempstone, the U.S. Ambassador to Kenya, stated that he now believes the U.S. embassy should have declared the 1992 elections invalid.[83] Many donor nations felt that the risks of annulling the vote were greater than the risks of accepting it. But by endorsing the elections, they actually delayed democracy by giving Moi new legitimacy and an additional decade of power.

CHAPTER 7

The Philippines' "Bloodless Revolution"

After ruling the Philippines for 20 years, Ferdinand Marcos had become arrogant about his ability to maintain power. His hubris led him to announce snap elections, which he was certain he could win through vote rigging. As campaigning got under way, he scoffed at his opponent, Corazon Aquino; he reproached her for "having the nerve to aspire to the presidency."[1] But Marcos underestimated Filipinos' desire for change and their ability to strategically organize. He also failed to recognize a key premise of civil resistance theory: dictators can only rule through intimidation if troops carry out orders to repress. When Filipino officers and soldiers defected en masse, Marcos was left without any sanctioning powers. With no means of enforcing his rule, he boarded a plane for Hawaii, where he lived out the rest of his days in exile.

MARCOS'S ASSENT TO POWER

Marcos wasn't always a dictator. When he first assumed the presidency in 1965, he had considerable popular support since he was perceived as a leader who could transform the Philippines into a powerful Asian force. Marcos was also a master at creating a compelling public image, to the point that his constituents overlooked his criminal record. When Marcos was 18 years old, he shot his father's political rival after a particularly humiliating electoral defeat. Police immediately suspected Ferdinand Marcos; not only did he have motive but also he was an expert sharpshooter. When he was finally arrested three years later, Marcos was about to graduate from law school as valedictorian. Since the evidence strongly implicated him, he was convicted. Marcos quickly appealed, acting as his own defense attorney.

Submitting an 830-page brief, he convinced the judges to overturn the verdict based on court errors. By 1940, Marcos was free to pursue his own political career.[2]

Shortly thereafter, the Japanese bombed Pearl Harbor and a U.S. military base in the Philippines. In response, General Douglas McArthur mobilized 80,000 Filipino troops, including reserve officer Marcos, to fight alongside the 22,000 U.S. soldiers stationed in the region. Eventually, American troops withdrew, as the United States concentrated its war efforts elsewhere, and Philippine troops battled the Japanese on their own. Marcos was wounded in the fighting, purportedly receiving 30 medals for bravery. Many years later, journalists discovered that the majority of these medals were fabricated. Moreover, as they investigated his military record, they learned that he had been arrested for illegally collecting funds from the American military. In his shrewd machinations, Marcos had transformed himself from a thief into the Philippines' most decorated war hero.[3]

Marcos used this fictitious war hero status to promote his political career. He was elected to the Philippine House of Representatives, where he served three terms, followed by an additional term in the Senate. By 1965, he made a bid for the presidency. He was a formidable candidate—a highly intelligent man and a skilled orator whose beauty queen wife, Imelda, accompanied him on the campaign trail. These factors, along with a huge amount of funds, secured Marcos's victory.[4]

Once in office, Marcos became the epitome of nepotism. He appointed his wife as governor of Manila and chair of roughly two dozen government agencies—a role that gave her unrestricted access to millions of dollars. Marcos offered his sister another governor position and appointed his brother to leadership roles in 20 private industries. His cousin, Fabian Ver, headed the National Intelligence Security Authority. Marcos also granted his friends the rights to timber, precious metals, and coconut sales. As a result, Marcos and those closest to him quickly became wealthy.[5]

Despite growing criticism of his nepotism, Marcos ran for re-election in 1969. Although there were allegations of fraud, most people accepted the outcome as Marcos declared himself the winner. But in 1971, as his second presidential term was ending, Marcos proposed a constitutional amendment that would permit him to run a third time. With generous bribes, Marcos persuaded Congress to approve the amendment, which provoked massive student demonstrations. When the demonstrations turned violent, Marcos suspended the right of habeas corpus for detainees and threatened to impose emergency measures. The result: more demonstrations. During these protests, one person came to embody the revolt: Senator Benigno "Ninoy" Aquino, Marcos's rival for the 1973 presidential elections.[6]

Marcos used the student riots, along with reports of a growing communist insurgency, to justify stronger security measures.[7] But as several sources reveal, Marcos actually had intelligence officers stage the violence so he could declare martial law,[8] which went into effect on September 21, 1972. Immediately thereafter, Marcos announced that elections would be suspended indefinitely, and he ordered the military to shut down all newspapers and broadcasting stations. Troops were also sent to arrest 100 "enemies of the state," including Senator Aquino, who was charged with rebellion, subversion, illegal possession of weapons, and murder. Over the next few years, the number of political detainees rose to 50,000.[9] To quell resistance and win support for these emergency measures, Marcos promised to build a "New Society" by curbing the drug trade, redistributing land, disarming private armies, and fighting crime. As he fulfilled some of these promises, his popular support grew during the first years of martial law.[10]

But this support quickly deteriorated in the late 1970s due to a stagnating economy,[11] growing national debt,[12] an unemployment rate of 20 percent, and an underemployment rate of up to 40 percent.[13] It also reflected public outrage at Marcos's misuse of his office for personal enrichment. Marcos had made much of his money by taking a portion of every major business transaction in the country, earning himself the nickname "Mr. Ten Percent." He reportedly siphoned almost $1.2 billion from the Philippine sugar industry alone. As a result of his unethical business dealings, the Marcoses had become one of the richest couples in the world, with an estimated fortune of $2 to 20 billion. Their wealth stood in sharp contrast to the rest of the Filipino population, 70 percent of whom lived beneath the poverty line—a dramatic increase from 1965, when 28 percent were indigent.[14]

Filipinos were also angered by the growing power and abuse of the armed forces. Marcos had significantly expanded his troops—from 55,000 in 1970 to more than 156,000 in 1975[15]—and built a cadre of loyal officers. He gave these officers a raise, a promotion, and an expanded set of benefits immediately following the imposition of martial law.[16] In return, the troops kept a lid on opposition activities through intimidation, terror, and torture. A 1976 Amnesty International report noted:

> Torture was widespread. Electrical shock was routinely applied to [political] prisoners' breasts or genitals. One common torture was to force a prisoner to lie with his feet on one bed, his head on another, arms held tight by the side; whenever his body fell or sagged, he was beaten and kicked. . . . [Some were] made to go without sleep for eight days and nights, forced to stand for hours at a time in front of a full-blast air conditioner. . . . [Others'] lips were burned with a cigarette.[17]

By 1982, Amnesty International released a report indicating the use of torture had increased.[18] According to the Philippine government's own accounts, an estimated 4,228 people had suffered from human rights abuses between 1972 and 1982.[19]

AQUINO'S ASSASSINATION AND THE EMERGENCE
OF MASS OPPOSITION

The declaration of martial law, the misuse of political power for personal enrichment, and the escalation of human rights abuses led to the formation of various opposition groups. But they had little impact, as Marcos continued to plunder and rule. But everything changed on August 21, 1983—the day Ninoy Aquino was assassinated. After martial law was imposed, Aquino had been sentenced to death by a military tribunal. He served nearly eight years on death row before he was given a medical leave in 1980 to receive surgical treatment in the United States. The Aquino family remained in the United States for three years, but when Marcos announced that legislative elections would be held in the spring of 1984, Aquino was compelled to return home. He was convinced that he could provide strong leadership to the fledgling opposition and, after studying Gandhi, he was certain that a nonviolent strategy could topple Marcos.[20]

Repatriating to the Philippines was dangerous, and numerous individuals tried to dissuade Aquino. Minister of Defense Juan Ponce Enrile warned that he would most certainly be killed. Even Imelda Marcos met with Aquino in New York to inform him of potential threats. But Aquino was not deterred. His hope of ousting Marcos was greater than his fear of prison or death, and he thus began planning his return.[21] His preparations included writing a speech that he would deliver to the Filipino people when he arrived. It read:

> We can be united only if all the rights and freedoms enjoyed before September 21, 1972 are fully restored. The Filipino asks for nothing more, but will surely accept nothing less.
>
> 1. [For the settlement of my dispute with Marcos], I shall define my terms: Order my immediate execution or set me free. I was sentenced to die for allegedly being the leading communist leader. I am not a communist, never was, and never will be.
>
> 2. National reconciliation and unity can be achieved but only with justice. . . . There can be no deal with a dictator. No compromise with a dictator.
>
> 3. In a [violent] revolution there can really be no victors, only victims. We do not have to destroy in order to build.
>
> 4. Subversion stemming from economic, social, and political causes will not be solved by purely military solutions; it can be curbed not with ever increasing repression, but with more equitable distribution of wealth, more democracy, more freedom.

5. For the economy to get going once again, the working-man must be given his just and rightful share of his labor, and to the owners and managers must be restored the hope where there is so much uncertainty if not despair. . . . I return from exile to an uncertain future with only determination and faith to offer—faith in our people and faith in God.[22]

Finally, Aquino boarded a flight to the Philippines. He wore a bulletproof vest and was accompanied by numerous international journalists and camera crews, whom he thought would provide a degree of protection. When his plane landed in Manila, he exited with three armed escorts. Despite these precautions, he was shot in the head just as he reached the tarmac. He died instantly. The next day, Marcos made a televised appearance to report that a communist assassin had killed Aquino. Given his history of deception and corruption, no one believed Marcos; the consensus was growing that the government was responsible.[23]

Aquino's body was placed in an open casket—still in its bloodied form, untouched by funeral cosmeticians—and roughly 100,000 people came to pay their respects. When the body was moved to a nearby Catholic church a few days later, 2 million Filipinos formed a processional behind the hearse.[24] In the weeks that followed, students, blue-collar workers, professionals, housewives, priests, and nuns participated in anti-Marcos demonstrations. According to government estimates, more than 265 demonstrations were held in the six months following Aquino's murder.[25]

The assassination was a turning point for many, including the nation's elites, who quickly severed their ties to the regime. This included business leaders from Binondo (Manila's Chinatown) and the Makati financial district. Although both the Makati and Binondo communities had largely prospered under martial law, they grew increasingly frustrated with Marcos as the economy spiraled downward in the beginning of the 1980s. Gross national product (GNP) growth had declined from an average of 6.4 percent in the late 1970s to just 1.1 percent in 1983.[26] Then Aquino's assassination caused massive capital flight, depleting the country's reserves. As a result, by October 1983, Marcos announced that the nation could not pay its foreign debts and requested a payment moratorium from nearly 500 creditors. The debt crisis in turn caused imports to drop precipitously, and the nation barely managed to import oil and food. By 1984, inflation had risen to 50 percent, unemployment stood at 36.5 percent, and investor confidence plummeted.[27] As one observer put it:

The Marcos regime had become very bad for business in the Philippines. Before the assassination, most business professionals were unwilling to take the financial risks involved in directly opposing the regime. . . . A feeling of class immunity had developed among the elite. Aquino's murder, however, shattered the self-assurance of the privileged. . . . The wealthy were shocked that one of their own could be killed on government orders.[28]

The business sector's resistance to Marcos took two forms. On a public level, weekly demonstrations were held in the Makati financial district, where approximately 100,000 office workers and executives marched to the privately owned Ugarte Field (to avoid the need for a government permit to demonstrate). Privately, many business leaders made large financial contributions to the opposition movement.[29]

Aquino's murder also created rifts within the military, mainly between those who remained loyal to Marcos and those who wanted change. One of the reformists was Defense Minister Juan Ponce Enrile.[30] Enrile organized a group of soldiers—mostly young, low-ranking officers frustrated by military corruption. Together they created the "Reform the Armed Forces of the Philippines Movement" (RAM), and RAM representatives quietly began to meet with opposition leaders.[31]

The assassination additionally strained Marcos's relationship to the U.S. government. Although some U.S. politicians argued that failure to fully back Marcos would lead to a communist victory, it became harder and harder for the Reagan administration to convince others that Marcos was really interested in democracy. When U.S. intelligence sources confirmed that high-ranking members of the Marcos regime were responsible for Aquino's death, the U.S. State Department began pressuring Marcos to hold elections. The United States was still willing to support Marcos, but they wanted him to improve his corrupt image.[32]

PREPARATIONS FOR A NONVIOLENT REVOLUTION

As business elites, some military personnel, and U.S. opinion turned against Marcos, civil resistance groups seized the opportunity, preparing for a full-scale revolt. They quickly agreed to use nonviolent methods, largely due to the influence of Manila's Cardinal Jaime Sin. Several religious orders, who were at the forefront of the movement, recognized that they needed training. Thus they asked the Cardinal's permission to invite leaders from the pacifist organization, the International Fellowship of Reconciliation, to teach them the art of civil resistance. Cardinal Sin agreed, and by 1984, 43 training seminars were held throughout the country, attended by lawyers, union organizers, peasants, students, business professionals, and clergy. Butz Aquino, Ninoy Aquino's brother, commented: "Unquestionably the seminars helped prepare people for a more active role and . . . prepared us for the kind of disciplined nonviolent struggle that was needed."[33]

The freshly trained activists put their new knowledge to work right away, launching hundreds of demonstrations. But it was not enough to force Marcos out of office. In fact, Marcos had a new plan for retaining power: hold National Assembly elections in 1984 to gain legitimacy and strengthen his claim to the presidential office. The opposition movement was divided over whether they should participate. Convinced that Marcos would rig it, some wanted to boycott the election. Others planned to participate in hopes of winning enough congressional seats to start an impeachment process. Still others decided to organize the National Citizens Movement for Free Elections (NAMFREL) to counter anticipated acts of election fraud. Cardinal Sin supported NAMFREL's efforts, encouraging priests and nuns to form and lead local chapters.

As soon as campaigning began, it was clear that Marcos had numerous advantages over the opposition. He was able to print $330 million in new currency, which he used for vote bribing. He ordered security forces to intimidate voters, killing 348 people and injuring 107 who attended opposition candidate rallies.[34] Marcos also controlled all television stations and most radio stations and newspapers, thereby enabling him to dominate the airwaves. Opposition candidates had little access to the media, and thus they relied heavily on the Catholic radio station Veritas to get their message out.

Despite bribery and intimidation, opposition candidates won a significant number of seats on Election Day but not enough to impeach the president. Meanwhile, Marcos was proclaiming victory, telling television reporters, "We have presented the world an image of democracy" and promising to run again in 1987.[35] But the next election would happen earlier than planned. On November 3, 1985, Marcos made a live appearance on the U.S. news program *This Week with David Brinkley*. One of the program's guests, U.S. columnist George Will, pressed Marcos about Manila's mass demonstrations and accusations of electoral fraud. Will asked whether it would be possible to hold elections earlier to re-establish credibility. Indignant, Marcos replied, "If all these childish claims . . . have to be settled, I think we had better settle it by calling an election right now. I'm ready, I'm ready."[36] The date for the new presidential elections was set for February 1986.[37]

THE 1986 ELECTION

Once the snap election was announced, the opposition quickly selected their candidate: Ninoy Aquino's widow, Cory. At the urging of Cardinal Sin, she accepted the nomination and became a skillful campaigner, speaking frankly about Marcos's corruption.[38] She frequently invoked the words of her late husband who claimed, "We cannot fight Marcos with arms, because he has so many. We cannot fight him with money, because we do not have any. The only way we can fight him is with morality."[39] Filipinos loved her, donning the color yellow to symbolize the "people power movement." During each campaign event, Aquino made her intentions clear,: "I am asking for your help to topple the Marcos regime."[40]

Yet even though Cory Aquino's popular support expanded rapidly, Marcos never took her candidacy seriously, perhaps because he was taking extensive measures to ensure his victory. As usual, he used intimidation, issuing weapons to loyal warlords and sending them into opposition stronghold areas. As a result, 264 Aquino supporters were assassinated and another 227 injured during the campaign period. Moreover, as in the 1984 election, Marcos resorted to vote buying. By some estimates, he spent $500 million on bribes in the 1986 election. Individual voters were paid between $2.50 and $5.00 to cast their ballot for Marcos. Those who allowed voter tabulation sheets to be altered were paid $50, and election inspectors were given $500 if they permitted Marcos's party to cheat. The regime also disenfranchised a large number of voters by removing names from registration lists and changing polling station locations on short notice. Through these tactics, an estimated 8 to 12 percent of eligible voters were denied their right to vote.[41]

Marcos was so confident in his ability to rig the election that he gave the National Citizen Movement for Free Elections (NAMFREL) considerable freedom to organize. When election day arrived on February 7, 1986, NAMFREL volunteers—numbering 500,000—accompanied voters to polling stations and guarded ballot boxes to avoid tampering. While NAMFREL helped ensure fairness as ballots were cast, the organization was not able to ensure fairness as the ballots were counted. NAMFREL vote counters quickly realized that their vote tally did not match the statistics being reported by the government's Commission on Elections (COMELEC), who claimed that Marcos was leading. The rigging was so blatant that 35 COMELEC computer operators walked off the job, stating that the vote counts they submitted were being dramatically altered. Even the U.S. election observers conceded that Marcos had stolen the election, although President Reagan, a longtime friend of the Marcoses, was more reluctant to do so, claiming that both sides had cheated.[42]

After election day ended, the Bishops' Conference of the Philippines released a pastoral letter denouncing the election. The bishops proclaimed that Marcos had lost all legitimacy and thus had lost the right to rule. The letter read:

> The people have spoken. Or have tried to. Despite the obstacles thrown in the way . . . we, the bishops, believe that on the basis of our assessment of the recently concluded polls, what they attempted to say is clear enough. In our considered judgment, the polls were unparalleled in fraudulence. . . . A government that assumes or retains power through

fraudulent means has no moral basis. For such an access to power is tantamount to a forcible seizure and cannot command the allegiance of the citizenry. . . .

If such a government does not of itself freely correct the evil it has inflicted on the people, then it is our serious moral obligation as a people to make it do so. We are not going to effect the change we seek by doing nothing. . . . Neither do we advocate a bloody, violent means of righting this wrong. If we did, we would be sanctioning the enormous sin of fratricidal strife. Killing to achieve justice is not within the purview of our Christian vision. . . . The way indicated to us now is the way of nonviolent struggle for justice. This means active resistance to evil by peaceful means. . . .

Now is the time to repair the wrong. The wrong was systematically organized. So must its correction be. But as in the election itself, that depends fully on the people, on what they are willing and ready to do. We, the bishops, stand in solidarity with them in the common discernment for the good of the nation. But we insist: Our acting must always be according to the Gospel of Christ, that is, in a peaceful, nonviolent way.[43]

Despite the bishops' denunciation and international condemnation, on February 15 the Philippine government declared that Marcos had won the election. Anticipating a backlash, Marcos once again used acts of terror to silence his critics. Within days, the bodies of 30 Aquino supporters were found. Many had been mutilated and decapitated and some bore signs of sexual assault.[44]

THE FALL OF MARCOS

The stolen election was the proverbial last straw. Cory Aquino declared that she was the legitimate winner and demanded that Marcos step down immediately. When he refused, she announced on February 16 that she was launching the Tagumpay ng Bayan (triumph of the people) civil disobedience campaign. Addressing a crowd of 2 million people in downtown Manila, Aquino called for a boycott of all government-controlled companies, banks, and newspapers. She also asked people to delay paying their water and light bills. These were just first steps, she said, and they were deliberately limited. Over the ensuing days, she would initiate additional protest measures, culminating in a nationwide general strike on February 26, Marcos's inauguration day. If Marcos still refused to transfer power at that point, she would ask businesses to withhold corporate income taxes—a key source of government revenue.[45]

But just as Aquino's civil resistance campaign started, the Reform the Armed Forces of the Philippines Movement (RAM) began planning a coup. Two key players were behind the plot: Juan Ponce Enrile, Marcos's defense minister, and Lieutenant General Fidel Ramos, deputy chief of staff of the armed forces and commander of the Philippine constabulary. When Marcos learned about the planned coup, he sent troops to detain RAM's leaders.

Someone tipped off Enrile, who called Ramos on February 22. The two agreed to hold a press conference that evening at Camp Aguinaldo to announce their resignations. In his televised appearance, Enrile stated, "I believe that the mandate of the people does not belong to the present regime."[46] And Ramos said that he was compelled to resign after he heard the bishops' statement.[47]

As the press conference concluded, Enrile and Ramos knew that Marcos's troops would arrive soon. Although a couple hundred RAM soldiers and roughly 60 citizens came to Camp Aguinaldo to support them, they knew it was not enough. But the situation changed when Butz Aquino made an appeal on Radio Veritas for citizens to protect the rebels.[48] And around midnight, Cardinal Sin announced, "I am deeply concerned about the situation of General Ramos and Minister Enrile. I am calling all our people to support our two good friends . . . and show your solidarity with them at this crucial period."[49] The cardinal asked people to protect the defected military leaders and bring food for the soldiers. As the head of the Filipino Catholic Church, Cardinal Sin's moral authority evoked a strong response. Although only 60 citizens had shown up after the press conference, nearly 20,000 gathered within a few hours of the cardinal's call, even though it was the middle of the night. By the next day, February 23, nearly 1 million people had come out, carrying crucifixes, statues of the Virgin Mary, and posters appealing for nonviolence.[50] The showdown with Marcos had begun.

As people gathered outside Camp Aguinaldo, religious orders quickly took charge of the situation. Their nonviolence training and NAMFREL experience had turned these nuns and priests into skilled organizers who readily commanded the crowd's attention. Bryan Johnson noted:

> The various religious orders lent immediate form to the human barricades, turning potential chaos into a well-ordered campground. Taking charge of the sacks of rice, bread, crackers, sardines, and doughnuts that helpful civilians had [brought], they quickly set up food brigades that became the crowd's life support system, and used their religious robes to gently coerce the grocers and merchants. . . . The nuns served as cooks, dishwashers, first-aid workers, and dispensers of courage.[51]

As the number of civil resisters outside Camp Aguinaldo expanded, the gathering acquired a carnival-like atmosphere. The tone changed quickly, however, when tanks arrived. Ramos and Enrile implored the troops to not harm unarmed people. Butz Aquino spoke to the soldiers through a megaphone, stating that the people were nonviolent and there was no need for bloodshed. Many demonstrators carried pocket radios, listening closely to Radio Veritas for instructions. They were told, "Pray to God that you will not have to follow these instructions, but just in case, they are important.

[If] the tanks . . . start firing, lie down and roll to the side out of the path. . . . Keep as low as you can. Keep praying!"[52]

When the tanks stopped in front of the human barricade, a commander told civil resisters that they had 30 minutes to disband. After that, the tanks would force their way through. When the allotted time passed and the people still stood their ground, the tension was almost unbearable. At that moment, a group of nuns dropped to their knees in front of the armored vehicles and began praying the rosary. Someone else hung a rosary on a tank's gun barrel.[53] Soon, others were praying on their knees, too. Given that roughly 90 percent of the population was Catholic,[54] the emotional and moral impact of these actions was compelling. Still no one knew how the soldiers would respond. One participant described the situation:

> Panic sweeps over us. Unthinking, I drop to my knees. Looking up I see only the general and his marines, disciplined, hard-eyed. . . . I shout and raise my hands, daring them: "Go on, kill us!" . . . The metal mountain jerks forward. Defiant, nervous shouts all around. The praying voices rise another key. I wonder what it is like to be crushed under tons of metal. Then the engine stops. There is an astounding split second of silence. The crowd erupts into wild cheers and applause.[55]

But it was not over yet. One of the marines drew his weapon and ordered the drivers to proceed. As the tanks' engines started up again, the nuns continued to pray. Then an 81-year-old woman in a wheelchair held up a crucifix and stated, "Stop! I am an old woman. You can kill me but don't kill the young people here." Unwilling to harm her, one soldier climbed out of the tank and embraced the handicapped grandmother. The crowd cheered, passing food and water to other soldiers, stating: "You are one of us. You belong to the people. Come back to those to whom you belong." Someone even placed a three-year-old girl on top of the armored personnel carrier; the girl kissed the driver, causing him to turn the engine off.[56] Soon, more soldiers joined the crowd. Finally, an officer announced that they would not kill anyone. Shortly thereafter, the tanks retreated.

Marcos fumed over the situation most of the night. In the predawn hours of February 24, he declared a state of emergency and announced that his policy of "maximum tolerance" was over. Under the cover of darkness, anti-riot soldiers threw tear gas into the crowd, sending the first line of resisters running while the subsequent lines remained in place. But then priests and nuns handed out towels with lemon water to neutralize the tear gas. Covering their faces, the protesters regrouped and once again appealed to the soldiers to defect. But just as the soldiers launched more tear gas, the wind shifted direction, causing the tear gas to engulf the troops.[57] One observer recalled, "We stood there until the soldiers were able to form a line again.

The sergeant had a hard time convincing them to line up again. They were reluctant. . . . They moved slowly. I knew we had won."[58] At that moment, the people began to embrace the soldiers, many of whom joined the crowd.

As the day progressed, more and more troops defected. In fact, so many soldiers were deserting that someone posted a banner in the nearby parade grounds that read "DEFECTION CENTER."[59] The tide had turned. Nevertheless, Marcos was adamant that he would not resign or flee the country. "We will defend the republic unto the last breath of our lives and to the last drop of our blood."[60] He ordered his troops back to their tanks with clear instructions to disperse the crowd by any means necessary. But the same scene played out, as nuns and others appealed to the soldiers, and the tanks eventually retreated. By nightfall, roughly 80 percent of soldiers had defected, and Marcos received a phone call from the White House encouraging him to step down.[61]

By February 25—the day of his presidential inauguration—Marcos realized that he had no power. Employees at the television networks refused to give him airtime. Civil resisters refused to disperse. Soldiers were not carrying out orders. Even the elite palace guards retreated, fearing that the palace would be bombed or stormed by the masses. Marcos had no capacity to enforce his rule, and thus he phoned the U.S. ambassador to request a military escort. At 9:00 P.M., Marcos and his family departed the palace in U.S. helicopters, headed for Hawaii.[62]

WHY THE MOVEMENT WON

There are numerous parallels between the nonviolent revolts in Kenya and the Philippines. In both cases, an uprising emerged to oust long-standing dictators who had manipulated elections to prolong their presidential terms. Both movements faced potentially brutal repression and had the support of religious institutions. Moreover, activists in both nations benefited from favorable structural conditions, including a declining economy and divided elites. One of the key structural differences between these cases is the ethnic diversity in Kenya versus the relative ethnic homogeneity in the Philippines, which made it easier for Filipino civil resisters to generate a united front. But this is not the only reason the Philippine movement succeeded while the Kenyan uprising failed. To fully understand these differential outcomes, we must look not only at existing structural conditions but also at the Philippine movement's strategy.

The "people power" strategy included the withdrawal of several types of citizen support First, Filipinos withheld *authority* from Marcos by refusing to recognize the outcome of the 1986 election. Second, the

Catholic Church helped transform citizens' *attitudes of obedience* to the state by offering religious justification for resistance. Third, the boycott of Marcos's crony businesses, along with the withholding of payments to government utility companies, had the potential to undercut the regime's *material resources*; however, since the boycott lasted only a week, the effect was minimal. Fourth, civil resisters withheld their *cooperation and obedience*, refusing to follow orders to disperse during the confrontation with troops outside Camp Aguinaldo. Fifth, during the last days of the struggle, television station employees withheld their *skills and labor* when they refused to put Marcos on the air. Sixth, the movement successfully undermined the regime's *sanctioning powers* by encouraging soldiers to defect.

Of these six strategic actions, promoting military mutiny was the most important in securing the movement's victory. While this process was encouraged by the movement, it began with the highly publicized defection of two top-ranking military leaders. While Enrile and Ramos's defections may have happened because of internal military politics and their own self-interests, the people power movement quickly made it clear that the two men needed the movement for survival.[63] Without the protection of citizens, Enrile and Ramos would have been quickly arrested and probably killed.

But why did so many other soldiers follow Enrile and Ramos's example? Why did so many troops risk their own lives by defecting? Certainly, civil resisters' nonviolent demeanor made it hard for soldiers to justify the use of force. Moreover, Enrile and Ramos's highly publicized defections revealed that there was a divide within the military. This gave an opening to soldiers who were reluctant to harm the protesters. Additionally, as civil resisters calmly appealed to the soldiers, offering them food and drink, it made it easier for troops to defect without fear of crowd retaliation. Many credit the nuns for creating an atmosphere that facilitated mutiny. Carlos Guiyab recalled: "The [nuns] were the real heroes. They were the front-liners. When the tanks started to move, they didn't budge. They just kept praying. They were cool. They talked to the soldiers . . . offered them water or cigarettes. They pacified the people who were hot-tempered."[64] But it was also the nature of the confrontation—and the prospect of repressing children, the elderly, and nuns—that made soldiers realize that this was not simply a job that they must execute but a moral dilemma. One soldier confessed:

> I was trained to deal with enemy soldiers and rebels and I know exactly how to handle them. But when my men and I approached these unarmed, friendly people, I did not know what to do. There were pregnant women and little children there that reminded us

of our own families. I knew that if I didn't clear the road and follow orders, I would be shot. But I also knew that if I did that, I would have to violate my conscience.[65]

In short, widespread defections occurred because civil resisters remained nonviolent, they minimized troops' fear of retaliation, and they appealed to soldiers' moral conscience.

Clearly, the movement's strategy was effective. Yet to complete our understanding of why civil resisters won, we must also assess Marcos's counterstrategy. During the four-day standoff, Marcos did very little: he repeatedly ordered his remaining troops to disperse protesters, and he made televised appearances to emphasize that he was still in power. Why was his response, in the words of one analyst, so "inexplicably lame?"[66] We can only speculate, since Marcos never publicly spoke about his overthrow. It may have reflected his arrogance; after 20 years in power, he likely assumed that his fraudulent electoral activities would work as well as they had in the past and that repression would quell any resistance. The role of religious orders may have also complicated his ability to crack down on the movement, since crushing nuns with tanks would have surely provoked an international outcry. Additionally, because Marcos did not anticipate that his agents of repression would turn on him, he was unprepared to deal with mass defections and unable to come up with new strategies to reinforce troops' loyalty. In short, Marcos relied on his old tactics of repression and fraud. When they no longer worked, he no longer knew how to hold onto power.

CHAPTER 8

How Civil Resistance Works

As the 1980s began, few anticipated that nonviolent revolutionary movements would instigate significant political changes throughout the world. Cold War animosities and the escalating arms race created a bellicose global dynamic, which was used to justify all sorts of totalitarian measures. And yet within a few years, citizens rose up to challenge some of these authoritarian regimes. Many did so nonviolently—facing down tanks, embarking on hunger strikes, filling the streets with protesters, and refusing to support unjust leaders any longer. Some of these revolts produced spectacular results, ousting long-standing dictatorships in a short time. Others failed to instigate change, sometimes ending tragically. Given the number of unarmed insurrections in recent history, we have a rich opportunity to expand our knowledge of why some nonviolent revolts succeed while others fail.

To discern the factors that shaped the outcomes of the six nonviolent revolts examined here, we need to answer a number of questions. What structural factors helped or hurt these movements? Which civil resistance techniques had the greatest impact on regimes? What problems arose that undermined these movements' potential? And what strategies helped regime leaders retain power? In this chapter, I offer some answers to these questions by systematically comparing the civil resistance movements in China, East Germany, Panama, Chile, Kenya, and the Philippines.

STRUCTURAL FACTORS

Structural conditions and changing political circumstances are important because they can generate widespread dissatisfaction with a regime or strengthen the belief that change is now attainable. This, in turn, creates a large pool of potential civil resisters, making it possible to launch a revolt. Table 8.1 indicates that several structural factors contributed to mobilization. First, economic downturns occurred in all six cases. In some places, such as the Philippines, the country's financial troubles were severe. But other countries, such as Chile, had more modest problems that were reversed in a relatively short period of time. Regardless of the extent of the economic problems, the prevalence of this factor across all cases suggests that financial hardships were at least initially important in making citizens sympathetic to a revolutionary cause and ripe for recruitment.

Second, in several cases, mobilization was spurred by a blatant act of repression or a state-sanctioned atrocity—what some researchers refer to as a "moral shock"[1] or a "suddenly-imposed grievance."[2] Such events expose the state's brutality and unleash public outrage, pushing many to act on their belief that regime change is imperative. The mobilizing capacity of moral shocks can be seen in the murders of Philippine opposition leader Ninoy Aquino, Kenya's Bishop Alexander Muge, and former Panamanian Minister of Health Hugo Spadafora.

In other cases, resistance erupted not from an assassination but from new political opportunities. In China, student dissidents had been meeting for some time but had not yet initiated any protest campaigns. But when the former secretary general of the Chinese Communist Party died unexpectedly, they knew they could transform public acts of mourning into public acts of dissent. In East Germany, Hungary's decision to open its border to the West was the political shift that catalyzed the movement. When 100,000 fled the German Democratic Republic, the government was financially devastated; this, in turn, inspired remaining

Table 8.1: STRUCTURAL FACTORS AND POLITICAL OPPORTUNITIES AT THE TIME OF MOVEMENT EMERGENCE

Structural Factors	Successful Cases			Unsuccessful Cases		
	GDR	Chile	Philippines	China	Panama	Kenya
Economic decline	+	+	+	+	+	+
Moral shock or new political opportunity	+	+	+	+	+	+
Divided elites	*	+	+	+	+	+
Free space	+	+	+	+	+	+

+ = factor was present
— = factor was absent
* = factor was primarily caused by movement activity

citizens to directly challenge the weakened regime. In Chile, several campaigns against Pinochet had failed. But when Pinochet announced the plebiscite vote, it created a new opportunity that helped focus organizing efforts.

A third factor contributing to the emergence of these movements was elite defections. Consistent with the armed revolutions literature, this study finds that the combination of a bad economy and moral shocks can lead many elites to rethink their loyalty to regime leaders. For some—such as business leaders in the Philippines, Panama, and Kenya—it was no longer lucrative to support corrupt leaders whose policies harmed local businesses, and thus they began to assist opposition movements. For others, such as some Chinese political elites, divisions arose when reformists advocated modernization measures but found themselves in conflict with hardliners who were unwilling to make such changes. As regimes lost their traditional supporters or found factions emerging within their party ranks, the balance of power tipped more favorably toward the opposition, causing more people to join the movement since the perceived chances of winning were stronger with elites on their side.

Yet none of these favorable structural conditions would have produced an uprising if there had not been free spaces where activists could strategize and develop oppositional cultures. In all six cases, free spaces were available—predominantly in religious institutions.[3] Although religion has often perpetuated attitudes of submission to government leaders, religious institutions typically have a degree of autonomy from the state and thus have the potential to be sites where people discuss grievances and criticize state practices.[4] In addition, the sacred nature of these institutions makes it more difficult for dictators to take repressive action against them, thereby giving them a degree of protection.[5] In the cases examined here, protected spaces provided an array of opportunities for dissent and resistance—from the Leipzig churches' peace prayer services, to Kenyan pastors' sermons, to the Chilean Catholic Church's formation of human rights organizations.

These four factors—economic decline, new political opportunities or moral shocks, divided elites, and the availability of free spaces—were present in all six cases and preceded the emergence of wide-scale, massive civil resistance movements. Since they were present in both the successful and the failed revolts, they appear to be necessary for mobilization but not necessarily influential in determining movement outcomes. Thus we can conclude that initially favorable structural conditions may open the door for resistance to erupt but strategic factors—the tactics and maneuvers that activists and regime leaders employ—will heavily shape the movements' outcome.

To assess the effects of movements' strategic actions, I focus on the six techniques of civil resistance. As indicated in Table 8.2., participants in all six nonviolent revolts refused to acknowledge or accept regime authority. This is not surprising since people must first view a regime as illegitimate before they mobilize against it.[6] Additionally, in all the cases, civil resisters withheld their cooperation. Some acts of noncooperation were primarily symbolic, such as Chileans attending concerts when Pinochet had banned public singing; other instances entailed bold acts of defiance, such as refusing to disperse as Marcos's troops attempted to arrest defected military leaders. Finally, in five of the cases, cultural mentalities of obedience were challenged as religious leaders sided with civil resisters, denounced regime abuses, and called for change. In China, protesters used the communist party's ideology to argue that the state and its military must be working for the interests of the people, not party elites. However, since all six movements used these civil resistance techniques, this indicates that such strategic actions may not be sufficient to bring about regime demise.

In several cases, civil resisters additionally withdrew skills from the state, restricting its ability to carry out daily services and functions. This was true in East Germany, where mass emigration led to a shortage of factory workers, health care providers, transportation operators, and communication specialists. However, the withholding of skills is not an essential

Table 8.2: TYPES OF CIVIL RESISTANCE TECHNIQUES USED

Techniques	Successful Cases			Unsuccessful Cases		
	GDR	Chile	Philippines	China	Panama	Kenya
Refusal to acknowledge regime authority	+	+	+	+	+	+
Refusal to cooperate or comply with laws	+	+	+	+	+	+
Challenging mentalities of obedience	+	+	+	+	+	+
Withholding skills	+	–	–	–	+	
Withholding material resources	+	–	–	–	+	+
Undermining states' sanctioning power	+	+	+	–	–	–

+ = power source was successfully withdrawn from the regime
– = power source was not successfully withheld from the regime

component of a winning strategy, since Chileans and Filipinos were able to oust their dictators without doing so on a large scale. Moreover, Panama's National Civic Crusade did use general strikes but was not able to topple Noriega.

The withholding of material resources can also undermine rulers' ability to govern but does not inevitably lead to their demise. In East Germany, the economic drain of mass emigration had a devastating effect, causing political elites to divide over the situation. But neither the Chilean nor the Filipino movement undercut their states' material resources, and yet they still succeeded. Moreover, these cases indicate that rulers can counter the loss of material resources in a couple of ways. First, as we saw with Kenya's President Moi, dictators may make limited concessions to get aid restored and sanctions repealed. Moi's decision to hold multiparty elections enabled him to keep Kenya's economy afloat without actually implementing any real changes, since he ensured the election would favor him. A second strategy is evident in Panama, where General Noriega survived financial losses by soliciting aid from other nations and by generating illicit revenue through drug trafficking. Thus the withdrawal of material resources can destabilize authoritarian leaders, but rulers may have alternative sources of money that can sustain them.

As Table 8.2 reveals, there is only one factor that distinguishes the successful cases from the failed ones: the regime's loss of sanctioning power. In short, where defections occurred or troops became unreliable, movements prevailed. But when troops remained loyal, regime leaders held on to power. Given the significance of this factor, we need to examine how mutiny occurs and when defections are most likely to happen.

SECURITY FORCE DEFECTIONS AND MUTINY

In the three successful cases examined here, security force defections occurred in different ways. In East Germany, defections started from below: a sizable number of low-ranking soldiers deserted or informed commanding officers that they would not carry out orders to repress protesters. This had a trickle-up effect on mid-level and high-ranking officers, who became reluctant to order violent sanctions when troops were on the verge of mass insubordination. In contrast, mutiny in Chile occurred at the top, as the navy, air force, and police commanders refused to impose martial law after the plebiscite vote. They refused to issue the orders—not because their troops were unreliable but because they did not believe that Pinochet could steal the election without major domestic and international backlash. Finally, the Philippine case reflects an interactive effect between high-ranking officers and lower-ranking troops. When two high-profile military leaders defected, they publicized a rift in the armed forces that opened opportunities for low-ranking soldiers to defect. As low-ranking troops deserted en masse, this in turn led more officers to mutiny since they had virtually no one to carry out their orders. As Defense Minister Enrile put it, "Marcos was relying too much on his generals. And the generals thought by simply issuing commands they would be obeyed. That is the greatest error of a leader: to only deal with the top. Many of those generals were already washed out so far as their commands were concerned."[7] Regardless of how defections occur, these three cases indicate that victory may happen shortly after rulers lose the capacity to impose sanctions.[8]

But precisely which factors facilitated troops' decision to shift their allegiance from the regime to the movement? In these three cases, we see that troops were less willing to repress when resisters remained nonviolent. In East Germany, resisters' peaceful behavior contradicted government propaganda that depicted them as malcontents who could be brought under control only through force. In contrast, when Chinese resisters became hostile toward the People's Army, troops found the Chinese government's claims more credible and hence were more likely to follow orders. Protester hostility also created a polarizing dynamic that made Chinese troops feel that it was "us against them." As sociologist Lewis Coser argued, external threats generate in-group cohesion,[9] making defections less likely.

Defections occurred in some instances because troops shared a collective identity with civil resisters. In East Germany, many soldiers were not military careerists; a sizable number were conscripts who had friends and family members in the movement. Moreover, these soldiers often supported demonstrators' goals, such as fewer travel restrictions and more political freedoms; this made it difficult for troops to view civil resisters as unreasonable radicals. A shared identity was also important in the Philippine struggle as Catholic soldiers faced Catholic resisters. This collective religious identity made it easier for troops to be sympathetic to the movement and difficult for them to attack the crowd of protesters, which included many nuns and priests.

The Kenyan and Chinese cases serve as counterpoints. Historical tensions among Kenya's ethnic groups meant that troops and resisters did not share a common identity or set of interests. President Moi exploited this dynamic, filling the armed forces with ethnic minorities when many oppositional leaders were members of ethnic majority groups, thereby decreasing the chance of defections. In the Chinese case, party leaders recognized the danger of a shared identity as some troops sided with the protesters. To break this solidarity, political leaders brought in troops from remote regions who did not identify with resisters and, in some cases, did not even speak the same dialect.

Another condition that contributed to defections, at least in the Philippines, was that civil resisters were able to make regime loyalty a moral issue. The religious nature of the Filipino revolt made obedience to Marcos an ethical dilemma. The bishops' denunciation of Marcos as a fraudulent leader and their call for faithful Catholics to nonviolently remove him from power made it difficult for Catholic soldiers to continue supporting the dictator. But the most poignant ethical dilemma came when unarmed citizens—including nuns, priests, pregnant women, children, and the elderly—knelt before the tanks. Although the troops knew that Marcos would imprison and probably execute anyone who refused orders, many believed that killing these innocent civilians would have eternal ramifications. Marcos might take their life for defecting, but following his orders could jeopardize their salvation.

Finally, troops were more willing to defect when they were aware that other soldiers were doing so. In the East German case, entire units decided beforehand that they would refuse orders; then they jointly announced their decision to their commanding officers. A similar dynamic occurred in the Philippines, where troops who manned the tanks witnessed many of their fellow soldiers joining the crowd. And in Chile, when the leaders of each military branch refused to carry out Pinochet's plans for annulling the vote, they made that choice collectively. If Pinochet had met with each leader separately to explain his plans for martial law, they might have relented, not knowing if the other military commanders would support them. Collective acts of defiance are easier and safer than solitary action, where the individual is more vulnerable to punishment. As sociologist Mark Granovetter has argued, very few people are willing to be the first to act. But once they do, others will follow suit; hence a critical mass can develop, reaching a tipping point for wide-scale desertions and defiance.[10]

But understanding why troops defect is only one piece of the picture. We must also examine why some soldiers remain loyal. In Panama, few soldiers turned against General Noriega because they had financial interests at stake. While Panama's economy crumbled, Noriega's officers lived well because he permitted them to accept bribes and engage in other corrupt financial practices. If Noriega was removed, their source of wealth would have been drastically reduced, and thus they had a strong incentive to keep him in office. In Kenya, troops also had good reason to keep their regime intact. Kenyan soldiers, who were mostly ethnic minorities, largely supported President Moi because they feared ethnic retaliation if he were deposed. These cases suggest that troops are most likely to remain loyal when they have something to lose. If they do not derive any direct benefits from the regime, they have less reason to protect it.

FACTORS THAT CAN DERAIL NONVIOLENT UPRISINGS

While the undermining of states' sanctioning powers and other civil resistance techniques are at the heart of a nonviolent revolt, movement organizers must also pay careful attention to factors that can undermine their capacity to engage in strategic action. The cases of China, Panama, and Kenya provide insights into some of the factors, listed in Table 8.3, that can derail nonviolent revolutions.

Divided Leadership and Internal Movement Conflict

The Chinese and Kenyan cases indicate that a nonviolent uprising is more likely to founder if its leaders become divided. What are typical sources of tension? In China, leaders fought over strategy. One faction advocated negotiations; the other faction called for a more militant, confrontational approach. Thus they spent much time and energy battling one another, limiting their ability to launch new actions. Strategic disagreements also made it difficult for the Chilean opposition to succeed in its earliest campaigns; it was only when the communist branch of the movement gave up its armed struggle and backed the plebiscite campaign that unity finally occurred, providing the opposition with a united front.

Table 8.3: FACTORS THAT UNDERMINE MOVEMENTS' CHANCES OF WINNING

Factors	Successful Cases			Unsuccessful Cases		
	GDR	Chile	Philippines	China	Panama	Kenya
Divided leadership or internal factions	–	–	–	+	–	+
Inability to remain nonviolent	–	–	–	+	+	+
External sanctions that backfired	–	–	–	–	+	+

– = problem did not exist
+ = problem did exist

Divisions can also stem from ethnic, class, and regional tensions among civil resisters. In the Chinese case, students disdained the thousands of workers who joined the Tiananmen Square occupation. Rather than forming a coalition that would have broadened the movement's base, the students largely rejected and ignored the workers. In addition, Beijing students—who initiated the movement—found themselves fighting with students from outside provinces. These tensions fragmented the movement, generated a high level of internal suspicion and distrust, and undermined the ability to act collectively.

While class and regional differences divided the Chinese movement, ethnic tensions divided the Kenyan uprising. When multiparty elections finally took place in Kenya, opposition leaders formed three different parties based on regional and ethnic affiliation. Thus the voting constituency was split, making it easier for Moi to win. Even if they had united, Moi would have probably still stolen the election, but the movement's lack of unity made it easier for him to give the appearance of being the legitimate winner, thereby extending his term in office.

Inability to Maintain Nonviolent Discipline

Another factor that derailed the uprisings in China, Panama, and Kenya was the inability to keep protesters nonviolent. In all three of these cases, there were moments when demonstrators became aggressive and sometimes rioted. This gave rulers the justification to declare martial law and use repression. It may have also made soldiers reluctant to defect, fearing retaliation at the hands of a hostile crowd.[11] While this is a potential problem for all civil resistance movements, a closer look at the successful cases in this study can provide insight into the factors that help resisters maintain nonviolent discipline.

The primary reason that the East German, Chilean, and Filipino movements refrained from violence is that movement leaders emphasized nonviolent discipline and prepared resisters to remain peaceful during moments of confrontation. Religious orders in the Philippines sponsored dozens of nonviolence training workshops. Similar workshops were held in East Germany by Protestant ministers and church-based activist groups[12] and in Chile by the faith-based organization Servicio Paz y Justicia.[13] Moreover, in East Germany and the Philippines, religious leaders were present at moments when massacres were about to happen. They provided direction to the protesters, strongly discouraged any hostility toward the troops, and reminded civil resisters of the strategic importance of remaining peaceful.

In the Philippines, religious leaders were a critical part of why the movement retained its nonviolent character. When Enrile and Ramos resigned, Filipino citizens were uncertain about whether to trust these men who had led a corrupt and repressive military for many years. One activist recalled, "My first reaction listening to the press conference of Enrile and Ramos ... was civil war was imminent. I also doubted the sincerity of the [military leaders'] revolt."[14] Others feared that the defectors would simply install a military regime once Marcos was ousted. Thus the potential for citizen rejection and retaliation against these men was strong. But this did not happen because Cardinal Sin called on Catholics to accept and protect the defectors. One observer recalled, "The moment they heard the confessions of Ramos and Enrile for their actions in the past *and the blessing conferred on them by the cardinal,* the people extended their trust to these once-feared men."[15]

Philippine religious leaders also reinforced protesters' discipline and courage when Marcos's tanks advanced. At that moment, as civil resisters faced the real prospect of a massacre, members of religious orders kept the situation calm. Priests and nuns initiated discussions with soldiers, calmed hostile individuals in the crowd, and yet refused to back down. Given the devoutly Catholic nature of the Philippine population, these religious authorities set an example that the crowd undoubtedly felt compelled to follow. As Butz Aquino stated, "I was scared. And then you see those ... nuns and you can't back off."[16]

In general, religious groups were important in all the cases except China. In addition to maintaining nonviolent discipline, religious groups offered these unarmed revolutionary movements other forms of support as well. Table 8.4 shows that in five cases, churches offered a free space where oppositional culture flourished and strategic organizing occurred. In some places—such as East Germany, Chile, and Kenya—the level of repression meant that there was no other place for activists to meet. Additionally, in each of these five uprisings, church leaders denounced regime abuses and supplied varied resources—from communications systems to financial assistance. But only the East German and Filipino churches undertook tasks that were critical to regime collapse: encouraging soldiers to defect and training resisters to remain calm during moments of crisis.

Negative Consequences of International Sanctions

The final factor that derailed some of these nonviolent uprisings was the imposition of international sanctions. In the Panama and Kenya cases, international actors who wanted to help civil resisters inadvertently

Table 8.4: FORMS OF RELIGIOUS SUPPORT GIVEN TO NONVIOLENT UPRISINGS

	Successful Cases			Unsuccessful Cases	
	GDR	*Chile*	*Philippines*	*Panama*	*Kenya*
Free space	yes	yes	yes	yes	yes
Denunciation of the regime	yes	yes	yes	yes	yes
Organizational resources*	yes	yes	yes	yes	yes
Encouraged mutiny	yes	no	yes	no	no
Offered nonviolence training	yes	yes[1]	yes	no	no
Directly helped to maintain nonviolent discipline	yes	no	yes	no	no

*These include financial contributions, recruitment networks, and communication channels.
[1] Many of the nonviolence training sessions in Chile were offered through the faith-based, ecumenical organization SERPAJ rather than the churches, but this training is noted since it appears to be critical in maintaining nonviolent discipline.

undermined them. This phenomenon merits closer examination since scholars, policy makers, and activists often assume that international support is unequivocally positive.[17] This assumption must be questioned since this study indicates that international sanctions against a regime can potentially backfire in two ways.

First, when a powerful nation such as the United States imposes sanctions on a dictatorship, their actions may create new allies for the regime. In Latin America, there is a long history of U.S. imperialism that has generated suspicion of American interests. Thus, as the United States began to sanction Noriega, countries that were politically opposed to U.S. policies—such as Nicaragua, Cuba, and Libya—offered assistance to Panama. These nations did not provide support to Noriega because they believed he was virtuous; they simply wanted to stop U.S. involvement in the region. Therefore, as Panama's revolutionary movement paralyzed industry through strikes and undermined the regime's financial base, an influx of assistance from new allies helped Noriega stay afloat.

The second potential problem with international sanctions can be seen in the Kenyan struggle against Daniel arap Moi. After donor nations withdrew $350 million in aid, Moi consented to donors' demands since he was highly dependent on this financial support, which would not be reinstated until multiparty elections were held. While this opened an opportunity to oust Moi, that opportunity was lost when donor nations endorsed an unfair election. Even though Moi had obstructed opposition groups' campaigning efforts and passed legislation that basically ensured his victory, international actors did not contest or reject the results. By accepting a flawed election, international donors thought they were helping Kenyans avoid a brutal civil conflict; in fact, they were prolonging an unjust system by giving Moi new legitimacy. Kenyan citizens, not developed nations in the Northern Hemisphere, should have decided whether to accept the elections. But since the donor nations controlled the purse strings, they had undue influence. In short, international actors may gain inappropriate levels of power and influence when they intervene in a struggle, and they do not always use that power effectively or appropriately.

Does this mean that international support is always harmful to nonviolent revolutionary movements? Not necessarily. Further research is needed to tease out the complexities of this dynamic: it might be that support from nongovernmental organizations and civil society groups has a profoundly different effect than support from nation-states.[18] Moreover, some scholars have argued for the development and use of "smart sanctions" that specifically undermine an authoritarian ruler's power while minimizing the harm done to the population.[19] While a full-scale examination of the differential effects of international sanctions is beyond the scope of this book, one thing is clear: whatever role international actors play in revolutionary situations, local civil resisters ought to have the greatest decision-making power in determining when, where, and how sanctions are applied.

IMPLICATIONS

What implications does this comparative analysis have for civil resisters seeking to overturn authoritarian regimes and for the international community aiming to support these movements? There are several insights we can draw from this study. However, I must emphasize that there is no formula that guarantees success. Even when movement leaders carefully construct a sound strategy, chance and contingency can add an element of unpredictability. Moreover, as Charles Kurzman noted in his study of the 1979 Iranian revolution, revolutionary participants often lack access to key pieces of information while the insurrection is occurring, making it difficult to evaluate the best course of action. Civil resisters may find it challenging to develop appropriate strategies since revolutions typically unfold in a rapidly changing environment. Thus social scientists who study revolutions have the advantage of identifying causal factors retrospectively and with access to a wide array of data sources. For those who are involved in a revolutionary struggle, assessing such factors in real time (with only limited information) is far more difficult, and thus misjudgments frequently occur.[20] Therefore, there will always be a degree of uncertainty involved as revolutionaries devise strategies and time their campaigns. Nonetheless, the six cases examined here may give civil resisters insight into the types of strategies that are worth pursuing and the types of problems they should try to avoid.

In terms of the best strategies to pursue, this study suggests that the techniques that have the most influence are those that undermine a regime's sanctioning power. In other words, civil resisters are more likely to win if they persuade troops to defect or refuse orders. This claim is supported by the research of Stephan and Chenoweth, who, using quantitative measures to assess a wider array of 20th-century cases, also found that security force defections are strongly correlated with movement success.[21] However, this does not imply that other civil resistance techniques are ineffective. It is likely that as resisters refuse to acknowledge the authority or legitimacy of a dictator, they raise the consciousness of others. This can transform a small movement into a critical mass. Similarly, as boycotts and general strikes weaken a nation's economy and limit public services, business elites may gain new understanding of the need for regime change and side with the movement. Thus these tactics may set the stage for defections by generating the perception that troops are futilely defending a crumbling regime. In short, civil resisters need to be aware that withholding their material resources, skills, cooperation, and support from a regime may not be enough to bring down a dictatorship. They might also need to encourage defections.

Another lesson we can derive from this study is that civil resisters should be judicious about the type of international support they solicit and accept. Activists need to assess whether external sanctions or the involvement of international groups is likely to produce a backlash that generates new aid and allies to the regime, as happened in Panama. If that is the case, a nonviolent movement may be better off working independently or seeking more neutral allies. Moreover, insurgent groups should carefully assess their regime's vulnerability to determine whether to request external sanctions. While certain sanctions—such as the discontinuation of aid—may have a strong effect on those regimes that are highly dependent on foreign assistance, other rulers may be less affected as they turn toward alternative sources of revenue, such as Noriega's access to illicit drug funds. When alternative funding is available to the regime, external sanctions are more likely to hurt citizens than the dictators they seek to oust. But if external sanctions are seen as potentially helpful to a nonviolent insurgency, then insurgents must insist that they hold the power to decide when those sanctions end.

Civil resisters may also consider alternative forms of international action. Although movements often propose the elimination of trade agreements, subsidies, and aid, such actions may not necessarily benefit the movement. It may be better to ask international actors to informally withdraw their influence from the situation. This was important in East Germany, where leaders were reluctant to crack down since they knew their own forces were unreliable and they could not rely on the intervention of Soviet troops. Although this was not a direct sanction against the regime, Gorbachev's unwillingness to get involved weakened the East German state. Similarly, President Reagan never cut aid to the Philippines, but his informal suggestion to Marcos that it was time to step down may well have contributed to the dictator's perception that he could no longer count on Reagan's support.

Finally, this study suggests that civil resisters and scholars must not take a one-sided view of the revolutionary process. Although theories of strategic nonviolence emphasize what citizens can do to undermine authoritarian regimes, these cases reveal that rulers also seek ways to reinforce their power. The revolts in China, Panama, and Kenya failed in large part because rulers implemented effective counterstrategies. When members of the Chinese People's Army grew insubordinate, military leaders found a way to fortify their sanctioning power. Similarly, Noriega and Moi made sure that their troops' interests were contingent upon keeping the regime intact, thereby decreasing the chance of defections. And Moi devised a plan to restore international aid to Kenya by conducting a "C-minus election" that would appease donors without making any real political changes. Therefore, just like champion chess players, civil resisters must not only plot their course to victory. Whenever possible, they must also anticipate their opponents' moves and find ways to neutralize or counter authoritarian leaders' strategies.

In short, the planning and execution of a nonviolent revolt is just as complex as planning a violent revolt. Leaders need to develop effective tactics that undermine a regime's ability to function. They must evaluate whether they want international support and which forms would benefit, rather than harm, their movement. They must ensure that international actors respect their decisions about how to proceed rather than imposing their own agendas. They need to prepare citizen insurgents to remain nonviolent, even in the face of potentially lethal repression. They must pay close attention to factors, such as internal divisions, that can derail their carefully orchestrated plans. And they must respond to rulers' attempts to prolong their power.

If nonviolent insurgents can accomplish this, the most remarkable changes are possible. Unarmed citizens can deflect tanks. Civil resisters can tear down walls that have held people captive for decades. Dictators who have never hesitated to torture or assassinate opponents find that their troops are not willing to torture any more. And most remarkable of all, these nonviolent revolts prove that entire political systems can be transformed without bloodshed.

NOTES

PREFACE

1. For an overview of these issues, see Ackerman, Peter. 2007. "Skills or Conditions? What Key Factors Shape the Success or Failure of Civil Resistance." Unpublished paper from the Conference on Civil Resistance and Power Politics, Oxford University, Oxford, Great Britain.

2. Schelling, Thomas C. 1967. "Some Questions on Civilian Defense." In *Civilian Resistance as a National Defense: Nonviolent Action against Aggression*, edited by Adam Roberts. Harrisburg, PA: Stackpole. Pages 351–352.

3. Such descriptive accounts include: Ackerman, Peter, and Jack DuVall. 2000. *A Force More Powerful: A Century of Nonviolent Conflict*. New York: St. Martin's; Zunes, Stephen, Lester R. Kurtz, and Sarah Beth Asher (eds.). 1999. *Nonviolent Social Movements: A Geographical Perspective*. Malden, MA: Blackwell. In addition to these descriptive works, there are three comparative studies of nonviolent movements: Ackerman, Peter, and Christopher Kruegler. 1994. *The Strategy of Nonviolent Conflict: The Dynamics of People Power in the Twentieth Century*. Westport, CT: Praeger; Schock, Kurt. 2005. *Unarmed Insurrections: People Power Movements in Nondemocracies*. Minneapolis: University of Minnesota Press. Stephan, Maria, and Erica Chenoweth. 2008. "Why Civil Resistance Works: The Strategic Conflict of Nonviolent Resistance." *International Security* 33(1): 7–44.

4. Goodwin, Jeff. 2001. *No Other Way Out: States and Social Revolutions, 1945–1991*. New York: Cambridge University Press. Pages 6–7; Lipsky, William E. 1976. "Comparative Approaches to the Study of Revolution: A Historiographic Essay." *Review of Politics* 38: 494–509.

5. Mill, John Stuart. 2002 [1843]. *A System of Logic*. Honolulu: University Press of the Pacific.

6. Arjomand, Said Amir. 1988. *The Turban for the Crown: The Islamic Revolution in Iran*. New York: Oxford University Press; Kurzman, Charles. 2004. *The Unthinkable Revolution in Iran*. Cambridge, MA: Harvard University Press.

7. A 2005 study, conducted by Adrian Karatnycky and Peter Ackerman, did find that those democracies established through nonviolent means were more stable and enduring than democracies put in place by violent methods. For the full results of this research, see: Karatnycky, Adrian, and Peter Ackerman. 2005. "How Freedom Is Won: From Civil Resistance to Durable Democracy." Washington, DC: Freedom House.

8. For an explanation of revolutionary typologies, see Goldstone, Jack. 2001. "Toward a Fourth Generation of Revolutionary Theory." *Annual Review of Political Science* 4: 139–187.

9. For further information on this method, see King, Gary, Robert Keohane, and Sidney Verba (eds.). 1994. *Designing Social Inquiry: Scientific Inference in Qualitative Research.* Princeton, NJ: Princeton University Press.

10. For a fascinating study of nonviolent resistance to occupying forces, see Semelin, Jacques. 1993. *Unarmed against Hitler: Civilian Resistance in Europe, 1939–1943.* Westport, CT: Praeger.

11. One point of clarification: all six cases in this study began in the 1980s. Five of these movements were over by 1990. The Kenyan uprising analyzed here continued until 1992, but the outcome was relatively unaffected by the Cold War's end.

12. See Jeff Goodwin's argument about the effects of state structure in his comparative study of anticommunist revolutions in Eastern Europe: *No Other Way Out.* 2001. New York: Cambridge University Press.

13. Eckstein, Harry. 1975. "Case Study and Theory in Political Science." In *Handbook of Political Science,* vol. 7, *Strategies of Inquiry,* edited by Fred Greenstein and Nelson Polsby. Reading, MA: Addison-Wesley; King, Keohane, and Verba, 1994, *Designing Social Inquiry.*

14. Marshall, T. H. (Thomas Humphrey). 1965. *Class, Citizenship, and Social Development.* Garden City, NY: Doubleday. Page 38.

15. For a useful discussion of the misconceptions of nonviolence, see Shock, Kurt. 2003. "Nonviolent Action and Its Misconceptions: Insights for Social Scientists." *PS: Political Science and Politics* 36: 705–712.

16. All six cases examined in this book were dedicated to using these methods to transform their governments. Although the movements in China, Panama, and Kenya were not always able to maintain nonviolent discipline, as actions occasionally digressed into rioting, these cases are nevertheless included because movement organizers intentionally rejected armed combat and purposefully selected civil resistance as their primary strategy.

17. Sharp, Gene (ed.). 2005. *Waging Nonviolent Struggle: 20ᵗʰ Century Practice and 21ˢᵗ Century Potential.* Boston: Porter Sargent. Page 41.

18. Roberts, Adam, and Timothy Garton Ash. 2009. *Civil Resistance and Power Politics: The Experience of Non-violent Action from Gandhi to the Present.* Oxford: Oxford University Press; Stephan, Maria, and Erica Chenoweth. 2008. "Why Civil Resistance Works: The Strategic Conflict of Nonviolent Resistance." *International Security* 33(1): 7–44.

19. Schock, 2005, *Unarmed Insurrections;* Zunes, Stephen. 1994. "Unarmed Insurrections against Authoritarian Governments in the Third World: A New Kind of Revolution?" *Third World Quarterly* 15: 403–426.

20. Zedong, Mao. 1927. "Report on an Investigation into the Peasant Movement in Hunan." *Selected Works of Mao Tse-tung, Volume 1.* Beijing: Beijing Foreign Language Press. Page 29.

21. Garton Ash, Timothy. 2009. "A Century of Civil Resistance: Some Lessons and Questions." In *Civil Resistance and Power Politics: The Experience of Non-Violent Action from Gandhi to the Present.* Oxford: Oxford University Press. Page 377.

22. This is consistent with the definition of revolution offered by Jack Goldstone in "Toward a Fourth Generation of Revolutionary Theory," page 142.

23. For further discussion of these differences, see Goldstone, Jack. 2009. "Rethinking Revolutions: Integrating Origins, Processes, and Outcomes." *Comparative Studies of South Asia, Africa and the Middle East* 29(1): 8–32.

24. Goldstone, Jack A. 2003. "Comparative Historical Analysis and Knowledge Accumulation in the Study of Revolutions." Pages 41–90 in *Comparative Historical Analysis in the Social Sciences,* edited by James Mahoney and Dietrich Rueschemeyer. New York:

Cambridge University Press; Kumar, Krishan. 2001. *1989: Revolutionary Ideas and Ideals.* Minneapolis: University of Minnesota Press.

25. Garton Ash, Timothy. 2009. "Velvet Revolution: The Prospects." *New York Review of Books* 56(19), December 3; Wheaton, Bernard, and Zdenek Kavan. 1992. *The Velvet Revolution: Czechoslovakia, 1988–1991.* Boulder, CO: Westview.

26. Kennedy, Michael D. 1999. "Contingencies and Alternatives of 1989: Toward a Theory and Practice of Negotiating Revolution. *Eastern European Politics and Societies* 13(2): 293–302; Lawson, George. 2005. *Negotiated Revolutions: The Czech Republic, South Africa and Chile.* Aldershot, UK: Ashgate; Stokes, Gale. 1993. *The Walls Came Tumbling Down: The Collapse of Communism in Eastern Europe.* New York: Oxford University Press.

27. This refers to political uprisings that reflect a combination of reform and revolution. For further discussion, see Garton Ash, Timothy. 1989. *The Uses of Adversity: Essays on the Fate of Central Europe.* Cambridge, UK: Granta.

CHAPTER 1

1. Wurfel, David. 1988. *Filipino Politics: Development and Decay.* Ithaca, NY: Cornell University Press.

2. Thompson, Mark. 1995. *The Anti-Marcos Struggle: Personalistic Rule and Democratic Transition in the Philippines.* New Haven, CT: Yale University Press.

3. Ibid.

4. C. A. Gambol, quoted on p. 116 in Jim and Nancy Forest's 1988 book, *Four Days in February: The Story of the Nonviolent Overthrow of the Marcos Regime* (London: Marshall Pickering).

5. Karatnycky, Adrian, and Peter Ackerman. 2005. *How Freedom Is Won: From Civil Resistance to Durable Democracy.* Washington, DC: Freedom House.

6. Stephan, Maria, and Erica Chenoweth. 2008. "Why Civil Resistance Works: The Strategic Logic of Nonviolent Conflict." *International Security* 33(1): 8.

7. Geddes, Barbara. 1999. "What Do We Know about Democratization after Twenty Years?" *Annual Review of Political Science* 2: 115–144; Goldstone, Jack. 2009. "Rethinking Revolutions: Integrating Origins, Processes, and Outcomes." *Comparative Studies of South Asia, Africa and the Middle East* 29(1): 18–32.

8. For an exceptional overview of the literature on revolutions, see Goldstone, Jack A. 2001. "Toward a Fourth Generation of Revolutionary Theory." *Annual Review of Political Science* 4: 139–187.

9. Goldstone, Jack. 1991. *Revolution and Rebellion in the Early Modern World.* Berkeley: University of California Press; Reykowski, Janusz. 1994. "Why Did the Collectivist State Fail?" *Theory and Society* 23(2): 233–252; Skocpol, Theda. 1979. *States and Social Revolutions.* Cambridge: Cambridge University Press.

10. Bunce, Valerie, and Sharon Wolchik. 2006. "International Diffusion and Postcommunist Electoral Revolutions." *Communist and Postcommunist Studies* 39: 283–304.

11. For further information about the role of elite divisions in revolutions, see the following: Arjomand, Said A. 1988. *The Turban for the Crown: The Islamic Revolution in Iran.* New York: Oxford University Press; Bunce, Valerie. 1989. "The Polish Crisis of 1980–1981 and Theories of Revolution." Pp. 167–188 in *Revolution in the World System*, edited by Terry Boswell. New York: Greenwood; DeFronzo, James. 1996. *Revolutions and Revolutionary Movements.* Boulder, CO: Westview; Dogan, Matthéi, and John Higley. 1998. *Elites, Crises, and the Origins of Regimes.* Lanham, MD: Rowman & Littlefield; Goldstone, 1991, *Revolutions and Rebellion in the Early Modern World*; Haggard, Stephen, and Robert R. Kaufman. 1995. *The Political Economy of Democratic Transitions.* Princeton, NJ: Princeton University Press; Higley, John, and Michael Burton. 1989. "The Elite Variable

in Democratic Transitions and Breakdowns." *American Sociological Review* 54: 17–32; Lachmann, Richard. 1997. "Agents of Revolution: Elite Conflicts and Mass Mobilization from the Medici to Yeltsin." Pp. 73–101 in *Theorizing Revolutions*, edited by John Foran. London: Routledge; Parsa, Misagh. 2000. *States, Ideologies, and Social Revolutions: A Comparative Analysis of Iran, Nicaragua, and the Philippines.* Cambridge: Cambridge University Press. Skocpol, 1979, *States and Social Revolutions*; Wood, Elisabeth Jean. 2000. *Forging Democracy from Below: Insurgent Transitions in South Africa and El Salvador.* New York: Cambridge University Press.

12. Oberschall, Anthony, and Hyojoung Kim. 1996. "Identity and Action." *Mobilization* 1: 63–86.

13. Goldstone, 2001, "Toward a Fourth Generation of Revolutionary Theory."

14. Shanin, Teodor. 1986. *The Roots of Otherness: Russia's Turn of the Century, Volume II: Revolution as a Moment of Truth.* New Haven, CT: Yale University Press. Pages 30–31.

15. Foran, John. 1997. *Theorizing Revolutions.* London: Routledge; Mansbridge, Jane. 2001. "The Making of Oppositional Consciousness." Pages 1–19 in *Oppositional Consciousness: The Subjective Roots of Social Protest*, edited by Jane Mansbridge and Aldon Morris. Chicago: University of Chicago Press; Wickham-Crowley, Timothy. 1992. *Guerrillas and Revolution in Latin America.* Princeton, NJ: Princeton University Press.

16. Snow, David, and Robert Benford. 1988. "Ideology, Frame Resonance, and Participant Mobilization." *International Social Movement Research* 1: 197–218; Cress, Daniel, and David Snow. 2000. "The Outcomes of Homeless Mobilization: The Influence of Organization, Disruption, Political Mediation, and Framing." *American Journal of Sociology* 105: 1063–1104.

17. Evans, Sarah M., and Harry C. Boyte. 1992. *Free Spaces.* Chicago: University of Chicago Press.

18. Foran, 1997, *Theorizing Revolutions.*

19. McAdam, Doug. 1982. *Political Process and the Development of Black Insurgency, 1930–1970.* Chicago: University of Chicago Press; Tarrow, Sidney. 1998. *Power in Movement: Social Movements and Contentious Politics*, 2nd ed. New York: Cambridge University Press.

20. Smith, Christian. 1996. *Resisting Reagan: The U.S.-Central America Peace Movement.* Chicago: University of Chicago Press.

21. Selbin, Eric. 1993. *Modern Latin American Revolutions.* Boulder, CO: Westview.

22. A classic example of how pre-existing structural features can affect movements is seen in Herbert Kitschelt's 1986 article, "Political Opportunity Structures and Political Protest: Anti-Nuclear Movements in Four Democracies." *British Journal of Political Science* 16: 57–85.

23. Schock, Kurt. 2005. *Unarmed Insurrections: People Power Movements in Nondemocracies.* Minneapolis: University of Minnesota Press.

24. Geddes, 1999. "What Do We Know about Democratization after Twenty Years?"; Way, Lucan. 2008. "The Real Causes of Color Revolutions." *Journal of Democracy* 19(3): 55–69.

25. For a full overview of the political process model, see McAdam, 1982, *Political Process and the Development of Black Insurgency, 1930–1970.*

26. Bunce, Valerie. 1999. *Subversive Institutions: The Design and Destruction of Socialism and the State.* Cambridge: Cambridge University Press.

27. Bunce, Valerie, and Sharon Wolchik. 2006. "Favorable Conditions and Electoral Revolutions." *Journal of Democracy* 17(4): 5–18.

28. Hale, Henry. 2006. "Democracy or Autocracy on the March? The Color Revolutions as Normal Dynamics of Patronal Presidentialism." *Communist and Post-Communist Studies* 39(3): 305–329.

29. Huntington, Samuel. 1991. *The Third Wave: Democratization in the Late Twentieth Century*. Norman: University of Oklahoma Press; Markoff, John. 1996. *Waves of Democracy: Social Movements and Political Change*. Thousand Oaks, CA: Pine Forge.

30. Jasper, James. 1997. *The Art of Moral Protest: Culture, Biography, and Creativity in Social Movements*. Chicago: University of Chicago Press.

31. On this point, also see Goodwin, Jeff. *No Other Way Out: States and Revolutionary Movements, 1945–1991*. New York: Cambridge University Press. Page 278.

32. I thank Clifford Bob for underscoring this point.

33. Ackerman, Peter, and Christopher Kruegler. 1994. *Strategic Nonviolent Conflict: The Dynamics of People Power in the Twentieth Century*. Westport, CT: Praeger. Pages xx–xxi.

34. My chosen definition is consistent with one offered by Marshall Ganz in his 2009 book, *Why David Sometimes Wins: Leadership, Organization, and Strategy in the California Farm Workers Movement* (New York: Oxford University Press). Other studies define *strategy* to include a much broader array of movement choices, including decisions over the type of movement organization and leadership system to implement, whether to forge alliances with other groups, which groups should be targeted for fund-raising, and so forth. (For a complete list of such strategic choices, see Jasper, James. 2004. "A Strategic Approach to Collective Action: Looking for Agency in Social Movement Choices." *Mobilization* 9:1–16.)

35. Sharp, Gene. 1973. *The Politics of Nonviolent Action*. Boston: Porter Sargent.

36. Sharp refers to this conception of power as "pluralist." However, Kurt Schock (2005) refers to this as a "relational" view to avoid confusion with political scientists' concept of pluralist power as depicted in studies of competing interest groups in democratic states.

37. Arendt, Hannah. 1970. *On Violence*. New York: Harcourt, Brace, and World; La Boétie, Etienne. 1997 [1548]. *The Politics of Obedience: The Discourse of Voluntary Servitude*. Montreal: Black Rose; Thoreau, Henry David. 2008. *On the Duty of Civil Disobedience*. Radford, VA: Wilder.

38. La Boétie, 1997, *The Politics of Obedience*, pages 52–53.

39. For further insights into Gandhi's strategic methods, see Bondurant, Joan. 1958. *Conquest of Violence: The Gandhian Philosophy of Conflict*. Princeton, NJ: Princeton University Press; Brown, Judith M. 1972. *Gandhi's Rise to Power*. Cambridge: Cambridge University Press; Brown, Judith M. 1977. *Gandhi and Civil Disobedience*. Cambridge: Cambridge University Press; Burrowes, Robert. 1996. *The Strategy of Nonviolent Defense: A Gandhian Approach*. Albany: State University of New York Press.

40. Gene Sharp, who popularized this theory, uses slightly different language. He argues that political power emerges from the interaction of the following popular power sources: (1) authority, (2) human resources (e.g., cooperation), (3) skills and knowledge, (4) intangible factors (psychological and ideological attitudes toward obedience), (5) material resources, and (6) sanctions. For further information about his theory, see Gene Sharp's 1973 book, *The Politics of Nonviolent Action* (Boston: Porter-Sargent).

41. Ibid., vol. 2, page 144.

42. Helvey, Robert L. 2004. *On Strategic Nonviolent Conflict: Thinking about Fundamentals*. Cambridge, MA: Albert Einstein Institution.

43. Sharp, 1990, *The Role of Power in Nonviolent Struggle*, page 9.

44. Ibid.

45. Bunce and Wolchik, 2006, "Favorable Conditions and Electoral Revolutions," page 6.

46. Ibid. Also see Bunce, Valerie, and Sharon Wolchik. 2009. "Getting Real about 'Real Causes.'" *Journal of Democracy* 20(1): 70.

47. Although *color revolutions* is an umbrella term for those movements that successfully used the electoral model, the movement in Georgia was actually dubbed the "Rose Revolution" and the uprising in Kyrgyzstan was called the "Tulip Revolution."

48. Seymour Martin Lipset first proposed this theory in his 1959 article, "Some Social Requisites of Democracy." *American Political Science Review* 53(1): 69–105. He later elaborated his theory in his 1963 book, *Political Man: The Social Bases of Politics*. Baltimore: Johns Hopkins University Press. More recent studies have also focused on the role of a nation's changing cultural attitudes. For more information, see Ronald Inglehart and Christian Welzel's 2005 book, *Modernization, Cultural Change, and Democracy: The Human Development Sequence*. New York: Cambridge University Press.

49. Prezworski, Adam, and Fernando Limongi. 1997. "Modernization: Theory and Facts." *World Politics* 49: 155–183.

50. For more insight into the structural approach to democratization, see Acemoglu, Daron, and James A. Robinson. 2005. *Economic Origins of Dictatorship and Democracy*. New York: Cambridge University Press; Rueschemeyer, Dietrich, Evelyn Huber Stephens, and John D. Stephens. 1992. *Capitalist Development and Democracy*. Chicago: University of Chicago Press.

51. For further information on the transition approach, refer to Di Palma, Guiseppe. 1990. *To Craft Democracies: An Essay on Democratic Transitions*. Berkeley: University of California Press; Higley, John, and Richard Gunther (eds.). 1992. *Elites and Democratic Consolidation in Latin America and Southern Europe*. Cambridge: Cambridge University Press; Mainwaring, Scott, Guillermo O'Donnell, and Arturo Valenzuela (eds.). 1992. *Issues in Democratic Consolidation*. Notre Dame, IN: University of Notre Dame Press; Shain, Yossi, and Juan Linz. 1995. *Between States: Interim Governments and Democratic Transitions*. Cambridge: Cambridge University Press.

52. The authors compiled this list of campaigns from several sources. For the nonviolent campaigns, they drew from encyclopedias and bibliographies such as: Carter, April, Howard Clark, and Michael Randel (eds.). 2006. *People Power and Protest since 1945: A Bibliography of Nonviolent Action*. London: Housmans; McCarthy, Ronald M., and Gene Sharp. 1997. *Nonviolent Action: A Research Guide*. New York: Garland. For a list of violent campaigns, the authors used Kristian Gleditsch's updates to the Correlates of War database on intrastate wars and from Kalev Sepp's list of counterinsurgency operations. For more information about these databases, see Gleditsch, Kristian. 2004. "A Revised List of Wars between and within Independent States, 1816–2002." *International Interactions* 30(3): 231–262; Sepp, Kalev. 2005. "Best Practices in Counterinsurgency." *Military Review* 85(3): 8–12.

53. For a more complete overview of their methodology, see Stephan and Chenoweth, 2008, "Why Civil Resistance Works."

54. Bob, Clifford. 2005. *The Marketing of Rebellion: Insurgents, Media, and International Activism*. New York: Cambridge University Press.

55. For an account of the effects of nongovernmental organizational financial support for the color revolutions, see Bunce and Wolchik, 2006, "Favorable Conditions and Electoral Revolutions."

56. This is also consistent with Jeffrey Record's findings in his 2006 article, "External Assistance: Enabler of Insurgent Success." *Parameters* 36(3): 36–49.

57. Stephan and Chenoweth, 2008, "Why Civil Resistance Works," pages 22–23.

58. Goodwin, Jeff, and Theda Skocpol. 1989. "Explaining Revolutions in the Contemporary Third World." *Political Sociology* 17: 489–507; Keck, Margaret, and Kathryn Sikkink. 1998. *Activists without Borders: Advocacy Networks in International Politics*. Ithaca, NY: Cornell University Press.

59. This is consistent with the argument put forth by Robert Pape in his 1997 article, "Why Economic Sanctions Do Not Work." *International Security* 22(2): 90–136.

60. Stephan and Chenoweth, 2008, "Why Civil Resistance Works," page 22.

61. Ibid.

62. Binnendijk, Anika Locke, and Ivan Marovic. 2006. "Power and Persuasion: Nonviolent Strategies to Influence State Security Forces in Serbia (2000) and Ukraine (2004)." *Communist and Post-Communist Studies* 39: 411–429.

63. Ibid.

64. Ibid.

65. For alternative explanations for why rulers resort to repression, see Earl, Jennifer. 2003. "Tanks, Tear Gas and Taxes: Toward a Theory of Movement Repression." *Sociological Theory* 21: 44–68.

66. Bob, Clifford, and Sharon Erickson Nepstad. 2007. "Kill a Leader, Murder a Movement? Leadership and Assassination in Social Movements." *American Behavioral Scientist* 50(10): 1370–1394.

67. Richard Gregg called this dynamic "moral jiu-jitsu" in his 1935 book, *The Power of Non-Violence* (London: George Routledge). Several decades later, Gene Sharp elaborated the concept in *The Politics of Nonviolent Action*, changing the term to "political jiu-jitsu" to underscore the strategic (rather than moral) nature of civil resistance and to emphasize the shifting balance of political force.

68. For further discussion of these paradoxical effects of repression, see Francisco, Ronald A. 2004. "After the Massacre: Mobilization in the Wake of Harsh Repression." *Mobilization* 9(2): 107–126; Hess, David, and Brian Martin. 2006. "Repression, Backfire, and the Theory of Transformative Events." *Mobilization* 11(2): 249–267; Lichbach, Mark. 1987. "Deterrent or Escalation? The Puzzle of Aggregate Studies of Repression and Dissent." *Journal of Conflict Resolution* 31: 266–297; Martin, Brian. 2007. *Justice Ignited: The Dynamics of Backfire*. Lanham, MD: Rowman & Littlefield; Schock, 2005, *Unarmed Insurrections*; Sharp, 2005, *Waging Nonviolent Struggle*; Smithey, Lee, and Lester R. Kurtz. 1999. "'We Have Bare Hands': Nonviolent Social Movements in the Soviet Bloc." Pp. 96–124 in *Nonviolent Social Movements: A Geographic Perspective*, edited by Stephen Zunes, Lester R. Kurtz, and Sarah Beth Asher. Malden, MA: Blackwell.

69. Almeida, Paul. 2003. "Opportunity Organization and Threat-Induced Contention: Protest Waves in Authoritarian Settings." *American Journal of Sociology* 109: 345–400.

70. Bob, 2005, *The Marketing of Rebellion*.

71. Stephan and Chenoweth, 2008, "Why Civil Resistance Works," page 20.

72. Jasper, James. Forthcoming. "Choice Points, Emotional Batteries, and Other Ways to Find Strategic Agency at the Micro Level." In *Strategy in Action*, edited by Gregory Maney, Rachel Kutz-Flamenbaum, Deana Rohlinger, and Jeff Goodwin. Minneapolis: University of Minnesota Press.

CHAPTER 2

1. Black, George, and Robin Munro. 1993. *Black Hands of Beijing: Lives of Defiance in China's Democracy Movement*. New York: John Wiley & Sons.

2. Xiaodong, Wang. 1993. "A Review of China's Economic Problems: The Industrial Sector." Pages 149–160 in *Chinese Democracy and the Crisis of 1989: Chinese and American Reflections*, edited by Roger V. Des Forges, Luo Ning, and Wu Yen-bo. Albany: State University of New York Press.

3. Lin, Nan. 1992. *The Struggle for Tiananmen: Anatomy of the 1989 Mass Movement*. Westport, CT: Praeger.

4. Xiadong, Wang, 1993, "A Review of China's Economic Problems."

5. Zhou, Xueguang. 1993. "Unorganized Interests and Collective Action in Communist China." *American Sociological Review* 58: 54–73.

6. Black and Munro, 1993, *Black Hands of Beijing*.

7. Ibid., page 50.

8. Black and Munro, 1993, *Black Hands of Beijing*.
9. Calhoun, Craig. 1994. *Neither Gods nor Emperors: Students and the Struggle for Democracy in China*. Berkeley: University of California Press.
10. Zhao, Dingxin. 2001. *The Power of Tiananmen: State-Society Relations and the 1989 Beijing Student Movement*. Chicago: University of Chicago Press.
11. Statement by Fang Lizhi as quoted in Brook, Timothy. 1992. *Quelling the People: The Military Suppression of the Beijing Democracy Movement*. New York: Oxford University Press, page 21.
12. Brook, 1992, *Quelling the People*.
13. Simmie, Scott, and Bob Nixon. 1989. *Tiananmen Square: An Eyewitness Account of the Chinese People's Passionate Quest for Democracy*. Seattle: University of Washington Press.
14. Calhoun, 1994, *Neither Gods nor Emperors*, pages 47–48.
15. Han, Minzhu. 1990. *Cries for Democracy: Writings and Speeches from the 1989 Chinese Democracy Movement*. Princeton, NJ: Princeton University Press, page 88.
16. Brook, 1992, *Quelling the People*, pages 27–29.
17. Statement by Shen Tong, quoted in Brook, 1992. *Quelling the People*, page 28.
18. Calhoun, 1994, *Neither Gods nor Emperors*.
19. Brook, 1992, *Quelling the People*, page 37.
20. Calhoun, 1994, *Neither Gods nor Emperors*, page 72.
21. Zhao, 2001, *The Power of Tiananmen*.
22. Calhoun, 1994, *Neither Gods nor Emperors*, page 67.
23. Zheng, Zhuyan. 1990. *Behind the Tiananman Square Massacre*. Boulder, CO: Westview.
24. Thomas, Gordon. 1991. *Chaos under Heaven: The Shocking Story of China's Search for Democracy*. New York: Birch Lane.
25. Han, 1990, *Cries for Democracy*, page 226.
26. Brook, 1992, *Quelling the People*, page 39.
27. Yu, Mok Chiu, and J. Frank Harrison. 1990. *Voices from Tiananmen Square: Beijing Spring and the Democracy Movement*. Montreal: Black Rose. Pages 129–130.
28. Brook, 1992, *Quelling the People*, page 39.
29. See "A Statement for the Soldiers," page 100 in Yu and Harrison, 1990, *Voices from Tiananmen Square*.
30. One letter to soldiers opens with the statement: "Dear soldiers, please ask yourselves how come in these days of wild inflation, your food stipend remains at 1.65 yuan. I suggest that you take a look at the profiteering going on among government officials!" Quoted on page 28 in Han's *Cries for Democracy*.
31. Yu and Harrison, 1990, *Voices from Tiananmen Square*, page 100.
32. Han, 1990, *Cries for Democracy*, pages 261–262.
33. Calhoun, 1994, *Neither Gods nor Emperors*.
34. Feigon, Lee. 1990. *China Rising: The Meaning of Tiananmen*. Chicago: Ivan R. Dee, page 203.
35. Black and Munro, 1993, *Black Hands of Beijing*, page 231.
36. Calhoun, 1994, *Neither Gods nor Emperors*, page 96.
37. Brook, 1992, *Quelling the People*.
38. Li, Lu. 1990. *Moving the Mountain: My Life in China from the Cultural Revolution to Tiananmen Square*. London: Macmillan.
39. Zhao, 2001, *The Power of Tiananmen*, pages 184–185.
40. Quoted in Brook, 1992, *Quelling the People*, page 63.
41. Some estimate that students from outside Beijing constituted roughly 80 percent of those occupying Tiananmen Square. For examples, see Khu, Jospehine M. T. 1993. "Student Organization in the Movement." Pages 161–175 in *Chinese Democracy and the Crisis*

of 1989: Chinese and American Reflections, edited by Roger V. Des Forges, Luo Ning, and Wu Yen-bo. Albany: State University of New York.

42. Calhoun, 1994, *Neither Gods nor Emperors*, pages 106–107.

43. Taso, Tsing-yuan. 1994. "The Birth of the Goddess of Democracy." Pages 140–147 in *Popular Protest and Political Culture in Modern China*, edited by Jeffrey N. Wasserstrom and Elizabeth H. Perry. Boulder, CO: Westview.

44. Calhoun, 1994, *Neither Gods nor Emperors*, page 110.

45. Scobell, Andrew. 1993. "Why the People's Army Fired on the People." Pages 191–221 in *Chinese Democracy and the Crisis of 1989: Chinese and American Reflections*, edited by Roger V. Des Forges, Luo Ning, and Wu Yen-bo. Albany: State University of New York Press.

46. Calhoun, 1994, *Neither Gods nor Emperors*, pages 113–114.

47. Calhoun, 1994, *Neither Gods nor Emperors*, pages 122–125.

48. Brook, 1992, *Quelling the People*, page 129.

49. Black and Munro, 1993, *Black Hands of Beijing*, page 241.

50. Gordon, 1991, *Chaos under Heaven*, page 290.

51. Both quotations from page 244–246 in Black and Munro, 1993, *Black Hands of Beijing*.

52. Black and Munro, 1993, *Black Hands of Beijing*, page 245.

53. Black and Munro, 1993, *Black Hands of Beijing*.

54. Brook, 1992, *Quelling the People*, pages 154–155, 167.

55. Calhoun, 1994, *Neither Gods nor Emperors*, page 145.

56. For further elaboration of the political opportunities that aided student mobilization, see Smith, Jackie, and Ronald Pagnucco. 1992. "Political Process and the 1989 Chinese Student Movement." *Studies in Conflict and Terrorism* 15: 169–184; Zuo, Jiping, and Robert Benford. 1995. "Mobilization Processes and the 1989 Chinese Democracy Movement." *Sociological Quarterly* 36(1): 131–156.

57. Ackerman and Kruegler, in their 1994 book, *Strategic Nonviolent Conflict*, argue that movements that employ multiple tactics are more likely to succeed than those who rely on one or two forms of resistance.

58. Chandra, Nirmal Humar. 1989. "Crisis in China: End of Socialism?" *Economic and Political Weekly* 24(46): 2551.

59. Perry, Elizabeth. 1994. "Casting a Chinese 'Democracy' Movement: The Role of Students, Workers, and Entrepreneurs." Pages 74–92 in *Popular Protest and Political Culture in Modern China*, edited by Jeffrey N. Wasserstrom and Elizabeth J. Perry. Boulder: Westview.

60. Chan, Anita, and Jonathan Unger. 1990. "Voices from the Protest Movement, Chongqing, Sichuan." *Australian Journal of Chinese Affairs* 24: 273.

61. Perry, 1994, "Casting a Chinese 'Democracy' Movement."

62. Ibid., pages 81–82.

63. Scobell, 1993, "Why the People's Army Fired on the People," page 197.

64. Ibid., page 201.

65. Calhoun, 1994, *Neither Gods nor Emperors*, page 122.

66. One of the student leaders, Li Lu, insisted that troops were intentionally promoting violence among resisters in order to justify their crackdown. See Zhao, 2001, *The Power of Tiananmen*, page 202 and footnote 163.

67. Ibid., page 203, footnote 169.

CHAPTER 3

1. Denitch, Bogdan. 1990. *The End of the Cold War: European Unity, Socialism, and the Shift in Global Power*. Minneapolis: University of Minnesota Press; Kuran, Timur. 1991. "Now out of Never: The Element of Surprise in the East European Revolutions in 1989." *World*

Politics 44(1): 7–48; Kuran, Timur. 1995. "The Inevitability of Future Revolutionary Surprises." *American Journal of Sociology* 100(6): 1528–1551.

2. Dale, Gareth. 2006. *The East German Revolution of 1989.* Manchester, UK: Manchester University Press.

3. Dennis, Mike. 2000. *The Rise and Fall of the German Democratic Republic, 1945–1990.* London: Longman, page 255.

4. Kuran, 1991, "Now out of Never," page 10.

5. Dennis, 2000, *The Rise and Fall of the German Democratic Republic.*

6. Ibid., page 59.

7. Ibid., page 63.

8. Dale, Gareth. 2003. "Like Wildfire? The East German Rising of June 1953." *Debatte: Review of Contemporary German Affairs* 11(2): 107–163.

9. Fullbrook, Mary. 1995. *Anatomy of a Dictatorship.* Oxford: Oxford University Press.

10. Dale, 2003, "Like Wildfire?"

11. Ibid.

12. Dennis, 2000, *The Rise and Fall of the German Democratic Republic,* page 67.

13. Kopstein, Jeffrey. 1997. *The Politics of Economic Decline in East Germany, 1945–1989.* Chapel Hill: University of North Carolina Press.

14. Dennis, 2000, *The Rise and Fall of the German Democratic Republic,* page 68.

15. Pfaff, Steven. 2006. *Exit-Voice Dynamics and the Collapse of East Germany: The Crisis of Leninism and the Revolution of 1989.* Durham, NC: Duke University Press.

16. Bleiker, Roland. 1993. *Nonviolent Struggle and the Revolution in East Germany.* Cambridge, MA: Albert Einstein Institution.

17. Dennis, 2000, *The Rise and Fall of the German Democratic Republic,* page 213.

18. Pond, Elizabeth. 1993. *Beyond the Wall: Germany's Road to Unification.* Washington, DC: Brookings Institution, page 80.

19. Pfaff, 2006, *Exit-Voice Dynamics.*

20. While open expressions of dissent were rare during this period, Jeffrey Kopstein makes a compelling argument that workers frequently engaged in various forms of "everyday resistance" that helped to undermine the state. For more information, see Kopstein, Jeffrey. 1996. "Chipping Away at the State: Workers' Resistance and the Demise of East Germany." *World Politics* 48(3): 391–423.

21. Statement by Klaus Kaden, quoted on page 158 in Philipsen, Dirk. 1993. *We Were the People: Voices from East Germany's Revolutionary Autumn of 1989.* Durham, NC: Duke University Press.

22. Burgess, John P. 1997. *The East German Church and the End of Socialism.* New York: Oxford University Press; Goeckel, Robert F. 1990. *The Lutheran Church and the East German State.* Ithaca, NY: Cornell University Press.

23. Pfaff, 2006 *Exit-Voice Dynamics,* page 84.

24. Here I have slightly altered the official name, Union of Evangelical-Lutheran Churches, in order to avoid confusion. In German, the term "Evangelical" denotes Protestant, not the born-again type of Christianity that the label is often associated with in the United States.

25. Pierard, Richard V. 1990. "Religion and the East German Revolution." *Journal of Church and State* 32(3): 501–509.

26. Grix, Jonathan. 2000. *The Role of the Masses in the Collapse of the GDR.* New York: St. Martin's Press, page 68.

27. Pfaff, 2006, *Exit-Voice Dynamics,* page 92.

28. Bartee, Wayne C. 2000. *A Time to Speak Out: The Leipzig Citizens Protests and the Fall of East Germany.* Westport, CT: Praeger.

29. Pierard, 1990, "Religion and the East German Revolution."

30. Opp, Karl-Dieter, Peter Voss, and Christine Gern. 1995. *Origins of a Spontaneous Revolution: East Germany, 1989*. Ann Arbor: University of Michigan Press.

31. Bartee, 2000, *A Time to Speak Out*, page 73.

32. Doellinger, David. 2002. *From Prayers to Protests: The Impact of Religious-Based Dissent on the Emergence of Civil Society in Slovakia and the GDR*. Ph.D. dissertation, University of Pittsburgh.

33. Bartee, 2000, *A Time to Speak Out*, page x.

34. Ibid., page 111.

35. Doellinger, 2002, *From Prayers to Protests*, page 314.

36. Bartee, 2000, *A Time to Speak Out*, page 177.

37. Pfaff, 2006, *Exit-Voice Dynamics*, page 97.

38. Ibid., pages 94–95.

39. Luxemberg, Rosa. 1961. *The Russian Revolution and Leninism or Marxism?* Ann Arbor: University of Michigan Press. Page 69.

40. Doellinger, 2002, *From Prayers to Protests*.

41. Maier, Charles S. 1997. *Dissolution: The Crisis of Communism and the End of East Germany*. Princeton, NJ: Princeton University Press.

42. Garton Ash, Timothy. 1990. *The Magic Lantern: The Revolution of '89 Witnessed in Warsaw, Budapest, Berlin, and Prague*. New York: Random House.

43. Joppke, Christian. 1995. *East German Dissidents and the Revolution of 1989: Social Movement in a Leninist Regime*. New York: New York University Press. Page 123.

44. Maier, 1997, *Dissolution*, page 59.

45. Joppke. 1995. *East German Dissidents*, page 124.

46. The terms *exit* (to denote emigration) and *voice* (in reference to demonstrations) were first used by Albert O. Hirschman in his influential 1993 article, "Exit, Voice and the Fate of the GDR: An Essay in Conceptual History." *World Politics* 45(2): 173–202.

47. Bleiker, 1993, *Nonviolent Struggle and the Revolution in East Germany*, page 8.

48. Pfaff, 2006, *Exit-Voice Dynamics*, page 109.

49. Dennis, 2000, *The Rise and Fall of the German Democratic Republic*, page 274; Joppke, 1995, *East German Dissidents*, page 138.

50. Bleiker, 1993, *Nonviolent Struggle and the Revolution in East Germany*, page 8.

51. Ibid., pages 11–12.

52. Dietrich, Christian, and Uwe Schwabe (eds.). 1994. *Freunde und Feinde: Dokumente zu den Friedensgebeten in Leipzig Zwischen 1981 und dem 9. Oktober 1989*. Leipzig: Evangelische Verlaganstalt.

53. Bartee, 2000, *A Time to Speak Out*, page 21.

54. Joppke, 1995, *East German Dissidents*, page 141.

55. Pfaff, 2006. *Exit-Voice Dynamics*, page 115.

56. Oldenburg, Fred S. 1990. "The October Revolution in the GDR—System, History, and Causes." *Eastern European Economics* 29(2): 55–77.

57. Pfaff, 2006, *Exit-Voice Dynamics*, page 122.

58. Chirot, Daniel. 1994. "What Happened in Eastern Europe in 1989?" Pages 218–245 in *Popular Protest and Political Culture in Modern China*, edited by Jeffrey Wasserstrom and Elizabeth Perry. Boulder, CO: Westview.

59. Opp, Karl-Dieter. 1994. "Repression and Revolutionary Action: East Germany in 1989." *Rationality and Society* 6(1): 129.

60. Pond, 1993, *Beyond the Wall*, page 112.

61. Hadjar, Andreas. 2003. "Non-Violent Political Protest in East Germany in the 1980s: Protestant Church, Opposition Groups, and the People." *German Politics* 12(3): 121.

62. Bartee, 2000, *A Time to Speak Out*, page 166.

63. Bleiker, 1993, *Nonviolent Struggle and the Revolution in East Germany*.

64. All quotations are from page 128 in Pfaff's 2006 account.

65. Pfaff, 2006, *Exit-Voice Dynamics*, page 129.

66. Pond, 1993, *Beyond the Wall*, page 188.

67. For more on these explanations, see Fulbrook, 1995, *Anatomy of a Dictatorship*; Opp, Voss, and Gern, 1995, *Origins of a Spontaneous Revolution*.

68. Hadjar, 2003, "Nonviolent Political Protest in East Germany," page 119.

69. Pfaff, 2006, *Exit-Voice Dynamics*, page 176.

70. Ibid., page 177.

71. Ibid.

72. Opp, Voss, and Gern, 1995, *Origins of a Spontaneous Revolution*, page 220.

73. Pond, 1993, *Beyond the Wall*, page 111.

74. Eberlein, Werner. 2000. *Geboren am 9. November: Erinnerungen.* [Born on November 9th: Memories]. Berlin: Das Neue Berlin, page 461.

75. Pond, 1993, *Beyond the Wall*, page 116.

76. Maier, 1997, *Dissolution*.

77. Bleiker, 1993, *Nonviolent Struggle and Revolution in East Germany*.

78. Dale, 2006, *The East German Revolution of 1989*, page 76.

79. Maier, 1997, *Dissolution*, pages 159–161.

80. As Steven Pfaff notes in his book *Exit-Voice Dynamics*, "Less than 10 percent of clergymen provided shelter or assistance to political groups. About the same percentage apparently served as [Stasi] informants." Page 87.

81. Bartee, 2000, *A Time to Speak Out*, page 112.

82. See the interview with Christian Führer on pages 177–178 in Bartee, 2000, *A Time to Speak Out*.

83. Pierard, 1990, "Religion and the East German Revolution."

84. Quoted in Bartee, 2000, *A Time to Speak Out*, page 177.

CHAPTER 4

1. Harding, Robert C. 2006. *The History of Panama*. Westport, CT: Greenwood, page 17.

2. LaRosa, Michael, and Germán Mejía. 2004. *The United States Discovers Panama: The Writings of Soldiers, Scholars, and Scoundrels, 1850–1905*. New York: Rowman & Littlefield; Schott, Joseph L. 1967. *The Story of the Building of the Panama Canal, 1849–1855*. Indianapolis: Bobbs-Merrill.

3. Harding, 2006, *The History of Panama*, page 21.

4. Lindsay-Poland, John. 2003. *Emperors in the Jungle: The Secret History of the U.S. in Panama*. Durham, NC: Duke University Press.

5. Harding, 2006, *The History of Panama*, pages 59–62.

6. Koster, R. M., and Guillermo Sánchez. 1990. *In the Time of the Tyrants, Panama: 1968–1990*. New York: W. W. Norton.

7. Harding, 2006, *The History of Panama*, page 71.

8. Ibid., page 74.

9. Greene, Graham. 1984. *Getting to Know the General*. Thorndike, ME: Thorndike.

10. Major, John. 2003. *Prize Possession: The United States Government and the Panama Canal 1903–1979*. New York: Cambridge University Press; Millett, Richard. 1988. "Looking beyond Noriega." *Foreign Policy* 71: 46–63.

11. Koster and Sánchez, 1990, *In the Time of the Tyrants*.

12. Kempe, Frederick. 1990. *Divorcing the Dictator: America's Bungled Affair with Noriega*. New York: G. P. Putnam's Sons.

13. Koster and Sánchez, 1990, *In the Time of the Tyrants*.

14. Harding, 2006, *The History of Panama*, page 100.

15. Conniff, Michael. 1992. *Panama and the United States: The Forced Alliance*. Athens: University of Georgia Press.
16. LaFeber, Walter. 1989. *The Panama Canal: The Crisis in Historical Perspective*. New York: Oxford University Press.
17. Kempe, 1990, *Divorcing the Dictator*.
18. Scranton, Margaret E. 1991. *The Noriega Years: U.S.-Panamanian Relations, 1981–1990*. Boulder, CO: Lynne Reiner. Page 110.
19. Buckley, Kevin. 1991. *Panama: The Whole Story*. New York: Simon & Schuster.
20. Guerrero, Alina. 1987. "Students, Police Clash over Allegations of Fraud and Murder." Associated Press, June 9, 1987.
21. Brown, Tom. 1987. "Panama Declares State of Emergency after Riots." Reuters News, June 11, 1987.
22. Kempe, 1990, *Divorcing the Dictator*, 213–214.
23. According to Scranton (*The Noriega Years*, 1991, page 109), groups in attendance that evening included medical and legal associations, agriculture and industry associations, Lions, Rotary, and Kiwanis clubs, the Children's Welfare Association, the Association of Panamanian Life Insurance Brokers, the Association of Automobile Spare Parts Distributors, the Association of Professors of the Republic of Panama, and the Association of Travel Agencies and Tourism.
24. Koster and Sánchez, 1990, *In the Time of the Tyrants*, pages 335–336.
25. Buckley, 1991, *Panama*.
26. Koster and Sánchez, 1990, *In the Time of the Tyrants*, page 336.
27. Koster and Sánchez, 1990, *In the Time of the Tyrants*.
28. Kempe, 1990, *Divorcing the Dictator*, page 214.
29. LaFeber, 1989, *The Panama Canal*.
30. Brennan, Bryna. 1987. "Crowd Attacked outside Church; Protesters Reportedly Fired Upon." Associated Press, June 13.
31. Harding, 2006, *The History of Panama*, page 104.
32. Knox, Paul. "Police Rout Student Rally in Panama." *Globe and Mail*, July 18.
33. Buckley, 1991, *Panama*, pages 85–87.
34. Golden, Arthur. 1987. "Opposing Panama Regime Has Its Costs." *San Diego Union-Tribune*, July 5.
35. Kempe, 1990, *Divorcing the Dictator*, 213–214.
36. Koster and Sánchez, 1990, *In the Time of the Tyrants*.
37. Rohter, Larry. 1987. "Panama Unrest Fails to Crack Noriega." *Sydney Morning Herald*, July 31.
38. Landrey, Wilbur G. 1987. "People's Power Comes Closer to Home." *St. Petersburg Times*, July 7.
39. Buckley, 1991, *Panama*.
40. Koster and Sánchez, 1990, *In the Time of the Tyrants*, pages 343–344.
41. Kempe, 1990, *Divorcing the Dictator*, page 225.
42. Harding, 2006. *The History of Panama*, page 105.
43. Branigin, William. 1987. "Political Problems Undermine Panama's Economic Foundations." *Toronto Star*, 3 August. Also see "Panama Official Appeals to Bankers on Eve of Strike." Reuters News, July 27.
44. Lombard, Joseph C. 1990. "The Survival of Noriega: Lessons from the U.S. Sanctions against Panama." *Stanford Journal of International Law* 26: 269–323.
45. Harding, 2006, *The History of Panama*, page 105.
46. Ibid., pages 105–106.
47. Koster and Sánchez, 1990, *In the Time of the Tyrants*, page 349.
48. Ardito-Barletta, Nicolás. 1997. "The Political and Economic Transition of Panama, 1978–1991." Pages 32–66 in *Democratic Transitions in Central America*, edited by Jorge I. Dominguez and Marc Lindenberg. Gainesville: University Press of Florida.

49. Buckley, 1991, *Panama*, page 96.

50. Scranton, 1991, *The Noriega Years*, page 108.

51. Koster and Sánchez, 1990, *In the Time of the Tyrants*, page 350.

52. Ropp, Steve. 1992. "Explaining the Long-Term Maintenance of a Military Regime: Panama before the U.S. Invasion." *World Politics* 44(2): 228.

53. Koster and Sánchez, 1990, *In the Time of the Tyrants*, pages 351–352.

54. Rohter, 1987, "Panama Unrest."

55. Trequesser, Gilles. 1987. "Lawyer for Dissident Panamanian Colonel Questions Retractions." *Reuters News*, August 3.

56. Lombard, 1990, "The Survival of Noriega," page 276.

57. Ibid.

58. Harding, 2006, *The History of Panama*, page 107.

59. Zimbalist, Andrew, and John Weeks. 1991. *Panama at the Crossroads*. Berkeley: University of California Press.

60. Harding, 2006, *The History of Panama*, page 108.

61. Lombard, 1990, "The Survival of Noriega," page 277.

62. Ibid., pages 282, 278.

63. Marcus, David. 1988. "Panamanians Riot against Noreiga: Workers Take to the Streets after Government Fails to Meet Payroll." *Dallas Morning News*, March 15.

64. Houston Chronicle News Service. 1988. "Police Fire Tear Gas at Panama Demonstrators." March 14.

65. King, Katherine. 1998. "Panama and U.S. in Diplomatic Standoff as Tensions Mount." *Reuter News*, March 16.

66. Kempe, 1990, *Divorcing the Dictator*, page 281.

67. Lombard, 1990, "The Survival of Noriega," page 278.

68. Robinson, Linda. 1989/1990. "Dwindling Options in Panama." *Foreign Affairs* 68(5): 194.

69. Kempe, 1990, *Divorcing the Dictator*, pages 281–287.

70. DeWitt, Karen. 1988. "Taxes from USA Help Noriega." *USA Today*, April 1.

71. Kempe, 1990, *Divorcing the Dictator*, page 281.

72. Koster and Sánchez, 1990, *In the Time of the Tyrants*, page 361.

73. Harding, 2006, *The History of Panama*, page 111.

74. Millett, Richard. 1988. "Looking beyond Noriega." *Foreign Policy* 71: 54.

75. Zimbalist and Weeks, 1991, *Panama at the Crossroads*.

76. Harding, 2006, *The History of Panama*, page 112.

77. Ibid.

78. Koster and Sánchez, 1990, *In the Time of the Tyrants*, pages 369–370.

79. Harding, 2006, *The History of Panama*, page 113.

80. Donnelly, Thomas, Margaret Roth, and Caleb Baker. 1991. *Operation Just Cause: The Storming of Panama*. New York: Lexington.

81. Harding, 2006, *The History of Panama*, page 115.

82. Sabrosky, Alan Ned. 1990. "Panama 1989: Deposing a Dictator." *Small Wars & Insurgencies* 1(3): 303–306.

83. Harding, 2006, *The History of Panama*, page 116.

84. Leaders within the National Civic Crusade were divided over the question of whether to encourage or discourage the United States to invade. Some were unequivocally committed to nonviolent methods while others were intent on deposing Noriega by any means possible.

85. Ropp, Steve C. 1987. "Panama's Struggle for Democracy." *Current History* 86: 422.

86. Muschett Ibarra, Stanley. 1992. *Church and Politics in Time of Crisis: Noriega's Panama*. Ph.D. Dissertation, Department of Government and International Studies, University of Notre Dame.

87. Eisenmann, Roberto. 1990. "The Struggle against Noriega." *Journal of Democracy* 1(1): 42. While this estimate may be high, numerous sources confirm that at least 100,000 people participated in the July 10 demonstration, revealing widespread opposition to Noriega.

88. Muschett Ibarra. 1992. *Church and Politics in Time of Crisis*; Ropp, Steve. 1990. "Military Retrenchment and Decay in Panama." *Current History* 89: 17–40.

89. Ropp, 1987, "Panama's Struggle for Democracy."

90. Buckley, 1991, *Panama*, page 96.

91. Millett, 1988, "Looking beyond Noriega," page 54.

92. For further discussion of Noriega's efforts to retain troops' loyalty, see Millett, 1988, "Looking beyond Noriega"; and Ropp, 1990, "Military Retrenchment and Decay in Panama."

93. Eisenmann, Roberto. 1990. "The Struggle against Noriega." *Journal of Democracy* 1(1): 43–44.

94. Buckley, 1991, *Panama*, page 97.

95. Eisenmann, 1990, "The Struggle against Noriega," page 44.

CHAPTER 5

1. Arriagada, Genero. 1988. *Pinochet: The Politics of Power*. Boston: Unwin Hyman.

2. Lowden, Pamela. 1996. *Moral Opposition to Authoritarian Rule in Chile, 1973–1990*. New York: St. Martin's, page 27.

3. Skidmore, Thomas E., and Peter H. Smith. 2001. *Modern Latin America*. New York: Oxford University Press.

4. Oppenheim, Lois Hecht. 1993. *Politics in Chile: Democracy, Authoritarianism, and the Search for Development*. Boulder, CO: Westview.

5. Blum, William. 1986. *The CIA: A Forgotten History. U.S. Global Interventions since World War II*. London: Zed. Page 232.

6. O'Shaughnessy, Hugh. 2000. *Pinochet: The Politics of Torture*. New York: New York University Press.

7. Spooner, Mary Helen. 1994. *Soldiers in a Narrow Land: The Pinochet Regime in Chile*. Berkeley: University of California Press.

8. Burbach, Roger. 2003. *The Pinochet Affair: State Terrorism and Global Justice*. London: Zed. Page 9.

9. Burbach, 2003, *The Pinochet Affair*.

10. Skidmore and Smith, 2001, *Modern Latin America*.

11. Burbach, 2003, *The Pinochet Affair*.

12. Spooner, 1994, *Soldiers in a Narrow Land*, page 270, footnote 21.

13. Fleet, Michael. 1985. *The Rise and Fall of Chilean Christian Democracy*. Princeton, NJ: Princeton University Press. Pages 165–167.

14. Oppenheim, 1993, *Politics in Chile*.

15. For further discussion of pre-coup deliberations among military officers, see Arriagada, 1988, *Pinochet: The Politics of Power*.

16. Muñoz, Heraldo. 2008. *The Dictator's Shadow: Life under Augusto Pinochet*. New York: Basic Books. Page 11.

17. Burbach, 2003, *The Pinochet Affair*, page 18.

18. As Pamela Constable and Arturo Valenzuela note, "The confusion surrounding Allende's death remained the subject of passionate debate for years. Admirers insisted he died fending off military attackers, while detractors claimed that he committed suicide rather than face defeat. Although the evidence suggests the president did take his own life, the event acquired an enduring mythical stature and an intense personal meaning for Chileans." See Constable and Valenzuela. 1991. *A Nation of Enemies: Chile under Pinochet*. New York: W. W. Norton. Page 17.

19. Burbach, 2003, *The Pinochet Affair*, page 20.
20. Ensalaco, Mark. 2000. *Chile under Pinochet: Recovering the Truth*. Philadelphia: University of Pennsylvania Press. Pages 32–33.
21. Verdugo, Patricia. 2001. *Chile, Pinochet, and the Caravan of Death*. Miami: North-South Center.
22. Ensalaco, 2000, *Chile under Pinochet*, page 46.
23. Burbach, 2003, *The Pinochet Affair*.
24. Constable and Valenzuela, 1991, *A Nation of Enemies*.
25. Lowden, 1996, *Moral Opposition to Authoritarian Rule in Chile*, page 38.
26. Ackerman, Peter, and Jack DuVall. 2000. *A Force More Powerful: A Century of Nonviolent Conflict*. New York: Palgrave.
27. Arriagada, 1988, *Pinochet*.
28. Spooner, 1994, *Soldiers in a Narrow Land*, page 144.
29. Petras, James, and Steve Vieux. 1988. "The Chilean 'Economic Miracle': An Empirical Critique." *Critical Sociology* 17: 57–72.
30. Lowden, 1996, *Moral Opposition*, page 39.
31. Bouvier, Virginia Marie. 1983. *Alliance or Compliance: Implications of the Chilean Experience for the Catholic Church in Latin America*. New York: Syracuse University. Pages 65–66.
32. Ensalaco, 2000, *Chile under Pinochet*.
33. Smith, Brian. 1982. *The Church and Politics in Chile*. Princeton. NJ: Princeton University Press. Page 318.
34. Loveman, Mara. 1998. "High Risk Collective Action Defending Human Rights in Chile, Uruguay, and Argentina." *American Journal of Sociology* 104(2): 477–525.
35. Chuchryk, Patricia. 1993. "Subversive Mothers: The Opposition to the Military Regime in Chile." Pages 86–97 in *Surviving beyond Fear: Women, Children, and Human Rights in Latin America*, edited by Marjorie Agosín. Fredonia, NH: White Pines; Krause, Wanda C. 2004. "The Role and Example of Chilean and Argentinian Mothers in Democratisation." *Development in Practice* 14(3): 366–380.
36. Smith, 1982, *The Church and Politics in Chile*.
37. Lowden, 1996, *Moral Opposition*; Smith, 1982, *Church and Politics in Chile*.
38. Spooner, 1994, *Soldiers in a Narrow Land*.
39. Ibid.
40. Ibid., pages 175–184.
41. Garretón, Manuel Antonio. 2001. "Popular Mobilization and the Military Regime in Chile: The Complexities of the Invisible Transition." Pages 259–277 in *Power and Popular Protest: Latin American Social Movements*, edited by Susan Eckstein. Berkeley: University of California Press.
42. Ensalaco, 2000, *Chile under Pinochet*, pages 136–137.
43. Ibid., page 252, footnote 32.
44. Arriagada, 1988, *Pinochet*.
45. Spooner, 1994, *Soldiers in a Narrow Land*.
46. Arriagada, 1988, *Pinochet*.
47. Constable and Valencia, 1991, *A Nation of Enemies*.
48. Christian, Shirley. 1986. "Chile's Army Reacting to Attack, Arrests Foes and Shuts Magazines." *New York Times*, May 16.
49. Arriagada, 1988, *Pinochet*, page 71.
50. Ibid., page 74.
51. Arriagada, 1988, *Pinochet*.
52. Muñoz, 2008, *The Dictator's Shadow*.
53. Constable and Valencia, 1991, *A Nation of Enemies*.

54. Muñoz, 2008, *The Dictator's Shadow.*

55. Spooner, 1994, *Soldiers in a Narrow Land.*

56. Ensalaco, 2000, *Chile under Pinochet,* page 176.

57. Christian, 1986, "Chile's Army Reacting to Attack."

58. Timerman, Jacobo. 1987. *Chile: Death in the South.* New York: Alfred A. Knopf. Page 44.

59. Constable and Valenzuela, 1991, *A Nation of Enemies,* page 304.

60. Ackerman and Duvall, 2000, *A Force More Powerful,* page 297.

61. Constable and Valenzuela, 1991, *A Nation of Enemies,* page 306.

62. Power, Margaret. 2004. "More Than Mere Pawns: Right-Wing Women in Chile." *Journal of Women's History* 16(3): 138–151.

63. Constable and Valenzuela, 1991, *A Nation of Enemies,* pages 302–303.

64. Spooner, 1999, *Soldiers in a Narrow Land,* page 244.

65. Ensalaco, 2000, *Chile under Pinochet.*

66. Constable and Valenzuela, 1991, *A Nation of Enemies,* page 310.

67. Muñoz, 2008, *The Dictator's Shadow.*

68. Silva, Eduardo. 1991. "The Political Economy of Chile's Regime Transition: From Radical to 'Pragmatic' Neo-Liberal Policies." Pages 98–127 in *The Struggle for Democracy in Chile, 1982–1990,* edited by Paul W. Drake and Iván Jaksic. Lincoln: University of Nebraska Press. Pages 107, 110.

69. Silva, 1991, "The Politic Economy of Chile's Regime Transition," pages 113, 102.

70. Constable and Valenzuela, 1991, *A Nation of Enemies,* page 172.

71. Ackerman and DuVall, 2000, *A Force More Powerful.*

72. Constable and Valenzuela, 1991, *A Nation of Enemies.*

73. Valenzuela, Arturo. 1991. "The Military in Power: The Consolidation of One-Man Rule." Pages 21–72 in *The Struggle for Democracy in Chile, 1982–1990,* edited by Paul W. Drake and Iván Jaksic. Lincoln: University of Nebraska Press. Page 35.

74. Varas, Augusto. 1991. "The Crisis of Legitimacy of Military Rule in the 1980s." Pages 73–97 in *The Struggle for Democracy in Chile, 1982–1990,* edited by Paul W. Drake and Iván Jaksic. Lincoln: University of Nebraska Press. Page 85.

75. Valenzuela, 1991, "The Military in Power," page 33.

76. Arriagada, 1988, *Pinochet.*

77. Huneeus, Carlos. 2009. "Political Mass Mobilization against Authoritarian Rule: Pinochet's Chile, 1983–1988." Pages 197–212 in *Civil Resistance and Power Politics: The Experience of Nonviolent Action from Gandhi to the Present,* edited by Adam Roberts and Timothy Garton Ash. Oxford: Oxford University Press.

78. Varas, 1991, "The Crisis of Legitimacy of Military Rule in the 1980s."

79. Spooner, 1994, *Soldiers in a Narrow Land.*

80. Ibid.

81. Loveman, Brian. 1991. "Mision Cumplida? Civil Military Relations and the Chilean Political Transition." *Journal of Interamerican Studies and World Affairs* 33(3): 35–74.

82. Weeks, Gregory. 2003. *The Military and Politics in Postauthoritarian Chile.* Tuscaloosa: University of Alabama Press. Page 56.

CHAPTER 6

1. Gustafson, Lindsey. 1995. "Kenya: The Struggle to Create a Democracy." *Brigham Young University Law Review* 2: 647–671.

2. These statistics are derived from Kenyan Ministry of Economic Planning and Development, Central Bureau of Statistics, *Statistical Abstracts* 1981, Nairobi: Kenya. They are confirmed in Joel Barkan's 1993 article, "Kenya: Lessons from a Flawed Election." *Journal of Democracy* 4(3): 85–99.

3. Haugerud, Angelique. 2008. *The Culture of Politics in Modern Kenya*. Cambridge: Cambridge University Press.

4. Anderson, David. 2005. *Histories of the Hanged: The Dirty War in Kenya and the End of Empire*. New York: W. W. Norton.

5. Edgerton, Robert. 1989. *Mau Mau: An African Crucible*. New York: Ballantine.

6. Miller, Norman, and Rodger Yeager. 1993. *Kenya: The Quest for Prosperity*. Boulder, CO: Westview.

7. Grindle, Merilee. 1996. *Challenging the State: Crisis and Innovation in Latin America and Africa*. New York: Cambridge University Press.

8. Mueller, Susanne D. 1984. "Government and Opposition in Kenya, 1966–69." *Journal of Modern African Studies* 22(3): 399–427.

9. Murunga, Godwin Rapando. 2002. "A Critical Look at Kenya's Non-Transition to Democracy." *Journal of Third World Studies* 19(2): 89–111.

10. Throup, David. 1989. "The Construction and Deconstruction of the Kenyatta State." Pages 33–74 in *The Political Economy of Kenya*, edited by Michael G. Schatzberg. Baltimore: Johns Hopkins University Press.

11. Widner, Jennifer A. 1992. *The Rise of a Party-State in Kenya: From "Harambee!" to "Nyayo!"* Berkeley: University of California Press.

12. Grindle, 1996, *Challenging the State*.

13. Widner, 1992, *The Rise of a Party-State in Kenya*, page 130.

14. Murunga, 2002, "A Critical Look at Kenya's Non-Transition to Democracy."

15. Murungi, Kiraitu. 1991. "President Moi and the Decline of Democracy in Kenya." *Trans-Africa Forum* 8(4): 3–18.

16. Widner, 1992, *The Rise of a Party-State in Kenya*.

17. Grindle, 1996, *Challenging the State*, page 67.

18. Currie, Kate, and Larry Ray. 1985. "State and Class in Kenya—Notes on the Cohesion of the Ruling Class." *Journal of Modern African Studies* 22(4): 559–593.

19. Barkan, Joel D. 2004. "Kenya after Moi." *Foreign Affairs* 83(1): 87–100.

20. Widner, 1992, *The Rise of a Party-State in Kenya*.

21. Rule, Sheila. 1985. "Clampdown on Students Reflects Kenyan Unease." *New York Times*, March 20, page A15.

22. Ibid.

23. Fitzgerald, Mary Anne. 1986. "Kenya's Leadership Grows Increasingly Vulnerable to Unrest." *Christian Science Monitor*, June 17, International section, page 14.

24. Sabar, Galia. 2002. *Church, State, and Society in Kenya: From Mediation to Opposition, 1963–1993*. London: Frank Cass. Pages 194–195.

25. Murungi, 1991, "President Moi and the Decline of Democracy in Kenya."

26. Widner, 1992, *The Rise of a Party-State in Kenya*.

27. Harden, Blaine. 1986. "Third World Review (Kenya): Pulpit Politics/The Clash between Church and State." *Guardian* (London), October 31.

28. Sabar, 2002, *Church, State, and Society in Kenya*.

29. Harden, Blaine. 1986. "Voice of Dissent in Kenya Comes from Pulpit; Vocal Pastor Relies on President's Christian Charity to Stay out of Jail." *Washington Post*, October 26, page A29.

30. Vallely, Paul. 1987. "Kenya's Changing Image: Church a Lonely Voice on Moi's Totalitarian Drift." *Times* (London), May 26, issue 62778.

31. "Kenyans Accused of Water Torture." 1987. *Globe and Mail*, April 8.

32. Robertson, Claire. 1987. "Rights Group Links Kenya with Torture." *Washington Post*, page A15.

33. Harden, Blaine. 1988. "Kenya Releases Political Prisoners in Move to Improve Human Rights Record; Following Pressure from Aid Donors, Moi Shakes Up Police." *Washington Post*, February 6, page A19.

34. Thiong'o, Ngugi Wa. 1987. "Third World Review: Kenya Breaks through the Circle of Fear—A Lie to Moi's Myth That Kenya Is a Model Democracy." *Guardian*, December 18.

35. Ibid.

36. "Kenya's Restless Students." 1987. *Times* (London), November 24, issue 62934.

37. Holmquist, Frank, and Michael Ford. "Kenya: Slouching toward Democracy." *Africa Today* 39(3): 97–111.

38. Buckoke, Andrew. 1988. "Unrest Brews in Moi's Land of Milk and Honey; Kenya's Political Volcano." *Times* (London), June 23, issue 63115.

39. Vallely, Paul. 1988. "Church Editor Falls Victim to Moi's War on Democracy." *Times* (London), August 22, issue 63166.

40. Murungi, 1991, "President Moi and the Decline of Democracy in Kenya."

41. Vallely, 1988, "Church Editor Falls Victim."

42. Murungi, 1991, "President Moi and the Decline of Democracy in Kenya."

43. Widner, 1992, *The Rise of a Party-State in Kenya*.

44. Montgomery, Charlotte. 1990. "Fear Raised of Crackdown on Critics." *Globe and Mail*, February 23.

45. Widner, 1992, *The Rise of a Party-State in Kenya*.

46. Sabar, 2002, *Church, State, and Society in Kenya*.

47. Widner, 1992, *The Rise of a Party-State in Kenya*, page 194.

48. Stamp, Patricia. 1991. "The Politics of Dissent in Kenya." *Current History* 90(May): 205–208.

49. Widner, 1992, *The Rise of a Party-State in Kenya*.

50. "Three More Kenyans Seized Calling for Opposition." 1990. *New York Times*, July 6, page A2.

51. Perlez, Jane. 1990. "Democracy Rally Crushed in Kenya." *New York Times*, July 8, page A3; Shields, Todd. 1990. "Nairobi Tense as Violent Opposition to Moi Increases." *Independent* (London), July 9, foreign news section, page 11.

52. Shields, Todd. 1990. "Death Toll in Kenya Rises to 28." *Independent* (London), July 12, foreign news section, page 14.

53. Grosh, Barbara, and Stephen Orvis. 1996/1997. "Democracy, Confusion, or Chaos: Political Conditionality in Kenya." *Studies in Comparative International Development* 31(4): 46–65.

54. Holmquist and Ford, 1992, "Slouching toward Democracy."

55. Henry, Neil. 1990. "Crackdown in Kenya Strains Ties with U.S.; Congress to Review Foreign Aid to Nairobi." *Washington Post*, July 9, page A13.

56. Widner, 1992, *The Rise of the Party-State in Kenya*.

57. Barkan, Joel. 1993. "Kenya: Lessons from a Flawed Election." *Journal of Democracy* 4(3): 85–99.

58. Africa Watch. 1993. *Divide and Rule: State-Sponsored Ethnic Violence in Kenya*. New York: Human Rights Watch Report, page 1.

59. Brown, Stephen. 2001. "Authoritarian Leaders and Multiparty Elections in Africa: How Foreign Donors Help to Keep Kenya's Daniel arap Moi in Power." *Third World Quarterly* 22(5): 725–739.

60. Holmquist and Ford, 1992, "Slouching toward Democracy," pages 103–104.

61. Barkan, 1993, "Kenya: Lessons from a Flawed Election," page 92.

62. Barkan, 1993, "Kenya: Lessons from a Flawed Election."

63. Mutua, Makau. 2008. *Kenya's Quest for Democracy: Taming Leviathan*. Boulder, CO: Lynne Reinner.

64. Foeken, Dick, and Ton Dietz. 2000. "Of Ethnicity, Manipulation, and Observation: The 1992 and 1997 elections in Kenya." Pages 122–149 in *Election Observation and*

Democratization in Africa, edited by Jon Abbink and Gerti Hesseling. New York: Palgrave Macmillan. Page 135.

65. Brown, 2001, "Authoritarian Leaders," page 728.
66. For instance, see Barkan, 1993, "Lessons from a Flawed Election"; Holmquist, Frank, and Michael Ford. 1995. "Stalling Political Change: Moi's Way in Kenya." *Current History* 94 (591): 177–181; Steeves, Jeffrey. 2006. "Beyond Democratic Consolidation in Kenya: Ethnicity, Leadership, and Unbounded Politics." *African Identities* 4(2): 195–211.
67. Throup, David, and Charles Hornsby. 1998. *Multi-Party Politics in Kenya: The Kenyatta and Moi States and the Triumph of the System in the 1992 Elections.* Oxford: James Curry.
68. Barkan, 2004, "Kenya after Moi."
69. Widner, 1992, *The Rise of a Party-State in Kenya*, page 181.
70. Mutua, 2008, *Kenya's Quest for Democracy.*
71. Grindle, 1996, *Challenging the State.*
72. Brown, 2001, "Authoritarian Leaders."
73. Grindle, 1996, *Challenging the State.*
74. Grosh and Orvis, 1996, "Democracy, Confusion, or Chaos."
75. Schedler, Andreas. 2002. "The Menu of Manipulation." *Journal of Democracy* 13(2): 36–50.
76. Sabar, 2002, *Church, State, and Society in Kenya*; Throup and Hornsby, 1998, *Multi-Party Politics in Kenya.*
77. Holmquist and Ford, 1992, "Kenya Slouching toward Democracy."
78. Hempstone, Smith. 1997. *Rogue Ambassador: An African Memoir.* Sewanee, TN: University of the South Press.
79. Barkan, 1993, "Kenya: Lessons from a Flawed Election," page 95.
80. Brown, 2001, "Authoritarian Leaders," page 732.
81. Barkan, Joel D., and Njuguna Ng'ethe. 1999. "Kenya Tries Again." Pages 184–200 in *Democratization in Africa*, edited by Larry Diamond and Marc F. Plattner. Baltimore: Johns Hopkins University Press.
82. Brown, 2001, "Authoritarian Leaders."
83. Hempstone, 1997, *Rogue Ambassador.*

CHAPTER 7

1. Romulo, Beth Day. 1987. *Inside the Palace: The Rise and Fall of Ferdinand and Imelda Marcos.* New York: G. P. Putnam's Sons. Page 216.
2. Bonner, Raymond. 1987. *Waltzing with a Dictator: The Marcoses and the Making of American Policy.* New York: Times.
3. Burton, Sandra. 1989. *Impossible Dream: The Marcoses, the Acquinos, and the Unfinished Revolution.* New York: Warner.
4 Bonner, 1987, *Waltzing with a Dictator.*
5. Forest, Jim, and Nancy Forest. 1988. *Four Days in February: The Story of the Nonviolent Overthrow of the Marcos Regime.* London: Marshall Pickering.
6. Lyons, John, and Karl Wilson. 1987. *Marcos and Beyond: The Philippines Revolution.* Kenthurst, Australia: Kangaroo.
7. At the moment when martial law was imposed, there were fewer than 800 communist guerrillas in the Philippines. See Overhalt, William H. 1986. "The Rise and Fall of Ferdinand Marcos." *Asian Survey* 26(11): 1137–1163.
8. Alex Bello Brillantes Jr., in his 1987 book *Dictatorship and Martial Law: Philippine Authoritarianism in 1972* (Quezon City, Philippines: Great Books), interviews two of Marcos's aides who claim that the president financed student protests (page 49). This claim has also been substantiated by Raymond Bonner (*Waltzing with the Dictator*, page 125) and Sandra Burton (*Impossible Dream*, page 76).

9. Burton, 1989, *Impossible Dream*, page 88.

10. Bonner, 1987, *Waltzing with the Dictator*.

11. Villegas, Bernardo. 1986. "The Economic Crisis." Pages 145–175 in *Crisis in the Philippines: The Marcos Era and Beyond*, edited by John Bresnan. Princeton, NJ: Princeton University Press.

12. Stanley, Peter W. 1986. "Toward Democracy in the Philippines." *Proceedings of the Academy of Political Science* 36(1): 129–141.

13. Kessler, Richard J. 1986. "Marcos and the Americans." *Foreign Policy* 63: 41.

14. Thompson, Mark R. 1995. *The Anti-Marcos Struggle: Personalistic Rule and Democratic Transition in the Philippines*. New Haven, CT: Yale University Press. Page 52.

15. Kessler, Richard J. 1989. *Rebellion and Repression in the Philippines*. New Haven: Yale University Press. Pages 108–109.

16. Lande, Carl H. 1986. "The Political Crisis." Pages 114–144 in *Crisis in the Philippines: The Marcos Era and Beyond*, edited by John Bresnan. Princeton, NJ: Princeton University Press.

17. Bonner, 1987, *Waltzing with a Dictator*, page 166.

18. Ibid., page 315.

19. Gregor, A. James. 1984. *Crisis in the Philippines: A Threat to U.S. Interests*. Washington, D.C.: Ethics and Public Policy Center. Page 31.

20. Burton, 1989, *Impossible Dream*.

21. Wurfel, David. 1988. *Filipino Politics: Death and Decay*. Ithaca, NY: Cornell University Press.

22. Buss, Claude A. 1987. *Cory Aquino and the People of the Philippines*. Stanford, CA: Stanford Alumni Association. Page 13.

23. Bonner, 1987, *Waltzing with a Dictator*.

24. Ibid.

25. Thompson, 1995, *The Anti-Marcos Struggle*, page 116.

26. Ibid., page 119.

27. Villegas, Bernardo. 1986. "The Economic Crisis." Pages 145–175 in *Crisis in the Philippines: The Marcos Era and Beyond*, edited by John Bresnan. Princeton, NJ: Princeton University Press.

28. Thompson, 1995, *The Anti-Marcos Struggle*, page 120.

29. Burton, 1989, *Impossible Dream*.

30. The available evidence suggests that General Fabian Ver, Marcos's cousin, and Imelda Marcos were the ones who orchestrated the murder.

31. Johnson, Bryan. 1987. *The Four Days of Courage: The Untold Story of the People Who Brought Marcos Down*. New York: Free Press.

32. Bonner, 1987, *Waltzing with a Dictator*.

33. Forest and Forest, 1988, *Four Days in February*, page 45.

34. Thompson, 1995, *The Anti-Marcos Struggle*, page 126.

35. Buss, 1987, *Cory Aquino*, page 21.

36. Burton, 1989, *Impossible Dream*, page 291.

37. Lande, 1986, "The Political Crisis."

38. Buss, 1987, *Cory Aquino*, page 30.

39. Burton, 1989, *Impossible Dream*, page 313.

40. Komisar, Lucy. 1987. *Corazon Aquino: The Story of a Revolution*. New York: George Braziller. Page 78.

41. Thompson, 1995, *The Anti-Marcos Struggle*, pages 142–144.

42. Forest and Forest, 1988, *Four Days in February*.

43. Ibid., pages 73–75.

44. Bonner, 1987, *Waltzing with a Dictator*, page 426.

45. Burton, 1989, *Impossible Dream*, page 368.

46. Forest and Forest, 1988, *Four Days in February*, page 78.
47. Bonner, 1987, *Waltzing with a Dictator*.
48. Simons, Lewis M. 1987. *Worth Dying For*. New York: William Morrow.
49. Forest and Forest, 1988, *Four Days in February*, page 82.
50. Burton, 1989, *Impossible Dream*, pages 388–391.
51. Johnson, 1987, *Four Days of Courage*, pages 83–84.
52. Forest and Forest, 1988, *Four Days in February*, page 94.
53. Buss, 1987, *Cory Aquino*.
54. Stanley, 1986, "Toward Democracy," page 138.
55. Burton, 1989, *Impossible Dream*, page 393.
56. Forest and Forest, 1988, *Four Days in February*, pages 98–100.
57. Romulo, 1987, *Inside the Palace*.
58. Forest and Forest, 1988, *Four Days in February*, page 114.
59. Romulo, 1987, *Inside the Palace*, page 236.
60. Buss, 1987, *Cory Aquino*, page 40.
61. Ibid, page 40.
62. Johnson, 1987, *The Four Days of Courage*.
63. Zunes, Stephen. 1999. "The Origins of People Power in the Philippines." Pages 129–157 in *Nonviolent Social Movements: A Geographical Perspective*, edited by Stephen Zunes, Lester R. Kurtz, and Sarah Beth Asher. Malden, MA: Blackwell.
64. Forest and Forest, 1988, *Four Days in February*, page 102.
65. Ibid., page 103.
66. Mendoza, Amado. 2009. "'People Power' in the Philippines, 1983–1986." Pages 179–196 in *Civil Resistance and Power Politics*, edited by Adam Roberts and Timothy Garton Ash. Oxford: Oxford University Press. Page 192.

CHAPTER 8

1. Jasper, James M. 1997. *The Art of Moral Protest: Culture, Biography, and Creativity in Social Movements*. Chicago: University of Chicago Press.
2. Walsh, Edward. 1981. "Resource Mobilization and Citizen Protest in Communities around Three Mile Island." *Social Problems* 29: 1–21.
3. Churches were the primary free spaces available to activists in five cases. In the sixth case, China, the democracy salons and universities served this function initially.
4. This, of course, is consistent with the theory of neo-Marxist Antonio Gramsci, who argued that religious groups are often semi-autonomous from the state and are therefore a key location for the development of counter-hegemonic views.
5. There are, of course, exceptions to this trend. For instance, many churches in Central America during the 1970s and 1980s were actually targeted by the state since they were seen as the location for oppositional activities and the source of insurgent ideas. Sacred institutions, therefore, are not always immune to state repression.
6. For more on this process, see Piven, Francis Fox, and Richard Cloward. 1977. *Poor People's Movements: How They Succeed, Why They Fail*. New York: Pantheon.
7. Romulo, Beth Day. 1987. *Inside the Palace: The Rise and Fall of Ferdinand and Imelda Marcos*. New York: G. P. Putnam's Sons. Pages 230–231.
8. This was also true for many of the early-21st-century nonviolent revolutions. For example, in the orange revolution, civil resisters held a series of meetings with members of the Ukrainian army and secret service, encouraging them to refuse orders to repress. This dialogue contributed to military leaders' decision to not crack down on protesters who had gathered in Kiev. Shortly thereafter, civil resisters seized government offices, and the Supreme Court conceded to their demands to annul the fraudulent election. For further

information about the role of security force defections in this situation, see Binnendijk, Anika Locke, and Ivan Marovic. 2006. "Power and Persuasion: Nonviolent Strategies to Influence State Security Forces in Serbia (2000) and Ukraine (2004)." *Communist and Post Communist Studies* 39(3): 411–429.

9. Coser, Lewis. 1956. *The Functions of Social Conflict*. New York: Free Press.

10. Granovetter, Mark. 1978. "Threshold Models of Collective Behavior." *American Journal of Sociology* 83(6): 1420–1443.

11. For further discussion of this issue, see Stephan, Maria, and Erica Chenoweth. 2008. "Why Civil Resistance Works: The Strategic Logic of Nonviolent Conflict." *International Security* 33(1): 7–44.

12. Hadjar, Andreas. 2003. "Non-Violent Political Protest in East Germany in the 1980s: Protestant Church, Opposition Groups, and the People." *German Politics* 12(3): 121; Pierard, Richard V. 1990. "Religion and the East German Revolution." *Journal of Church and State* 32(3): 501–509.

13. Barahona de Brito, Alexandra. 1997. *Human Rights and Democratization in Latin America: Uruguay and Chile*. New York: Oxford University Press.

14. Forest, Jim, and Nancy Forest. 1988. *Four Days in February: The Story of the Nonviolent Overthrow of the Marcos Regime*. London: Marshall Pickering. Page 82.

15. Burton, Sandra. 1989. *Impossible Dream: The Marcoses, the Aquinos, and the Unfinished Revolution*. New York: Warner. Page 391, italics mine.

16. Romulo, 1987, *Inside the Palace*, page 231.

17. For more on this issue, see Bob, Clifford. 2005. *The Marketing of Rebellion: Insurgents, Media, and International Activism*. New York: Cambridge University Press.

18. I thank Lester Kurtz for drawing my attention to this point.

19. Cortright, David, and George A. Lopez (eds.). 2002. *Smart Sanctions: Targeting Economic Statecraft*. Lanham, MD: Rowman & Littlefield.

20. For further discussion of these points, see Kurzman, Charles. 2004. *The Unthinkable Revolution in Iran*. Cambridge, MA: Harvard University Press.

21. Stephan and Chenoweth, 2008, "Why Civil Resistance Works," page 20.

REFERENCES

Acemoglu, Daron, and James A. Robinson. 2005. *Economic Origins of Dictatorship and Democracy*. New York: Cambridge University Press.

Ackerman, Peter. 2007. "Skills or Conditions: What Key Factors Shape the Success or Failure of Civil Resistance?" Unpublished paper presented at the Conference on Civil Resistance and Power Politics, Oxford University, Oxford, Great Britain.

Ackerman, Peter, and Jack DuVall. 2000. *A Force More Powerful: A Century of Nonviolent Conflict*. New York: Praeger.

Ackerman, Peter, and Christopher Kruegler. 1994. *Strategic Nonviolent Conflict: The Dynamics of People Power in the Twentieth Century*. Westport, CT: Praeger.

Africa Watch. 1993. *Divide and Rule: State-Sponsored Ethnic Violence in Kenya*. New York: Human Rights Watch Report.

Almeida, Paul. 2003. "Opportunity, Organization and Threat-Induced Contention: Protest Waves in Authoritarian Settings." *American Journal of Sociology* 109: 345–400.

Anderson, David. 2005. *Histories of the Hanged: The Dirty War in Kenya and the End of Empire*. New York: W. W. Norton.

Ardito-Barletta, Nicols. 1997. "The Political and Economic Transition of Panama, 1978–1991." Pages 32–66 in *Democratic Transitions in Central America*, edited by Jorge I. Dominguez and Marc Lindenberg. Gainesville: University Press of Florida.

Arendt, Hannah. 1970. *On Violence*. New York: Harcourt, Brace, and World.

Arjomand, Said A. 1988. *The Turban for the Crown: The Islamic Revolution in Iran*. New York: Oxford University Press.

Arriagada, Genero. 1988. *Pinochet: The Politics of Power*. Boston: Unwin Hyman.

Barahona de Brito, Alexandra. 1997. *Human Rights and Democratization in Latin America: Uruguay and Chile*. New York: Oxford University Press.

Barkan, Joel. 1993. "Kenya: Lessons from a Flawed Election." *Journal of Democracy* 4(3): 85–99.
——. 2004. "Kenya after Moi." *Foreign Affairs* 83(1): 87–100.

Barkan, Joel D., and Njuguna Ng'ethe. 1999. "Kenya Tries Again." Pages 184–200 in *Democratization in Africa*, edited by Larry Diamond and Marc F. Plattner. Baltimore: Johns Hopkins University Press.

Bartee, Wayne C. 2000. *A Time to Speak Out: The Leipzig Citizens Protests and the Fall of East Germany*. Westport, CT: Praeger.

Binnendijk, Anika Locke, and Ivan Marovic. 2006. "Power and Persuasion: Nonviolent Strategies to Influence State Security Forces in Serbia (2000) and Ukraine (2004)." *Communist and Post Communist Studies* 39(3): 411–429.

Black, George, and Robin Munro. 1993. *Black Hands of Beijing: Lives of Defiance in China's Democracy Movement*. New York: John Wiley & Sons.

Bleiker, Roland. 1993. *Nonviolent Struggle and the Revolution in East Germany*. Cambridge, MA: Albert Einstein Institution.

Blum, William. 1986. *The CIA, A Forgotten History: U.S. Global Interventions since World War II.* London: Zed.

Bob, Clifford. 2005. *The Marketing of Rebellion: Insurgents, Media, and International Activism.* New York: Cambridge University Press.

Bob, Clifford, and Sharon Erickson Nepstad. 2007. "Kill a Leader, Murder a Movement? Leadership and Assassination in Social Movements." *American Behavioral Scientist* 50(10): 1370–1394.

Bondurant, Joan. 1958. *Conquest of Violence: The Gandhian Philosophy of Conflict.* Princeton, NJ: Princeton University Press.

Bonner, Raymond. 1987. *Waltzing with a Dictator: The Marcoses and the Making of American Policy.* New York: Times Books.

Bouvier, Virginia Marie. 1983. *Alliance or Compliance: Implications of the Chilean Experience for the Catholic Church in Latin America.* New York: Syracuse University.

Branigin, William. 1987. "Political Problems Undermine Panama's Economic Foundations." *Toronto Star,* 3 August.

Brennan, Bryna. 1987. "Crowd Attacked outside Church; Protesters Reportedly Fired Upon." *Associated Press,* June 13.

Brillantes, Alex B., Jr. 1987. *Dictatorship and Martial Law: Philippine Authoritarianism in 1972.* Manila: Great Books.

Brook, Timothy. 1992. *Quelling the People: The Military Suppression of the Beijing Democracy Movement.* New York: Oxford University Press.

Brown, Judith M. 1972. *Gandhi's Rise to Power.* Cambridge: Cambridge University Press.

———. 1977. *Gandhi and Civil Disobedience.* Cambridge: Cambridge University Press.

Brown, Stephen. 2001. "Authoritarian Leaders and Multiparty Elections in Africa: How Foreign Donors Help to Keep Kenya's Daniel arap Moi in Power." *Third World Quarterly* 22(5): 725–739.

Brown, Tom. 1987. "Panama Declares State of Emergency after Riots." *Reuters News,* June 11, 1987.

Buckley, Kevin. 1991. *Panama: The Whole Story.* New York: Simon & Schuster.

Buckoke, Andrew. 1988. "Unrest Brews in Moi's Land of Milk and Honey; Kenya's Political Volcano." *Times* (London), June 23, issue 63115.

Bunce, Valerie. 1989. "The Polish Crisis of 1980–1981 and Theories of Revolution." Pages 167–188 in *Revolution in the World System,* edited by Terry Boswell. New York: Greenwood.

———. 1999. *Subversive Institutions: The Design and Destruction of Socialism and the State.* Cambridge: Cambridge University Press.

Bunce, Valerie, and Sharon Wolchik. 2006. "Favorable Conditions and Electoral Revolutions." *Journal of Democracy* 17(4): 5–18.

———. 2009. "Getting Real about 'Real Causes.'" *Journal of Democracy* 20(1): 69–73.

Burbach, Roger. 2003. *The Pinochet Affair: State Terrorism and Global Justice.* London: Zed.

Burgess, John P. 1997. *The East German Church and the End of Socialism.* New York: Oxford University Press.

Burrowes, Robert J. 1996. *The Strategy of Nonviolent Defense: A Gandhian Approach.* Albany: State University of New York Press.

Burton, Sandra. 1989. *Impossible Dream: The Marcoses, the Aquinos, and the Unfinished Revolution.* New York: Warner.

Buss, Claude A. 1987. *Cory Aquino and the People of the Philippines.* Stanford, CA: Stanford Alumni Association.

Calhoun, Craig. 1994. *Neither Gods nor Emperors: Students and the Struggle for Democracy in China.* Berkeley: University of California Press.

Carter, April, Howard Clark, and Michael Randel (eds.). 2006. *People Power and Protest since 1945: A Bibliography of Nonviolent Action.* London: Housmans.

Chan, Anita, and Jonathan Unger. 1990. "Voices from the Protest Movement, Chongqing, Sichuan." *Australian Journal of Chinese Affairs* 24: 273.

Chandra, Nirmal Humar. 1989. "Crisis in China: End of Socialism?" *Economic and Political Weekly* 24(46): 2551.

Chirot, Daniel. 1994. "What Happened in Eastern Europe in 1989?" Pages 218–245 in *Popular Protest and Political Culture in Modern China*, edited by Jeffrey Wasserstrom and Elizabeth Perry. Boulder, CO: Westview.

Christian, Shirley. 1986. "Chile's Army Reacting to Attack, Arrests Foes and Shuts Magazines." *New York Times*, September 9.

Chuchryk, Patricia. 1993. "Subversive Mothers: The Opposition to the Military Regime in Chile." Pages 86–97 in *Surviving beyond Fear: Women, Children, and Human Rights in Latin America*, edited by Marjorie Agosín. Fredonia, NH: White Pines.

Conniff, Michael. 1992. *Panama and the United States: The Forced Alliance*. Athens: University of Georgia Press.

Constable, Pamela, and Arturo Valenzuela. 1991. *A Nation of Enemies: Chile under Pinochet*. New York: W. W. Norton.

Cortright, David, and George A. Lopez (eds.). 2002. *Smart Sanctions: Targeting Economic Statecraft*. Lanham, MD: Rowman & Littlefield.

Coser, Lewis. 1956. *The Functions of Social Conflict*. New York: Free Press.

Cress, Daniel, and David Snow. 2000. "The Outcomes of Homeless Mobilization: The Influence of Organization, Disruption, Political Mediation, and Framing." *American Journal of Sociology* 105: 1063–1104.

Currie, Kate, and Larry Ray. 1985. "State and Class in Kenya—Notes on the Cohesion of the Ruling Class." *Journal of Modern African Studies* 22(4): 559–593.

Dale, Gareth. 2003. "Like Wildfire? The East German Rising of June 1953." *Debatte: Review of Contemporary German Affairs* 11(2): 107–163.

———. 2006. *The East German Revolution of 1989*. Manchester, UK: Manchester University Press.

Davenport, Christian. 1995. "Multi-dimensional Threat Perception and State Repression: An Inquiry into Why States Apply Negative Sanctions." *American Journal of Political Science* 3: 683–713.

DeFronzo, James. 1996. *Revolutions and Revolutionary Movements*. Boulder, CO: Westview.

Denitch, Bogdan. 1990. *The End of the Cold War: European Unity, Socialism, and the Shift in Global Power*. Minneapolis: University of Minnesota Press.

Dennis, Mike. 2000. *The Rise and Fall of the German Democratic Republic, 1945–1990*. London: Longman.

DeWitt, Karen. 1988. "Taxes from USA Help Noriega." *USA Today*, April 1.

Dietrich, Christian, and Uwe Schwabe (eds.). 1994. *Freunde und Feinde: Dokumente zu den Friedensgebeten in Leipzig Zwischen 1981 und dem 9. Oktober 1989*. Leipzig: Evangelische Verlaganstalt.

Di Palma, Guiseppe. 1990. *To Craft Democracies: An Essay on Democratic Transitions*. Berkeley: University of California Press.

Doellinger, David. 2002. *From Prayers to Protests: The Impact of Religious-Based Dissent on the Emergence of Civil Society in Slovakia and the GDR*. Ph.D. dissertation, University of Pittsburgh.

Dogan, Mattéi, and John Higley, 1998. *Elites, Crises, and the Origins of Regimes*. Boulder, CO: Rowman & Littlefield.

Donnelly, Thomas, Margaret Roth, and Caleb Baker. 1991. *Operation Just Cause: The Storming of Panama*. New York: Lexington.

Earl, Jennifer. 2003. "Tanks, Tear Gas and Taxes: Toward a Theory of Movement Repression." *Sociological Theory* 21: 44–68.

Eberlein, Werner. 2000. *Geboren am 9. November: Erinnerungen.* [Born on November 9th: Memories]. Berlin: Das Neue Berlin.

Eckstein, Harry. 1975. "Case Study and Theory in Political Science." In *Handbook of Political Science,* vol. 7, *Strategies of Inquiry,* edited by Fred Greenstein and Nelson Polsby. Reading, MA: Addison-Wesley.

Edgerton, Robert. 1989. *Mau Mau: An African Crucible.* New York: Ballantine.

Eisenmann, Roberto. 1990. "The Struggle against Noriega." *Journal of Democracy* 1(1): 41–46.

Ensalaco, Mark. 2000. *Chile under Pinochet: Recovering the Truth.* Philadelphia: University of Pennsylvania Press.

Evans, Sarah M., and Harry C. Boyte. 1992. *Free Spaces.* Chicago: University of Chicago Press.

Feigon, Lee. 1990. *China Rising: The Meaning of Tiananmen.* Chicago: Ivan R. Dee.

Fitzgerald, Mary Anne. 1986. "Kenya's Leadership Grows Increasingly Vulnerable to Unrest." *Christian Science Monitor,* June 17, International section, page 14.

Fleet, Michael. 1985. *The Rise and Fall of Chilean Christian Democracy.* Princeton, NJ: Princeton University Press.

Foeken, Dick, and Ton Dietz. 2000. "Of Ethnicity, Manipulation, and Observation: The 1992 and 1997 Elections in Kenya." Pages 122–149 in *Election Observation and Democratization in Africa,* edited by Jon Abbink and Gerti Hesseling. New York: St. Martin's.

Foran, John. 1997. *Theorizing Revolutions.* London: Routledge.

Forest, Jim, and Nancy Forest. 1988. *Four Days in February: The Story of the Nonviolent Overthrow of the Marcos Regime.* London: Marshall Pickering.

Francisco, Ronald. 2004. "After the Massacre: Mobilization in the Wake of Harsh Repression." *Mobilization* 9(2): 107–126.

Fullbrook, Mary. 1995. *Anatomy of a Dictatorship.* Oxford: Oxford University Press.

Ganz, Marshall. 2009. *Why David Sometimes Wins: Leadership, Organization, and Strategy in the California Farm Worker Movement.* New York: Oxford University Press.

Garretón, Manuel Antonio. 2001. "Popular Mobilization and the Military Regime in Chile: The Complexities of the Invisible Transition." Pages 259–277 in *Power and Popular Protest: Latin American Social Movements,* edited by Susan Eckstein. Berkeley: University of California Press.

Garton Ash, Timothy. 1989. *The Uses of Adversity: Essays on the Fate of Central Europe.* Cambridge, UK: Granta.

———. 1990. *The Magic Lantern: The Revolution of '89 Witnessed in Warsaw, Budapest, Berlin, and Prague.* New York: Random House.

———. 2009. "A Century of Civil Resistance: Some Lessons and Questions." In *Civil Resistance and Power Politics: The Experience of Non-Violent Action from Gandhi to the Present.* Oxford: Oxford University Press.

———. 2009. "Velvet Revolution: The Prospects." *New York Review of Books* 56 (19), December 3.

Geddes, Barbara. 1999. "What Do We Know about Democratization after Twenty Years?" *Annual Review of Political Science* 2: 115–144.

Gilbert, Martin. 2001. *A History of the Twentieth Century.* New York: W. Morrow.

Gleditsch, Kristian. 2004. "A Revised List of Wars between and within Independent States, 1816–2002." *International Interactions* 30(3): 231–262.

Goeckel, Robert F. 1990. *The Lutheran Church and the East German State.* Ithaca, NY: Cornell University Press.

Golden, Arthur. 1987. "Opposing Panama Regime Has Its Costs." *San Diego Union-Tribune,* July 5.

Goldstone, Jack A. 1991. *Revolutions and Rebellion in the Early Modern World.* Berkeley: University of California Press.

———. 2001. "Toward a Fourth Generation of Revolutionary Theory." *Annual Review of Political Science* 4: 139–187.

———. 2003. "Comparative Historical Analysis and Knowledge Accumulation in the Study of Revolutions." Pages 41–90 in *Comparative Historical Analysis in the Social Sciences*, edited by James Mahoney and Dietrich Rueschemeyer. New York: Cambridge University Press.

———. 2009. "Rethinking Revolutions: Integrating Origins, Processes, and Outcomes." *Comparative Studies of South Asia, Africa and the Middle East* 29(1): 18–32.

Goodwin, Jeff. 2001. *No Other Way Out: States and Revolutionary Movements, 1945–1991*. New York: Cambridge University Press.

Goodwin, Jeff, and Theda Skocpol. 1989. "Explaining Revolutions in the Contemporary Third World." *Political Sociology* 17: 489–507.

Granovetter, Mark. 1978. "Threshold Models of Collective Behavior." *American Journal of Sociology* 83(6): 1420–1443.

Greene, Graham. 1984. *Getting to Know the General*. Thorndike, ME: Thorndike.

Gregg, Richard. 1935. *The Power of Non-Violence*. London: George Routledge.

Gregor, A. James. 1984. *Crisis in the Philippines: A Threat to U.S. Interests*. Washington, DC: Ethics and Public Policy Center.

Grindle, Merilee. 1996. *Challenging the State: Crisis and Innovation in Latin America and Africa*. New York: Cambridge University Press.

Grix, Jonathan. 2000. *The Role of the Masses in the Collapse of the GDR*. New York: St. Martin's.

Grosh, Barbara, and Stephen Orvis. 1996/1997. "Democracy, Confusion, or Chaos: Political Conditionality in Kenya." *Studies in Comparative International Development* 31(4): 46–65.

Guerrero, Alina. 1987. "Students, Police Clash over Allegations of Fraud and Murder." Associated Press, June 9, 1987.

Gustafson, Lindsey. 1995. "Kenya: The Struggle to Create a Democracy." *Brigham Young University Law Review* 2: 647–671.

Hadjar, Andreas. 2003. "Non-Violent Political Protest in East Germany in the 1980s: Protestant Church, Opposition Groups, and the People." *German Politics* 12(3): 121.

Haggard, Stephen, and Robert R. Kaufman. 1995. *The Political Economy of Democratic Transitions*. Princeton, NJ: Princeton University Press.

Hale, Henry. 2006. "Democracy or Autocracy on the March? The Color Revolutions as Normal Dynamics of Patronal Presidentialism." *Communist and Post-Communist Studies* 39(3): 305–329.

Han, Minzhu. 1990. *Cries for Democracy: Writings and Speeches from the 1989 Chinese Democracy Movement*. Princeton, NJ: Princeton University Press.

Harden, Blaine. 1986. "Voice of Dissent in Kenya Comes from Pulpit; Vocal Pastor Relies on President's Christian Charity to Stay out of Jail." *Washington Post*, October 26, page A29.

———. 1986. "Third World Review (Kenya): Pulpit Politics/the Clash between Church and State." *Guardian* (London), October 31.

———. 1988. "Kenya Releases Political Prisoners in Move to Improve Human Rights Record; Following Pressure from Aid Donors, Moi Shakes Up Police." *Washington Post*, February 6, page A19.

Harding, Robert C. *The History of Panama*. Westport, CT: Greenwood.

Haugerud, Angelique. 2008. *The Culture of Politics in Modern Kenya*. Cambridge: Cambridge University Press.

Helvey, Robert L. 2004. *On Strategic Nonviolent Conflict: Thinking about Fundamentals*. Cambridge, MA: Albert Einstein Institution.

Hempstone, Smith. 1997. *Rogue Ambassador: An African Memoir*. Sewanee, TN: University of the South Press.

Henry, Neil. 1990. "Crackdown in Kenya Strains Ties with U.S.; Congress to Review Foreign Aid to Nairobi." *Washington Post*, July 9, page A13.

Hess, David, and Brian Martin. 2006. "Repression, Backfire, and the Theory of Transformative Events." *Mobilization* 11(2): 249–267.

Higley, John, and Michael Burton. 1989. "The Elite Variable in Democratic Transitions and Breakdowns." *American Sociological Review* 54: 17–32.

Higley, John, and Richard Gunther (eds.). 1992. *Elites and Democratic Consolidation in Latin America and Southern Europe.* Cambridge: Cambridge University Press.

Hirschman, Albert O. 1993. "Exit, Voice and the Fate of the GDR: An Essay in Conceptual History." *World Politics* 45(2): 173–202.

Holmquist, Frank, and Michael Ford. 1992. "Kenya: Slouching toward Democracy." *Africa Today* 39(3): 97–111.

Holmquist, Frank, and Michael Ford. 1995. "Stalling Political Change: Moi's Way in Kenya." *Current History* 94(591): 177–181.

Huneeus, Carlos. 2009. "Political Mass Mobilization against Authoritarian Rule: Pinochet's Chile, 1983–1988." Pages 197–212 in *Civil Resistance and Power Politics: The Experience of Nonviolent Action from Gandhi to the Present,* edited by Adam Roberts and Timothy Garton Ash. Oxford: Oxford University Press.

Huntington, Samuel. 1991. *The Third Wave: Democratization in the Late Twentieth Century.* Norman: University of Oklahoma Press

Ingelhart, Ronald, and Christian Welzel. 2005. *Modernization, Cultural Change, and Democracy: The Human Development Sequence.* New York: Cambridge University Press.

Jasper, James M. 1997. *The Art of Moral Protest: Culture, Biography, and Creativity in Social Movements.* Chicago: University of Chicago Press.

———. 2004. "A Strategic Approach to Collective Action: Looking for Agency in Social Movement Choices." *Mobilization* 9: 1–16.

———. Forthcoming. "Choice Points, Emotional Batteries, and Other Ways to Find Strategic Agency at the Micro Level." In *Strategy in Action,* edited by Gregory Maney, Rachel Kutz-Flamenbaum, Deana Rohlinger, and Jeff Goodwin. Minneapolis: University of Minnesota Press.

Johnson, Bryan. 1987. *The Four Days of Courage: The Untold Story of the People Who Brought Marcos Down.* New York: Free Press.

Joppke, Christian. 1995. *East German Dissidents and the Revolution of 1989.* New York: New York University Press.

Karatnycky, Adrian, and Peter Ackerman. 2005. *How Freedom Is Won: From Civil Resistance to Durable Democracy.* Washington, DC: Freedom House.

Keck, Margaret, and Kathryn Sikkink. 1998. *Activists beyond Borders: Advocacy Networks in International Politics.* Ithaca, NY: Cornell University Press.

Kempe, Frederick. 1990. *Divorcing the Dictator: America's Bungled Affair with Noriega.* New York: G. P. Putnam's Sons.

Kennedy, Michael D. 1999. "Contingencies and Alternatives of 1989: Toward a Theory and Practice of Negotiating Revolution." *Eastern European Politics and Societies* 13(2): 293–302.

Kenyan Ministry of Economic Planning and Development, Central Bureau of Statistics. 1981. *Statistical Abstracts.* Nairobi, Kenya: Author.

"Kenyans Accused of Water Torture." 1987. *Globe and Mail,* April 8.

"Kenya's Restless Students." 1987. *Times* (London), November 24, issue 62934.

Kessler, Richard J. 1986. "Marcos and the Americans." *Foreign Policy* 63: 40–57.

———. 1989. *Rebellion and Repression in the Philippines.* New Haven, CT: Yale University Press.

Khu, Josephine M. T. 1993. "Student Organization in the Movement." Pages 161–175 in *Chinese Democracy and the Crisis of 1989: Chinese and American Reflections,* edited by Roger V. Des Forges, Luo Ning, and Wu Yen-bo. Albany: State University of New York Press.

King, Gary, Robert Keohane, and Sidney Verba (eds.). 1994. *Designing Social Inquiry: Scientific Inference in Qualitative Research.* Princeton, NJ: Princeton University Press.

King, Katherine. 1998. "Panama and U.S. in Diplomatic Standoff as Tensions Mount." *Reuter News,* March 16.

Kitschelt, Herbert. 1986. "Political Opportunity Structures and Political Protest: Anti-Nuclear Movements in Four Democracies." *British Journal of Political Science* 16: 57–85.

Knox, Paul. "Police Rout Student Rally in Panama." *Globe and Mail*, July 18.

Komisar, Lucy. 1987. *Corazon Aquino: The Story of a Revolution.* New York: George Braziller.

Kopstein, Jeffrey. 1996. "Chipping Away at the State: Workers' Resistance and the Demise of East Germany." *World Politics* 48(3): 391–423.

———. 1997. *The Politics of Economic Decline in East Germany, 1945–1989.* Chapel Hill: University of North Carolina Press.

Koster, R. M., and Guillermo Sánchez. 1990. *In the Time of the Tyrants, Panama: 1968–1990.* New York: W. W. Norton.

Krause, Wanda C. 2004. "The Role and Example of Chilean and Argentinian Mothers in Democratisation." *Development in Practice* 14(3): 366–380.

Kumar, Krishan. 2001. *1989: Revolutionary Ideas and Ideals.* Minneapolis: University of Minnesota Press.

Kuran, Timur. 1991. "Now out of Never: The Element of Surprise in the East European Revolutions in 1989." *World Politics* 44(1): 7–48.

———. 1995. "The Inevitability of Future Revolutionary Surprises." *American Journal of Sociology* 100(6): 1528–1551.

Kurzman, Charles. 2004. *The Unthinkable Revolution in Iran.* Cambridge, MA: Harvard University Press.

La Boétie, Etienne. 1997 [1548]. *The Politics of Obedience: Discourse of Voluntary Servitude.* Montreal: Black Rose.

Lachmann, Richard. 1997. "Agents of Revolution: Elite Conflicts and Mass Mobilization from Medici to Yeltsin." Pages 73–101 in *Theorizing Revolutions,* edited by John Foran. London: Routledge.

LaFeber, Walter. 1989. *The Panama Canal: The Crisis in Historical Perspective.* New York: Oxford University Press.

Lande, Carl H. 1986. "The Political Crisis." Pages 114–144 in *Crisis in the Philippines: The Marcos Era and Beyond,* edited by John Bresnan. Princeton, NJ: Princeton University Press.

Landrey, Wilbur G. 1987. "People's Power Comes Closer to Home." *St. Petersburg Times,* July 7.

LaRosa, Michael, and Germán Mejía. 2004. *The United States Discovers Panama: The Writings of Soldiers, Scholars, and Scoundrels, 1850–1905.* New York: Rowman & Littlefield.

Lawson, George. 2005. *Negotiated Revolutions: The Czech Republic, South Africa and Chile.* Aldershot, UK: Ashgate.

Li, Lu. 1990. *Moving the Mountain: My Life in China from the Cultural Revolution to Tiananmen Square.* London: Macmillan.

Lichbach, Mark. 1987. "Deterrence or Escalation? The Puzzle of Aggregate Studies of Repression and Dissent." *Journal of Conflict Resolution* 31: 266–297.

Lin, Nan. 1992. *The Struggle for Tiananmen: Anatomy of the 1989 Mass Movement.* Westport, CT: Praeger.

Lindsay-Poland, John. 2003. *Emperors in the Jungle: The Secret History of the U.S. in Panama.* Durham, NC: Duke University Press.

Lipset, Seymour Martin. 1959. "Some Social Requisites of Democracy." *American Political Science Review* 53(1): 69–105.

———. 1963. *Political Man: The Social Bases of Politics.* Baltimore: Johns Hopkins University Press.

Lipsky, William E. 1976. "Comparative Approaches to the Study of Revolution: A Historiographic Essay." *Review of Politics* 38: 494–509.

Lombard, Joseph C. 1990. "The Survival of Noriega: Lessons from the U.S. Sanctions against Panama." *Stanford Journal of International Law* 26: 269–323.

Loveman, Brian. 1991. "Mision Cumplida? Civil Military Relations and the Chilean Political Transition." *Journal of Interamerican Studies and World Affairs* 33(3): 35–74.

Loveman, Mara. 1998. "High-Risk Collective Action: Defending Human Rights in Chile, Uruguay, and Argentina." *American Journal of Sociology* 104(2): 477–525.

Lowden, Pamela. 1996. *Moral Opposition to Authoritarian Rule in Chile, 1973–1990.* New York: St. Martin's.

Luxemberg, Rosa. 1961. *The Russian Revolution and Leninism or Marxism?* Ann Arbor: University of Michigan Press.

Lyons, John, and Karl Wilson. 1987. *Marcos and Beyond: The Philippines Revolution.* Kenthurst, Australia: Kangaroo.

Maier, Charles S. 1997. *Dissolution: The Crisis of Communism and the End of East Germany.* Princeton, NJ: Princeton University Press.

Mainwaring, Scott, Guillermo O'Donnell, and Arturo Valenzuela (eds.). 1992. *Issues in Democratic Consolidation.* Notre Dame, IN: University of Notre Dame Press.

Major, John. 2003. *Prize Possession: The United States Government and the Panama Canal, 1903–1979.* New York: Cambridge University Press.

Mansbridge, Jane. 2001. "The Making of Oppositional Consciousness." Pages 1–19 in *Oppositional Consciousness: The Subjective Roots of Social Protest*, edited by Jane Mansbridge and Aldon Morris. Chicago: University of Chicago Press.

Marcus, David. 1988. "Panamanians Riot against Noriega: Workers Take to the Streets after Government Fails to Meet Payroll." *Dallas Morning News*, March 15.

Markoff, John. 1996. *Waves of Democracy: Social Movements and Political Change.* Thousand Oaks, CA: Pine Forge.

Marshall, T. H. (Thomas Humphrey). 1965. *Class, Citizenship, and Social Development.* Garden City, NY: Doubleday.

Martin, Brian. 1989. "Gene Sharp's Theory of Power." *Journal of Peace Research* 26: 213–222.

———. 2007. *Justice Ignited: The Dynamics of Backfire.* Lanham, MD: Rowman & Littlefield.

Martin, Brian, and Wendy Varney. 2003. "Nonviolence and Communication." *Journal of Peace Research* 40(2): 213–232.

McAdam, Doug. 1982. *Political Process and the Development of Black Insurgency, 1930–1970.* Chicago: University of Chicago Press.

McCarthy, Ronald M., and Gene Sharp. 1997. *Nonviolent Action: A Research Guide.* New York: Garland.

Mendoza, Amado. 2009. "'People Power' in the Philippines, 1983–1986." Pages 179–196 in *Civil Resistance and Power Politics*, edited by Adam Roberts and Timothy Garton Ash. Oxford: Oxford University Press.

Mill, John Stuart. 2002 [1843]. *A System of Logic.* Honolulu: University Press of the Pacific.

Miller, Norman, and Rodger Yeager. 1993. *Kenya: The Quest for Prosperity.* Boulder, CO: Westview.

Millett, Richard. 1988. "Looking beyond Noriega." *Foreign Policy* 71: 46–63.

Montgomery, Charlotte. 1990. "Fear Raised of Crackdown on Critics." *Globe and Mail*, February 23.

Mueller, Susanne D. 1984. "Government and Opposition in Kenya, 1966–69." *Journal of Modern African Studies* 22(3): 399–427.

Muñoz, Heraldo. 2008. *The Dictator's Shadow: Life under Augusto Pinochet.* New York: Basic Books.

Murunga, Godwin Rapando. 2002. "A Critical Look at Kenya's Non-Transition to Democracy." *Journal of Third World Studies* 19(2): 89–111.

Murungi, Kiraitu. 1991. "President Moi and the Decline of Democracy in Kenya." *TransAfrica Forum* 8(4): 3–18.

Muschett Ibarra, Stanley M. 1992. *Church and Politics in Time of Crisis: Noriega's Panama.* Ph.D. Dissertation in Government and International Studies, University of Notre Dame.

Mutua, Makau. 2008. *Kenya's Quest for Democracy: Taming Leviathan.* Boulder, CO: Lynne Reinner.

Oberschall, Anthony, and Hyojoung Kim. 1996. "Identity and Action." *Mobilization* 1: 63–86.

Oldenburg, Fred S. 1990. "The October Revolution in the GDR—System, History, and Causes." *Eastern European Economics* 29(2): 55–77.

Opp, Karl-Dieter. 1994. "Repression and Revolutionary Action: East Germany in 1989." *Rationality and Society* 6(1): 129.

Opp, Karl-Dieter, and Wolfgang Roehl. 1990. "Repression, Micromobilization, and Political Protest." *Social Forces* 69: 521–547.

Opp, Karl-Dieter, Peter Voss, and Christine Gern. 1995. *Origins of a Spontaneous Revolution: East Germany, 1989.* Ann Arbor: University of Michigan Press.

Oppenheim, Lois Hecht. 1993. *Politics in Chile: Democracy, Authoritarianism, and the Search for Development.* Boulder, CO: Westview.

O'Shaughnessy, Hugh. 2000. *Pinochet: The Politics of Torture.* New York: University Press.

Overhalt, William H. 1986. "The Rise and Fall of Ferdinand Marcos." *Asian Survey* 26(11): 1137–1163.

Pape, Robert A. 1997. "Why Economic Sanctions Do Not Work." *International Security* 22(2): 90–136.

Parsa, Misagh. 2000. *States, Ideologies, and Social Revolutions: A Comparative Analysis of Iran, Nicaragua, and the Philippines.* Cambridge: Cambridge University Press.

Perlez, Jane. 1990. "Democracy Rally Crushed in Kenya." *New York Times*, July 8, section 1, page 3.

Perry, Elizabeth. 1994. "Casting a Chinese 'Democracy' Movement: The Role of Students, Workers, and Entrepreneurs." Pages 74–92 in *Popular Protest and Political Culture in Modern China*, edited by Jeffrey N. Wasserstrom and Elizabeth J. Perry. Boulder, CO: Westview.

Petras, James, and Steve Vieux. 1988. "The Chilean 'Economic Miracle': An Empirical Critique." *Critical Sociology* 17: 57–72.

Pfaff, Steven. 2006. *Exit-Voice Dynamics and the Collapse of East Germany: The Crisis of Leninism and the Revolution of 1989.* Durham, NC: Duke University Press.

Philipsen, Dirk. 1993. *We Were the People: Voices from East Germany's Revolutionary Autumn of 1989.* Durham, NC: Duke University Press.

Pierard, Richard V. 1990. "Religion and the East German Revolution." *Journal of Church and State* 32(3): 501–509.

Piven, Francis Fox and Richard Cloward. 1977. *Poor People's Movements: How They Succeed, Why They Fail.* New York: Pantheon.

Pond, Elizabeth. 1993. *Beyond the Wall: Germany's Road to Unification.* Washington, DC: Brookings Institution.

Power, Margaret. 2004. "More than Mere Pawns: Right-Wing Women in Chile." *Journal of Women's History* 16(3): 138–151.

Prezworski, Adam, and Fernando Limongi. 1997. "Modernization: Theory and Facts." *World Politics* 49: 155–183.

Record, Jeffrey. 2006. "External Assistance: Enabler of Insurgent Success." *Parameters* 36(3): 36–49.

Reykowski, Janusz. 1994. "Why Did the Collectivist State Fail?" *Theory and Society* 23(2): 233–252.

Roberts, Adam, and Timothy Garton Ash (eds.). 2009. *Civil Resistance and Power Politics: The Experience of Non-Violent Action from Gandhi to the Present.* Oxford: Oxford University Press.

Robertson, Claire. 1987. "Rights Group Links Kenya with Torture." *Washington Post*, page A15.

Robinson, Linda. 1989/1990. "Dwindling Options in Panama." *Foreign Affairs* 68(5): 187–205.

Rohter, Larry. 1987. "Panama Unrest Fails to Crack Noriega." *Sydney Morning Herald*, July 31.

Romulo, Beth Day. 1987. *Inside the Palace: The Rise and Fall of Ferdinand and Imelda Marcos.* New York: G. P. Putnam's Sons.

Ropp, Steve C. 1987. "Panama's Struggle for Democracy." *Current History* 86: 421–435.

———. 1990. "Military Entrenchment and Decay in Panama." *Current History* 89: 17–40.

———. 1992. "Explaining the Long-Term Maintenance of a Military Regime: Panama before the U.S. Invasion." *World Politics* 44(2): 228.

Rueschemeyer, Dietrich, Evelyn Huber Stephens, and John D. Stephens. 1992. *Capitalist Development and Democracy*. Chicago: University of Chicago Press.

Rule, Sheila. 1985. "Clampdown on Students Reflects Kenyan Unease." *New York Times*, March 20, page A15.

Sabar, Galia. 2002. *Church, State, and Society in Kenya: From Mediation to Opposition*. London: Frank Cass.

Sabrosky, Alan Ned. 1990. "Panama 1989: Deposing a Dictator." *Small Wars & Insurgencies* 1(3): 303–306.

Schedler, Andreas. 2002. "The Menu of Manipulation." *Journal of Democracy* 13(2): 36–50.

Schelling, Thomas C. 1967. "Some Questions on Civilian Defense." Pages 349–356 in *Civilian Resistance as a National Defense: Nonviolent Action against Aggression*, edited by Adam Roberts. Harrisburg, PA: Stackpole.

Schock, Kurt. 2003. "Nonviolent Action and Its Misconceptions: Insights for Social Scientists." *PS: Political Science and Politics* 36: 705–712.

———. 2005. *Unarmed Insurrections: People Power Movements in Nondemocracies*. Minneapolis: University of Minnesota Press.

Scobell, Andrew. 1993. "Why the People's Army Fired on the People." Pages 191–221 in *Chinese Democracy and the Crisis of 1989: Chinese and American Reflections*, edited by Roger V. Des Forges, Luo Ning, and Wu Yen-bo. Albany: State University of New York Press.

Scranton, Margaret. 1991. *The Noriega Years: U.S. Panamanian Relations, 1981–1990*. Boulder, CO: Lynne Rienner.

Selbin, Eric. 1993. *Modern Latin American Revolutions*. Boulder, CO: Westview.

Semelin, Jacques. 1993. *Unarmed against Hitler: Civilian Resistance in Europe, 1939–1943*. Westport, CT: Praeger.

Sepp, Kalev. 2005. "Best Practices in Counterinsurgency." *Military Review* 85(3): 8–12.

Shain, Yossi, and Juan Linz. 1995. *Between States: Interim Governments and Democratic Transitions*. Cambridge: Cambridge University Press.

Shanin, Teodor. 1986. *The Roots of Otherness: Russia's Turn of the Century, Volume 2: Revolution as a Moment of Truth*. New Haven, CT: Yale University Press.

Sharp, Gene. 1973. *The Politics of Nonviolent Action*. Boston: Porter Sargent.

———. 1990. *The Role of Power in Nonviolent Struggle*. Cambridge, MA: Albert Einstein Institute.

——— 2005. *Waging Nonviolent Struggle: 20th Century Practice and 21st Century Potential*. Boston: Porter Sargent.

Shields, Todd. 1990. "Nairobi Tense as Violent Opposition to Moi Increases," *Independent* (London), July 9, foreign news section, page 11.

———. 1990. "Death Toll in Kenya Rises to 28." *Independent* (London), July 12, foreign news section, page 14.

Silva, Eduardo. 1991. "The Political Economy of Chile's Regime Transition: From Radical to 'Pragmatic' Neo-Liberal Policies." Pages 98–127 in *The Struggle for Democracy in Chile, 1982–1990*, edited by Paul W. Drake and Iván Jaksic. Lincoln: University of Nebraska Press.

Simmie, Scott, and Bob Nixon. 1989. *Tiananmen Square: An Eyewitness Account of the People's Passionate Quest for Democracy*. Seattle: University of Washington Press.

Simons, Lewis M. 1987. *Worth Dying For*. New York: William Morrow.

Skidmore, Thomas E., and Peter H. Smith. 2001. *Modern Latin America*. New York: Cambridge University Press.

Skocpol, Theda. 1979. *States and Social Revolutions*. Cambridge: Cambridge University Press.

Smith, Brian. 1982. *The Church and Politics in Chile*. Princeton, NJ: Princeton University Press.

Smith, Christian. 1996. *Resisting Reagan: The U.S. Central America Peace Movement*. Chicago: University of Chicago Press.

Smith, Jackie, and Ronald Pagnucco. 1992. "Political Process and the 1989 Chinese Student Movement." *Studies in Conflict and Terrorism* 15: 169–184.

Smithey, Lee, and Lester R. Kurtz. 1999. "'We Have Bare Hands': Nonviolent Social Movements in the Soviet Bloc." Pages 96–124 in *Nonviolent Social Movements: A Geographic Perspective*, edited by Stephen Zunes, Lester R. Kurtz, and Sarah Beth Asher. Malden, MA: Blackwell.

Snow, David, and Robert Benford. 1988. "Ideology, Frame Resonance, and Participant Mobilization." *International Social Movement Research* 1: 197–218.

Spooner, Mary Helen. 1994. *Soldiers in a Narrow Land: The Pinochet Regime in Chile*. Berkeley: University of California Press.

Stamp, Patricia. 1991. "The Politics of Dissent in Kenya." *Current History* 90: 205–208.

Stanley, Peter W. 1986. "Toward Democracy in the Philippines." *Proceedings of the Academy of Political Science* 36(1): 129–141.

Steeves, Jeffrey. 2006. "Beyond Democratic Consolidation in Kenya: Ethnicity, Leadership, and 'Unbounded Politics.'" *African Identities* 4(2): 195–211.

Stephan, Maria, and Erica Chenoweth. 2008. "Why Civil Resistance Works: The Strategic Logic of Nonviolent Conflict." *International Security* 33(1): 7–44.

Stokes, Gale. 1993. *The Walls Came Tumbling Down: The Collapse of Communism in Eastern Europe*. New York: Oxford University Press.

Tarrow, Sidney. 1998. *Power in Movement: Social Movements and Contentious Politics*, 2nd ed. New York: Cambridge University Press.

Taso, Tsing-yuan. 1994. "The Birth of the Goddess of Democracy." Pages 140–147 in *Popular Protest and Political Culture in Modern China*, edited by Jeffrey N. Wasserstrom and Elizabeth J. Perry. Boulder, CO: Westview.

Thiong'o, Ngugi Wa. 1987. "Third World Review: Kenya Breaks through the Circle of Fear—A Lie to Moi's Myth That Kenya Is a Model Democracy." *Guardian*, December 18.

Thomas, Gordon. 1991. *Chaos under Heaven: The Shocking Story of China's Search for Democracy*. New York: Birch Lane.

Thompson, Mark R. 1995. *The Anti-Marcos Struggle: Personalistic Rule and Democratic Transition in the Philippines*. New Haven, CT: Yale University Press.

Thoreau, Henry David. 2008. *On The Duty of Civil Disobedience*. Radford, VA: Wilder.

"Three More Kenyans Seized Calling for Opposition." 1990. *New York Times*, July 6, page A2.

Throup, David. 1989. "The Construction and Deconstruction of the Kenyatta State." Pages 33–74 in *The Political Economy of Kenya*, edited by Michael G. Schatzberg. Baltimore: Johns Hopkins University Press.

Throup, David, and Charles Hornsby. 1998. *Multi-Party Politics in Kenya: The Kenyatta and Moi States and the Triumph of the System in the 1992 Elections*. Oxford: James Curry.

Timerman, Jacobo. 1987. *Chile: Death in the South*. New York: Alfred A. Knopf.

Trequesser, Gilles. 1987. "Lawyer for Dissident Panamanian Colonel Questions Retractions." *Reuters News*, August 3.

Valenzuela, Arturo. 1991. "The Military in Power: The Consolidation of One-Man Rule." Pages 21–72 in *The Struggle for Democracy in Chile, 1982–1990*, edited by Paul W. Drake and Iván Jaksic. Lincoln: University of Nebraska Press.

Vallely, Paul. 1987. "Kenya's Changing Image: Church a Lonely Voice on Moi's Totalitarian Drift." *Times* (London), May 26, issue 62778.

———. 1988. "Church Editor Falls Victim to Moi's War on Democracy." *Times* (London), August 22, issues 63166.

Varas, Augusto. 1991. "The Crisis of Legitimacy of Military Rule in the 1980s." Pages 73–97 in *The Struggle for Democracy in Chile, 1982–1990*, edited by Paul W. Drake and Iván Jaksic. Lincoln: University of Nebraska Press.

Verdugo, Patricia. 2001. *Chile, Pinochet, and the Caravan of Death*. Miami, FL: North-South Center.

Villegas, Bernardo. 1986. "The Economic Crisis." Pages 145–175 in *Crisis in the Philippines: The Marcos Era and Beyond*, edited by John Bresnan. Princeton, NJ: Princeton University Press.

Walsh, Edward. 1981. "Resource Mobilization and Citizen Protest in Communities around Three Mile Island." *Social Problems* 29: 1–21.

Way, Lucan. 2008. "The Real Causes of Color Revolutions." *Journal of Democracy* 19(3): 55–69.

Weeks, Gregory. 2003. *The Military and Politics in Postauthoritarian Chile*. Tuscaloosa: University of Alabama Press.

Wheaton, Bernard, and Zdenek Kavan. 1992. *The Velvet Revolution: Czechoslovakia, 1988–1991*. Boulder, CO: Westview.

Wickham-Crowley, Timothy. 1992. *Guerrillas and Revolution in Latin America*. Princeton, NJ: Princeton University Press.

Widner, Jennifer A. 1992. *The Rise of a Party-State in Kenya: From "Harambee!" to "Nyayo!"* Berkeley: University of California Press.

Wilson, Andrew. 2005. *Ukraine's Orange Revolution*. New Haven, CT: Yale University Press.

Wood, Elisabeth Jean. 2000. *Forging Democracy from Below: Insurgent Transitions in South Africa and El Salvador*. New York: Cambridge University Press.

Wurfel, David. 1988. *Filipino Politics: Death and Decay*. Ithaca, NY: Cornell University Press.

Xiaodong, Wang. 1993. "A Review of China's Economic Problems: The Industrial Sector." Pages 149–160 in *Chinese Democracy and the Crisis of 1989: Chinese and American Reflections*, edited by Roger V. Des Forges, Luo Ning, and Wu Yen-bo. Albany: State University of New York.

Yu, Mok Chiu, and J. Frank Harrison. 1990. *Voices from Tiananmen Square: Beijing Spring and the Democracy Movement*. Montreal: Black Rose.

Zedong, Mao. 1927. "Report on an Investigation into the Peasant Movement in Hunan." *Selected Works of Mao Tse-tung*, Vol. 1. Beijing: Beijing Foreign Language Press.

Zhao, Dingxin. 2001. *The Power of Tiananmen: State-Society Relations and the 1989 Beijing Student Movement*. Chicago: University of Chicago Press.

Zheng, Zhuyan. 1990. *Beyond the Tiananmen Square Massacre*. Boulder, CO: Westview.

Zhou, Xueguang. 1993. "Unorganized Interests and Collective Action in Communist China." *American Sociological Review* 58: 54–73.

Zimbalist, Andrew, and John Weeks. 1991. *Panama at the Crossroads*. Berkeley: University of California Press.

Zunes, Stephen. 1994. "Unarmed Insurrections against Authoritarian Governments in the Third World: A New Kind of Revolution?" *Third World Quarterly* 15: 403–426.

———. 1999. "The Origins of People Power in the Philippines." Pages 129–157 in *Nonviolent Social Movements: A Geographical Perspective*, edited by Stephen Zunes, Lester R. Kurtz, and Sarah Beth Asher. Malden, MA: Blackwell.

Zunes, Stephen, Lester R. Kurtz, and Sarah Beth Asher (eds.). 1999. *Nonviolent Social Movements: A Geographical Perspective*. Malden, MA: Blackwell.

Zuo, Jiping, and Robert Benford. 1995. "Mobilization Processes and the 1989 Chinese Democracy Movement." *Sociological Quarterly* 36(1): 131–156.

INDEX

velvet revolutions, xviii, 4, *See* nonviolent
revolutions
violent revolutions
causes of, 5–6
characteristics of, xviii
factors influencing the outcome of, 6–8
strategy of, 7–8

Wang Dan, 24, 28, 30
West Germany, xi, xiv, 45, 51–52
Wonneberger, Christoph, 42–43,
53–54
Wuer Kaixi, 24, 28, 32

Zhao Ziyang, 29, 33

CPSIA information can be obtained at www.ICGtesting.com
Printed in the USA
BVOW021552160812

298073BV00002B/27/P